The History of Egypt Under the Ptolemies

By Samuel Sharpe

ISBN: 978-1-63923-719-7

Printed: February 2023

Published and Distributed By:
Lushena Books
607 Country Club Drive, Unit E
Bensenville, IL 60106
www.lushenabks.com

ISBN: 978-1-63923-719-7

PREFACE

Professor Maspero closes his History of Egypt with the conquest of Alexander the Great. There is a sense of dramatic fitness in this selection, for, with the coming of the Macedonians, the sceptre of authority passed for ever out of the hand of the Egyptian. For several centuries the power of the race had been declining, and foreign nations had contended for the vast treasure-house of Egypt. Alexander found the Persians virtually rulers of the land. The ancient people whose fame has come down to us through centuries untarnished had been forced to bow beneath the yoke of foreign masters, and nations of alien blood were henceforth to dominate its history.

The first Ptolemy founded a Macedonian or Greek dynasty that maintained supremacy in Egypt until the year 30 B. C. His successors were his lineal descendants, and to the very last they prided themselves on their Greek origin; but the government which they established was essentially Oriental in character. The names of Ptolemy and Cleopatra convey an Egyptian rather than a Greek significance; and the later rulers of the dynasty were true Egyptians, since their ancestors had lived in Alexandria for three full centuries.

In the year 30 B. C. Augustus Cæsar conquered the last of the Ptolemies, the famous Cleopatra. Augustus made Egypt virtually his private province, and drew from it resources that were among the chief elements of

his power. After Augustus, the Romans continued in
control until the coming of the Saracens under Amr,
in the seventh century. Various dynasties of Moham-
medans, covering a period of several centuries, maintained control until the Mamluks, in 1250, overthrew the
legitimate rulers, to be themselves overthrown three
centuries later by the Turks under Selim I. Turkish
rule was maintained until near the close of the eighteenth century, when the French, under Napoleon Bona-
parte, invaded Egypt. In 1806, after the expulsion of
the French by the English, the famous Mehemet Ali
destroyed the last vestiges of Mamluk power, and set
up a quasi-independent sovereignty which was not disturbed until toward the close of the nineteenth century.
The events of the last twenty-five years, comprising a
short period of joint control of Egypt by the French and
English, followed by the British occupation, are fresh
in the mind of the reader.

What may be termed the modern history of Egypt
covers a period of more than twenty-two centuries.
During this time the native Egyptian can scarcely be
said to have a national history, but the land of Egypt,
and the races who have become acclimated there, have
passed through many interesting phases. Professor
Maspero completes the history of antiquity in that dramatic scene in which the ancient Egyptian makes his
last futile struggle for independence. But the Nile Valley has remained the scene of the most important events
where the strongest nations of the earth contended for
supremacy. It is most interesting to note that the

invaders of Egypt, while impressing their military stamp
upon the natives, have been mastered in a very real sense
by the spell of Egypt's greatness; but the language, the
key to ancient learning and civilisation, still remained
a well-guarded secret. Here and there one of the Ptolemies or Greeks thought it worth his while to master the
hieroglyphic writing. Occasionally a Roman of the later
period may have done the same, but such an accomplish-
ment was no doubt very unusual from the first. The
subordinated Egyptians therefore had no resource but
to learn the language of their conquerors, and presently
it came to pass that not even the native Egyptian remembered the elusive secrets of his own written language. Egyptian, as a spoken tongue, remained, in a
modified form, as Koptic, but at about the beginning of
our era the classical Egyptian had become a dead language. No one any longer wrote in the hieroglyphic,
hieratic, or demotic scripts; in a word, the hieroglyphic
writing was forgotten. The reader of Professor Maspero's pages has had opportunity to learn how this secret
was discovered in the nineteenth century. This information is further amplified in the present volumes, and we
see how in our own time the native Egyptian has regained
something of his former grandeur through the careful
and scientific study of monuments, inscriptions, and
works of art. Thus it will appear in the curious round-
ing out of the enigmatic story that the most ancient
history of civilisation becomes also the newest and most
modern human history.

PUBLISHER'S NOTE

It should be explained that Doctor Rappoport, in preparing these volumes, has drawn very largely upon the authorities who have previously laboured in the same field, and in particular upon the works of Creasy, Duruy, Ebers, Lavisse, Marcel, Michaud, Neibuhr, Paton, Rambaud, Sharp, and Weil. The results of investigations by Professor W. M. Flinders Petrie and other prominent Egyptologists have been fully set forth and profusely illustrated.

CONTENTS

CONTENTS

CHANGER V.

CHAPTER VI.

CHAPTER VII.

LIST OF ILLUSTRATIONS

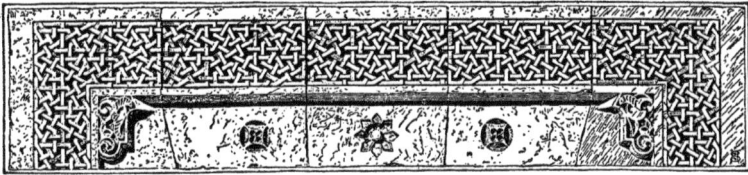

EGYPT UNDER THE PTOLEMIES

ALEXANDER THE GREAT AND THE CONQUEST OF EGYPT — THE REIGNS
OF THE PTOLEMIES — GRADUAL GROWTH OF ROMAN INFLUENCE
— INTRIGUES OF CLEOPATRA WITH POMPEY, CÆSAR, AND ANTONY

*Alexander the Great in Egypt — Alexandria founded — The
Greeks favour the Jews — Ptolemy Soter establishes himself in
Egypt and overcomes Perdiccas — Struggles for Syria — Beginning of
Egyptian coinage — Art and Scholarship — Ptolemy resigns in favour
of his son Philadelphus — First treaty with Rome — Building of the
Pharos — Growth of Commerce — Encouragement of Learning — The
library of Alexandria — Euclid the geometer — Poets, astronomers,
historians, and critics — The Septuagint — Marriage of Philadelphus
to his sister Arsinoë — Ptolemy Euergetes plunders Asia — Egyptian
temples enlarged — Religious tolerance — Annual tribute of the Jews —
Eratosthenes the astronomer — Philosophy and Science — Culmination
of Ptolemaic rule — The dynasty declines under Philopator — Syrians
invade Egypt; Philopator retaliates; visits Jerusalem — The Jews
persecuted — The king's follies — Riots at Alexandria — Inglorious
end of Philopator — The young Ptolemy Epiphanes protected by
Rome — Military revolt suppressed — Coronation of Epiphanes — The
Rosetta Stone — Marriage of Epiphanes and Cleopatra, daughter of
Antiochus the Great — A second rebellion repressed — Accession of
Ptolemy Philometer under the guardianship of Cleopatra — Antiochus
Epiphanes defeats Philometer — Euergetes seizes the throne and appeals
to Rome — Antiochus supports Philometor against his brother Euergetes*

— The brothers combine against Antiochus — Fraternal rivalry — Philometer appeals to the Romans who adjust the quarrel — Philometer arbitrates in a dispute between the Jews and the Samaritans — New temples built — Egyptian asceticism — Philometer's death; Euergetes reigns alone, and divorces his queen Cleopatra — Popular tumult in Alexandria — Euergetes flees — Cleopatra in power — Euergetes regains the throne; conquers Syria and makes peace with Cleopatra — The reign of Cleopatra Cocce with Lathyrus (Ptolemy Soter II.) — Cleopatra in the ascendent — She helps the Jews, while Lathyrus helps the Samaritans — Lathyrus flees to Cyprus — Ptolemy Alexander I rules with Cleopatra — Death of Alexander and restoration of Lathyrus — Accession of Cleopatra Berenicê — Ptolemy Alexander II. bequeaths Egypt to Rome, murders Berenicê, and is slain by his guards — Auletes succeeds — The Romans claim Egypt — Pompey assists Auletes who is expelled by the Egyptians — Cleopatra Tryphœna and Berenicê placed on the throne — Gabinius and Mark Antony march into Egypt and restore Auletes — The reign of Cleopatra — Pompey made governor — The Egyptian fleet aids Pompey — Pompey is slain — Cæsar besieged by the Alexandrians — He overcomes opposition, is captivated by Cleopatra and establishes her authority — The Queen's extravagance — Defeat of Antony — Death of Cleopatra — Octavianus annexes Egypt.

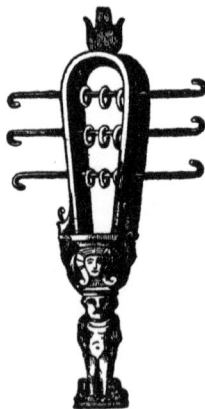

INTRODUCTORY ESSAY

HELLENISM AND HEBRÆISM IN EGYPT UNDER THE PTOLEMIES

WHEN Alexander the Great bridged the gulf dividing Occident and Orient, the Greeks had attained to a state of maturity in the development of their national art and literature. Greek culture and civilisation, passing beyond the boundaries of their national domain, crossed this bridge and spread over the Asiatic world. To perpetuate his name, the great Macedonian king founded a city, and selected for this purpose, with extraordinary prescience, a spot on the banks of the Nile, which, on account of its geographical position, was destined to become a centre, not only of international commerce and an entrepôt between Asia and Europe, but also a centre of intellectual culture. The policy of Alexander to remove the barriers between the Greeks and the Asiatics, and to pave the way for the union of the races of his vast empire, was continued by the Lagidæ dynasty in Egypt. With her independence and native dynasties, Egypt had also lost her political strength and

3

unity; she retained, however, her ancient institutions, her customs, and religious system. The sway of Persian dominion had passed over her without overthrowing this huge rock of sacerdotal power which, deeply rooted with many ramifications, seemed to mock the wave of time. Out of the ruins of political independence still towered the monuments of civilisation of a mighty past which gave to this country moral independence, and prevented the obliteration of nationality. It would have mattered very little in the vast empire of Alexander if one province had a special physiognomy. It was different, however, with the Lagidæ: their power was concentrated in Egypt, and they were therefore compelled to obliterate the separation existing between the conquering and the conquered races, and fuse them, if possible, into one. A great obstacle which confronted the Macedonian rulers in Egypt was the religion of the country. The interest and the policy of the Lagidæ demanded the removal of this obstacle, not by force but by diplomacy. Greek gods were therefore identified with Egyptian; Phtah became Hephæstos; Thot, Hermes; Ra, Helios; Amon, Zeus; and, in consequence of a dream which commanded him to offer adoration to a foreign god, Ptolemy Soter created a new Greek god who was of Egyptian origin. Osiris at that period was the great god of Egypt; Memphis was the religious centre of the cult of Apis, the representative of Osiris, and who, when living, was called Apis-Osiris, and when dead Osiris-Apis. Cambyses had killed the god or his representative: it was a bad move. Alexander made sacrifices to him:

Ptolemy Soter did more. He endeavoured to persuade the Egyptians that Osirapi or Osiris-Apis was also sacred to the Greeks, and to identify him with some Greek divinity. There was a Greek deity known as Serapis, identified with Pluton, the god of Hades. Serapis, by a clever manœuvre, *a coup de religion*, was identified with Osiris-Apis. The lingual similarity and the fact that Osirapi was the god of the Egyptian Hades made the identification acceptable.

Like true Greek princes, the Ptolemies had broad views and were very tolerant. Keeping the Greek religion themselves, they were favourably disposed towards the creeds of other nationalities under their dominion. Thanks to this broad-mindedness and tolerance which had become traditional in the Lagidæ family, and which has only rarely been imitated — to the detriment of civilisation — in the history of European dynasties, Oriental and Hellenic culture could flourish side by side. This benign government attracted many scholars, scientists, poets, and philosophers. Alexandria became the intellectual metropolis of the world; and it might truly be said to have been the Paris of antiquity. At the courts of the Ptolemies, the Medicis of Egypt, the greatest men of the age lived and taught. Demetrius Phalerius, one of the most learned and cultured men of an age of learning and knowledge, when driven from his luxurious palace at Athens, found hospitality at the court of Ptolemy Soter. The foundation of the famous Museion and library of Alexandria was most probably due to his influence. He advised the first Ptolemy to found a building where poets, scholars, and philosophers would have facilities for study, research, and speculation. The Museion was similar in some respects to the Academy of Plato. It was an edifice where scholars lived and worked together. Mental qualification was the only requirement for admission. Nationality and creed were no obstacles to those whose learning rendered them worthy of becoming members of this ideal academy and of being received among the immortals of antiquity. The Museion was in no sense a university, but an academy for the cultivation of the higher branches of learning. It might be compared in some respects to the Collège de France, ór regarded as a development of the system under which scholars had already lived and worked together in the Ramesseum under Ramses II. The generosity of the Lagidæ provided amply for this new centre of learning and study. Free from worldly cares, the scholars could leisurely gather information and hand down to posterity the fruits of their researches. From all parts of the world men flocked to this centre of fashionable learning, the birthplace of modern science. All that was brilliant and cultured, all the coryphées in the domain of intellect, were attracted by that splendid court.

In the shade of the Museion a brilliant assembly —Ptolemy, Euclid, Hipparchus, Apollonius, and Eratosthenes—made great discoveries and added materially to the sum of human knowledge. Here Euclid wrote his immortal " Elements; " and Herophilos, the father of surgery, added valuable information to the knowledge of anatomy. The art and process of embalming, in such vogue among the Egyptians, naturally fostered the advance of this science. Whilst Alexandria in abstract speculation could not rival Greece, yet it became the home of the pioneers of positive science, who left a great and priceless legacy to modern civilisation. The importance of this event (the foundation of the Museion), says Draper, in his *Intellectual Development of Europe*, though hitherto little understood, admits of no exaggeration so far as the intellectual progress of Europe is concerned. The Museum made an impression upon the intellectual career of Europe so powerful and enduring that we still enjoy its results.

If the purely literary productions of that age have sometimes been looked upon with contempt, European intellectual culture is still greatly indebted to Alexandria, and especially for the patronage she accorded to the works of Aristotle. Whilst the speculative mind was in later centuries allured by the supernatural, and the discussion of the criterion of truth and the principles of morality ended in the mystic doctrines of Neo-Platonism, the practical tendencies of the great Alexandrine scholars were instrumental in laying the foundations of science. To the Museion were attached the libraries: one in the Muscion itself, and another in the quarter Rhacotis in the temple of Serapis, which contained about 700,000 volumes. New books were continually acquired. The librarians had orders to pay any sum for the original of the works of great masters. The Ptolemies were not only patrons of learning but were themselves highly educated. Ptolemy Soter was an historian of no mean talent, and his son Philadelphus, as a pupil of the poet Philetas and the philosopher Strabo, was a man of great learning. Ptolemy III. was a mathematician, and Ptolemy Philopator, who had erected and dedicated a temple to Homer, was the writer of a tragedy. The efforts of the Ptolemies to bring the two nationalities, Hellenic and Egyptian, nearer to each other, to mould and weld them into one if possible, to mix and mingle the two civilisations and thus strengthen their own power, was greatly aided by the national character of the Greeks and the political position of the Egyptians.

The Greeks found in Egypt a national culture and especially a religious system. The pliant Hellenic genius could not remain insensible to that ancient and marvellous civilisation with its sphinxes and hieroglyphics, its pyramids and temples, its learning and thought, so strangely perplexing and interesting to the Greek mind. Not only the magnificence of Egyptian art, the majesty of her temples and palaces, but the wisdom of her social and political institutions impressed the conquerors. They made themselves acquainted with the institutions of the country; they studied its history and took an interest in its religion and mythology. Similarly, the conquered Egyptians, who had preferred the Macedonian ruler to their Persian oppressors, exhibited a natural desire to learn the languages and habits of their rulers, to make themselves acquainted with their knowledge and phases of thought, and art and science. The interest of the Greeks was strengthened by this, and the Egyptians were made to see their history in its proper light. To this endeavour we owe the history of Manetho. But, in spite of the policy of the Ptolemies, the impressionable nature of the Hellenic character and the interest of the Egyptians,—in spite of all that tended to a fusion of Hellenism and Orientalism, it never came to a proper amalgamation. The contradiction between the free-thought philosophy of Greece, which was fast outgrowing its polytheism and Olympian worship, and the deeply rooted sacerdotal system of the Pharaonian institutions, was too great and too flagrant. Thus there never was an Egypto-Hellenic phase of thought. But there was another civilisation of great antiquity, possessing peculiar features, not less interesting for the Greek mind than that of Egypt itself, with which Hellenism found itself face to face in the ancient land of the Pharaohs. It was the civilisation of Judæa, between which and Greek thought a greater fusion was effected.

II

From time immemorial the Hebrew race, with all its conservative tendencies in religious matters, has been amenable to the influence of foreign culture and civilisation. Egypt and Phœnicia, Babylonia and Assyria, Hellas and Rome have exercised an immense influence over it. It still is and always has been endeavouring to bring into harmony the exclusiveness of its national religion, with a desire to adopt the habits, culture, language, and manners of its neighbours; an attempt in which it may be apparently successful, for a certain period at least, but which must always have a tragic end. It is impossible to be conservative and progressive at the same time, to be both national and cosmopolitan. The attempts to reconcile religious formalism and free reasoning have never succeeded in the history of human thought. It soon led to the conviction that one factor must be sacrificed, and, as soon as this was perceived, the party of zealots was quickly at hand to preach reaction. In the times of the successors of Alexander, the Diadochæ and Epigones, the Seleucidæ and the Lagidæ, who had divided the vast dominion among them, Greek influence had spread all over Palestine. Greek towns were founded, theatres and gymnasia established; Greek art was admired and her philosophy studied. The Hellenic movement was paramount, and the aristocratic families did their best to further it. Even the high priests, like Jason and Menelaos, who were supposed to be the guardians of the national exclusive movement, favoured Greek culture and institutions.

In the mother country, however, the germ of reaction was always very strong. A constant opposition was directed against the influx of foreign modes of life and thought, which effaced and obliterated the intellectual movement. It was different, however, in the other countries of Macedonian dominion, and especially in Egypt. Alexander the Great, who seems to have been favourably inclined towards the Jews, settled a number of them in Alexandria. His policy was kept up by the descendants of Lagos, that great general of Alexander,

who made himself king of the province which was entrusted to the care of his administration. Egypt became
the resort of many refugees from Judæa, who gradually
came under the influence of the dazzling Greek thought
and culture, so new and therefore so attractive to the
Semitic mind. Hellenism and Hebraism had known each
other for some time, for Phœnician merchants and sea-
farers had carried the seed of Oriental wisdom to the
distant west. The acquaintance, however, was a slight
one. At the court of the Ptolemies, on the threshold of
Europe and Asia, they met at last. On the shores of the
Mediterranean, on the soil where lay the traces of the
ancient Egyptian civilisation, in the silent avenues of
mysterious sphinxes, amongst hieroglyphic-covered obelisks, Greek and Hebrew thought stood face to face. The
two civilisations embodied the principles of the Beautiful
and the Sublime, of Morality and Æstheticism, of religious and philosophic speculation. The result of this
meeting marks a glorious page in the annals of human
thought. Among the monuments of a great historic past,
the speculative spirit of the East made love to the plastic
beauty of the West, until, at last, they were united in
happy union. Hellenic taste and sense of beauty and
Semitic speculation not only evolved side by side in
Egypt but mixed and commingled; their thoughts were
intertwined and interwoven, giving rise to a new intellectual movement, a new philosophy of thought: the
Judæo-Hellenic. Alexandrian culture, during the reign
of the Ptolemies, is the offspring of a mixed marriage
between two parents belonging to two widely different

races, and, as a cross breed, is endowed with many qualities. It had the seriousness of the one parent and the delicacy of the other.

The Ptolemies encouraged the movement towards fusion. The result was that the Jews in Egypt, not being hampered by reactionary endeavours from the side of conservative parties, and with an adaptability peculiar to their race, soon acquired the language of the people in whose midst they dwelt. They conversed and wrote in Greek; they moulded and shaped their own thoughts into Greek form; they clothed the Semitic mode of thinking in Hellenic garb. The immediate result was the translation of the Pentateuch into Greek. Vanity, of which no individual or race is free, had embellished this literary production, which has acquired a high degree of importance alike among Jews and Christians, with many legends. This translation, known as the Septuaginta (LXX), was followed by independent histories relating to Biblical events. One of the best known authors is the chronographer Demetrius, who lived in the second half of the third century, and whose work Flavius Josephus is supposed to have utilised. Not to speak of the Greek authors in Judæa and Syria, we may mention Artapanos, who, following the fashion of the day, wrote history in the form of a romance, and showed traces of an apologetic character. He endeavoured to attribute all that was great in Egyptian civilisation to Moses. This was due to the fact that Manetho, the Egyptian historian, and others following his example, had spread fables and venomous tales about the ancient sojourn and exodus of the

Hebrews and their leader. To counterbalance these accusations, fables had to be interwoven into history, and history became romance. Moses was thus identified with Hermes, and made out to be the father of Egyptian wisdom. But, if the close acquaintanceship of Hebraism and Hellenism began with a mere flirtation, encouraged by the rulers of the land and kept up by the Jews, who wished to gain the favour of the conquering race and to show themselves and their history in as favourable a light as possible, it soon ended in a serious attachment. The Hebrews made themselves acquainted with Hellenic life and thought. They studied Homer and Hesiod, Empedocles and Parmenides, Plato and Aristotle, and they were startled by the discovery that in Greek thought there were many elements, moral and religious, familiar to them: this enhanced the attraction. The narrowness and exclusiveness to which strict nationality always gives rise, engendering contempt and hatred for everything foreign—which made even the Greeks, with all their intellectual culture, draw a line of demarcation between Greek and barbarian—gave way to a spirit of cosmopolitan breadth of view which has only very rarely been equalled in history. Hellenic and Hebrew forms of thought were brought into friendly union, and gave birth to ideas and aspirations of which humanity may always be proud. Greek æsthetic judgment and Semitic mysticism, different phases of thought in themselves, were welded into one. The religious conceptions of Moses and the Prophets were expressed in the language of the philosophical schools; an attempt was made to bring into harmony the dogmas of supernatural revelation and the fruits of human speculative thought. Such an attempt is a great undertaking, for, if sincerely and relentlessly pursued, it must end in breaking down the barriers of separation, in the establishment of a common truth, and in the sacrifice of cherished ideals and convictions which prove to be wrong. If carried to its logical conclusion, such a cosmopolitan broad-mindedness, such a cross-fertilisation of intellectual products, must give rise to the ennobling idea that there is only one truth, and that the external forms are only fleeting waves upon the vast ocean of human ideals. The attempt was made in Alexandria by the Judæo-Hellenic philosophers. Unfortunately, however, the Hebrews, with all their adaptability, have not yet carried this attempt to its logical conclusion. The spirit of reaction has ever and anon been ready to crush in its infancy the endeavour of truth and sincerity, of broad-mindedness and tolerance. When placed before the question to be or not to be, to be logical or illogical, it has chosen the latter, and striven after the impossible: the reconciliation of what cannot be reconciled without alterations, rejections, and selections. The happy marriage of Hellenism and Hebraism in Egypt had a tragic end. The union was dissolved, not, however, without having produced its issue: the Alexandrian culture, which was carried to Rome by Philo Judæus, and thus influenced later European thought and humanity at large.

ALEXANDRIA.

CHAPTER I

EGYPT CONQUERED BY THE GREEKS

Alexander the Great. — Cleomenes. — B. C. 332-323

THE way for the Grecian conquest of Egypt had been preparing for many years. Ever since the memorable march of Xenophon, who led, in the face of unknown difficulties, ten thousand Greeks across Asia Minor, the Greek statesman had suspected that the Hellenic soldier was capable of undreamed possibilities.

When the young Alexander, succeeding his father Philip on the throne of Macedonia, got himself appointed general by the chief of the Greek states, and marched against Darius Codomanus, King of Persia, at the head of the allied armies, it was not difficult to foresee the result. The Greeks had learned the weakness of the Persians by having been so often hired to fight for them. For a century past, every Persian army had had a body of ten or twenty thousand Greeks in the van, and without this guard the Persians were like a flock of sheep without the shepherd's dog. Those countries which had trusted to Greek mercenaries to defend them could hardly help falling when the Greek states united for their conquest.

Alexander defeated the Persians under Darius in a great and memorable battle near the town of Issus at the foot of the Taurus, at the pass which divides Syria from Asia Minor, and then, instead of marching upon Persia, he turned aside to the easier conquest of Egypt. On his way there he spent seven months in the siege of the wealthy city of Tyre, and he there punished with death every man capable of carrying arms, and made slaves of the rest. He was then stopped for some time before the little town of Gaza, where Batis, the brave governor, had the courage to close the gates against the Greek army. His angry fretfulness at being checked by so small a force was only equalled by his cruelty when he had overcome it; he tied Batis by the heels to his chariot, and dragged him round the walls of the city, as Achilles had dragged the body of Hector.

On the seventh day after leaving Gaza he reached Pelusium, the most easterly town in Egypt, after a march of one hundred and seventy miles along the coast of the Mediterranean, through a parched, glaring desert which forms the natural boundary of the country; while the fleet kept close to the shore to carry the stores for the army, as no fresh water is to be met with on the line of march. The Egyptians did not even try to hide their joy at his approach; they were bending very unwillingly under the heavy and hated yoke of Persia. The Persians had long been looked upon as their natural enemies, and in the pride of their success had added insults to the other evils of being governed by the satrap of a conqueror. They had not even gained the respect of the conquered by their warlike courage, for Egypt had in a great part been conquered and held by Greek mercenaries.

The Persian forces had been mostly withdrawn from the country by Sabaces, the satrap of Egypt, to be led against Alexander in Asia Minor, and had formed part of the army of Darius when he was beaten near the town of Issus on the coast of Cilicia. The garrisons were not strong enough to guard the towns left in their charge; the Greek fleet easily overpowered the Egyptian fleet in the harbour of Pelusium, and the town opened its gates to Alexander. Here he left a garrison, and, ordering his fleet to meet him at Memphis, he marched along the river's bank to Heliopolis. All the towns, on his approach, opened their gates to him. Mazakes, who had been left without an army, as satrap of Egypt, when Sabaces led the troops into Asia Minor, and who had heard of the

death of Sabaces, and that Alexander was master of Phœnicia, Syria, and the north of Arabia, had no choice but
to yield. The Macedonian army crossed the Nile near
Heliopolis, and then entered Memphis.

Memphis had long been the chief city of all Egypt,
even when not the seat of government. In earlier ages,
when the warlike virtues of the Thebans had made Egypt
the greatest kingdom in the world, Memphis and the low-
land corn-fields of the Delta paid tribute to Thebes; but,
with the improvements in navigation, the cities on the
coast rose in importance; the navigation of the Red Sea,
though always dangerous, became less dreaded, and
Thebes lost the toll on the carrying trade of the Nile.
Wealth alone, however, would not have given the sovereignty to Lower Egypt, had not the Greek mercenaries
been at hand to fight for those who would pay them. The
kings of Saïs had guarded their thrones with Greek
shields; and it was on the rash but praiseworthy attempt
of Amasis to lessen the power of these mercenaries that
they joined Cambyses, and Egypt became a Persian province. In the struggles of the Egyptians to throw off the
Persian yoke, we see little more than the Athenians and
Spartans carrying on their old quarrels on the coasts and
plains of the Delta; and the Athenians, who counted
their losses by ships, not by men, said that in their victories and defeats together Egypt had cost them two
hundred triremes. Hence, when Alexander, by his successes in Greece, had put a stop to the feuds at home,
the mercenaries of both parties flocked to his conquering
standard, and he found himself on the throne of Upper

TRANSPORTING GRAIN ON THE NILE.

and Lower Egypt without any struggle being made against him by the Egyptians. The Greek part of the population, who had been living in Egypt as foreigners, now found themselves masters. Egypt became at once a Greek kingdom, as though the blood and language of the people were changed at the conqueror's bidding.

Alexander's character as a triumphant general gains little from this easy conquest of an unwarlike country, and the overthrow of a crumbling monarchy. But as the founder of a new Macedonian state, and for reuniting the scattered elements of society in Lower Egypt after the Persian conquest, in the only form in which a government could be made to stand, he deserves to be placed

among the least mischievous of conquerors. We trace his march, not by the ruin, misery, and anarchy which usually follow in the rear of an army, but by the building of new cities, the more certain administration of justice, the revival of trade, and the growth of learning. On reaching Memphis, his first care was to prove to the Egyptians that he was come to re-establish their ancient monarchy. He went in state to the temple of Apis,

PHTAH, THE GOD OF MEMPHIS. and sacrificed to the sacred bull, as the native kings had done at their coronations; and gained the good-will of the crowd by games and music, performed by skilful Greeks for their amusement.

But though the temple of Phtah at Memphis, in which the state ceremonies were performed, had risen in beauty and importance by the repeated additions of the later kings, who had fixed the seat of government in Lower Egypt, yet the Sun, or Amon-Ra, or Kneph-Ra, the god of Thebes, or Jupiter-Ammon, as he was called by the Greeks, was the god under whose spreading wings Egypt had seen its proudest days. Every Egyptian king had called himself " the son of the Sun; " those who had reigned at Thebes had boasted that they were " beloved by Amon-Ra; " and when Alexander ordered the ancient titles to be used towards himself, he wished to lay his offerings in the temple of this god, and to be acknowledged by the priests as his son. As a reader of Homer, and the pupil of Aristotle, he must have wished to see the wonders of " Egyptian Thebes," the proper place for this ceremony; and it could only have been because, as a general, he had not time for a march of five hundred miles, that he chose the nearer and less known temple of Kneph-Ra, in the oasis of Ammon, one hundred and eighty miles from the coast.

Accordingly, he floated down the river from Memphis to the sea, taking with him the light-armed troops and the royal band of knights-companions. When he reached Canopus, he sailed westward along the coast, and landed at Rhacotis, a small village on the spot where Alexandria now stands. Here he made no stay; but, as he passed through it, he must have seen at a glance, for he was never there a second time, that the place was formed by nature to be a great harbour, and that with a little help from art it would be the port of all Egypt. The mouths of the Nile were too shallow for the ever increasing size of the merchant vessels which were then being built; and the engineers found the deeper water which was wanted, between the village of Rhacotis and the little island of Pharos. It was all that he had seen and admired at Tyre, but it was on a larger scale and with deeper water. It was the very spot that he was in search of; in every way suitable for the Greek colony which he proposed to found as the best means of keeping Egypt in obedience. Even before the time of Homer, the island of Pharos had given shelter to the Greek traders on that coast. He gave his orders to Dinocrates the architect to improve the harbour, and to lay down the plan of his new city; and the success of the undertaking proved the wisdom both of the statesman and of the builder, for the city of Alexandria subsequently became the most famous of all the commercial and intellectual centres of antiquity.

From Rhacotis Alexander marched along the coast to Parætonium, a distance of about two hundred miles through the desert; and there, or on his way there, he was met by the ambassadors from Cyrene, who were sent with gifts to beg for peace, and to ask him to honour their city with a visit. Alexander graciously received the gifts of the Cyrenæans, and promised them his friendship, but could not spare time to visit their city; and, without stopping, he turned southward to the oasis.

At Memphis Alexander received the ambassadors that came from Greece to wish him joy of his success; he reviewed his troops, and gave out his plans for the government of the kingdom. He threw bridges of boats over the Nile at the ford below Memphis, and also over the several branches of the river. He divided the country into two nomarchies or judgeships, and to fill these two offices of nomarchs or chief judges, the highest civil offices in the kingdom, he chose Doloaspis and Petisis, two Egyptians. Their duty was to watch over the due administration of justice, one in Upper and the other in Lower Egypt, and perhaps to hear appeals from the lower judges.

He left the garrisons in the command of his own Greek generals; Pantaleon commanded the counts, or knights-companions, who garrisoned Memphis, and Polemon was governor of Pelusium. These were the chief fortresses in the kingdom: Memphis overlooked the Delta, the navigation of the river, and the pass to Upper Egypt; Pelusium was the harbour for the ships of war, and the frontier town on the only side on which Egypt could be attacked. The other cities were given to other governors; Licidas commanded the mercenaries, Peucestes and Balacrus the other troops, Eugnostus was secretary, while Æschylus and Ephippus were left as overlookers, or perhaps, in the language of modern governments, as civil commissioners. Apollonius was made prefect of Libya, of which district Parætonium was the capital, and Cleomenes prefect of Arabia at Heroopolis, in guard of that frontier. Orders were given to all these generals that justice was to be administered by the Egyptian nomarchs according to the common law or ancient customs of the land. Petisis, however, either never entered upon his office or soon quitted it, and Doloaspis was left nomarch of all Egypt.

Alexander sent into the Thebaid a body of seven thousand Samaritans, whose quarrels with the Jews made them wish to leave their own country. He gave them lands to cultivate on the banks of the Nile which had gone out of cultivation with the gradual decline of Upper Egypt; and he employed them to guard the province against invasion or rebellion. He did not stay in Egypt longer than was necessary to give these orders, but hastened towards the Euphrates to meet Darius. In his absence Egypt remained quiet and happy. Peucestes soon followed him to Babylon with some of the troops that had been left in Egypt; and Cleomenes, the governor of Heroopolis, was then made collector of the taxes and prefect of Egypt. Cleomenes was a bad man; he disobeyed the orders sent from Alexander on the Indus, and he seems to have forgotten the mild feelings which guided his master; yet, upon the whole, after the galling yoke of the Persians, the Egyptians must have felt grateful for the blessings of justice and good government.

At one time, when passing through the Thebaid in his barge on the Nile, Cleomenes was wrecked, and one of his children bitten by a crocodile. On this plea, he called together the priests, probably of Crocodilopolis, where this animal was held sacred, and told them that he intended to revenge himself upon the crocodiles by having them all caught and killed; and he was only bought off from carrying his threat into execution by the priests giving him all the treasure that they could get

together. Alexander had left orders that the great
market should be moved from Canopus to his new city
of Alexandria, as soon as it should be ready to receive
it. As the building went forward, the priests and rich
traders of Canopus, in alarm at losing the advantages
of their port, gave Cleomenes a large sum of money for
leave to keep their market open. This sum he took, and,
when the building at Alexandria was finished, he again
came to Canopus, and because the traders would not or
could not raise a second and larger sum, he carried Alexander's orders into execution, and closed the market of
their city.

But instances such as these, of a public officer making
use of dishonest means to increase the amount of the
revenue which it was his duty to collect, might unfortunately be found even in countries which were for the
most part enjoying the blessings of wise laws and good
government; and it is not probable that, while Alexander
was with the army in Persia, the acts of fraud and wrong
should have been fewer in, his own kingdom of Macedonia. The dishonesty of Cleomenes was indeed equally
shown toward the Macedonians, by his wish to cheat
the troops out of part of their pay. The pay of the soldiers was due on the first day of each month, but on that
day he took care to be out of the way, and the soldiers
were paid a few days later; and by doing the same on
each following month, he at length changed the pay-day
to the last day of the month, and cheated the army out
of a whole month's pay.

Another act for which Cleomenes was blamed was not

so certainly wrong. One summer, when the harvest had been less plentiful than usual, he forbade the export of grain, which was a large part of the trade of Egypt, thereby lowering the price to the poor so far as they could afford to purchase such costly food, but injuring the landowners. On this, the heads of the provinces sent to him in alarm, to say that they should not be able to get in the usual amount of tribute; he therefore allowed

LIGHTHOUSE AT ALEXANDRIA.

the export as usual, but raised the duty; and he was reproached for receiving a larger revenue while the land-owners were suffering from a smaller crop.

At Ecbatana, the capital of Media, Alexander lost his friend Hephæstion, and in grief for his death he sent to Egypt to enquire of the oracle at the temple of Kneph in the oasis of Ammon, what honours he might pay to the deceased. The messengers brought him an answer, that he might declare Hephæstion a demigod, and order that he should be worshipped. Accordingly, Alexander then sent an express command to Cleomenes that he should build a temple to his lost favourite in his new city of Alexandria, and that the lighthouse which was to be built on the island of Pharos should be named after him; and as modern insurances against risks by sea usually begin with the words " In the name of God; Amen; " so all contracts between merchants in the port of Alexandria were to be written solemnly " In the name of Hephæstion." Feeling diffident of enforcing obedience at the mouth of the Nile, while he was himself writing from the sources of the Indus, he added that if, when he came to Egypt he found his wish carried into effect, he would pardon Cleomenes for those acts of misgovernment of which he had been accused, and for any others which might then come to his ears.

A somatophylax in the Macedonian army was no doubt at first, as the word means, one of the officers who had to answer for the king's safety; perhaps in modern language a colonel in the body-guards or household troops; but as, in unmixed monarchies, the faithful officer who was nearest the king's person, to whose watchfulness he trusted in the hour of danger, often found himself the adviser in matters of state, so, in the time of Alexander, the title of somatophylax was given to those generals on whose wisdom the king chiefly leaned, and by whose advice he was usually guided. Among these, and foremost in Alexander's love and esteem, was Ptolemy, the son of Lagus. Philip, the father of Alexander, had given Arsinoë, one of his relations, in marriage to Lagus; and her eldest son Ptolemy, born soon after the marriage, was always thought to be the king's son, though never so acknowledged. As he grew up, he was put into the highest offices by Philip, without raising in the young Alexander's mind the distrust which might have been felt if Ptolemy could have boasted that he was the elder brother. He earned the good opinion of Alexander by his military successes in Asia, and gained his gratitude by saving his life when he was in danger among the Oxydracæ, near the river Indus; and moreover, Alexander looked up to him as the historian whose literary powers and knowledge of military tactics were to hand down to the wonder of future ages those conquests which he witnessed.

Alexander's victories over Darius, and march to the river Indus, are no part of this history: it is enough to say that he died at Babylon eight years after he had entered Egypt; and his half-brother Philip Arridæus, a weak-minded, unambitious young man, was declared by the generals assembled at Babylon to be his successor. His royal blood united more voices in the army in his favour than the warlike and statesmanlike character of any one of the rival generals. They were forced to be content with sharing the provinces between them as his lieutenants; some hoping to govern by their power over the weak mind of Arridæus, and others secretly meaning to make themselves independent.

In this weighty matter, Ptolemy showed the wisdom and judgment which had already gained him his high character. Though his military rank and skill were equal to those of any one of Alexander's generals, and his claim by birth perhaps equal to that of Arridæus, he was not one of those who aimed at the throne; nor did he even aim at the second place, but left to Perdiccas the regency, with the care of the king's person, in whose name that ambitious general vainly hoped to govern the whole of Alexander's conquests. But Ptolemy, more wisely measuring his strength with the several tasks, chose the province of Egypt, the province which, cut off as it was from the rest by sea and desert, was of all others the easiest to be held as an independent kingdom against the power of Perdiccas. When Egypt was given to Ptolemy by the council of generals, Cleomenes was at the same time and by the same power made second in command, and he governed Egypt for one year before Ptolemy's arrival, that being in name the first year of the reign of Philip Arridæus, or, according to the chronologer's mode of dating, the first year after Alexander's death.

CHAPTER II

EGYPT UNDER PTOLEMY SOTER

Ptolemy governs Egypt, overcomes Perdiccas, and founds a dynasty.

PTOLEMY LAGUS was one of those who, at the death of Alexander, had raised their voices against giving the whole of the conquered countries to one king; he wished that they should have been shared equally among the generals as independent kingdoms. In this he was overruled, and he accepted his government as the lieutenant of the youthful Philip Arridæus, though no doubt with the fixed purpose of making Egypt an independent kingdom. On reaching Memphis, the seat of his government, his whole thoughts were turned towards strengthening himself against Perdiccas, who hoped to be obeyed, in the name of his young and weak-minded king, by all his fellow generals.

The Greek and foreign mercenaries of which the
army of Alexander was made up, and who were faithful
to his memory and to his family, had little to guide them
in the choice of which leader they should follow to his
distant province, beside the thought of where they should
be best treated; and Ptolemy's high character for wisdom, generosity, and warlike skill had gained many
friends for him among the officers; they saw that the
wealth of Egypt would put it in his power to reward
those whose services were valuable to him; and hence
crowds flocked to his standard. On reaching their provinces, the Greek soldiers, whether Spartans or Athenians,
forgetting the glories of Thermopylæ and Marathon, and
proud of their wider conquests under the late king,
always called themselves Macedonians. They pleased
themselves with the thought that the whole of the conquered countries were still governed by the brother of
Alexander; and no one of his generals, in his wildest
thoughts of ambition, whether aiming, like Ptolemy, at
founding a kingdom, or, like Perdiccas, at the government of the world, was unwise enough to throw off the
title of lieutenant to Philip Arridæus, and to forfeit the
love of the Macedonian soldiers and his surest hold on
their loyalty.

The first act of Ptolemy was to put to death Cleomenes, who had been made sub-governor of Egypt by the
same council of generals which had made Ptolemy governor. This act may have been called for by the dishonesty and crooked dealing which Cleomenes had been
guilty of in collecting taxes; but, though the whole tenor

of Ptolemy's life would seem to disprove the charge, we cannot but fear that he was in part led to this deed because he looked upon Cleomenes as the friend of Perdiccas, or because he could not trust him in his plans for making himself king of Egypt.

From the very commencement of his government, Ptolemy prepared for the war which he knew must follow a declaration of his designs. Perhaps better than any other general of Alexander, he knew how to win the favour of the people under his rule. The condition of the country quickly improved under his mild administration. The growing seaport of Alexandria was a good market for a country rich in natural produce, and, above all, Egypt's marvellously good geographical position stood her in good stead in time of war. Surrounded nearly on all sides by desert land, the few inhabitants, roving Bedouins, offered no danger. The land of the Nile was accessible to an enemy in one direction only, along the coast of Syria. This even teemed with difficulties. Transports there could only be managed with the greatest ingenuity, and, in case of defeat, retreat was almost impossible. On the other hand, the Egyptian army, helped by all the advantages of a land irrigated on the canal system, and which could be flooded at will, had only to act on the defensive to be certain of victory. The country is perhaps more open to an attack from the sea, but, by a moderately well-conducted defensive movement, the enemy could be kept to the coast. Even the landing there is scarcely possible, on account of the natural difficulties at the mouth of the Nile. The one easy

spot—Alexandria—was so well fortified that an invader
had but little chance of success.

About the time of Alexander's death (and to some
extent brought about by this event), civil war broke out
in Cyrenaica, in consequence of which the followers of
one party were forced out of the town of Cyrene. These
joined themselves with the exiles of the town of Barca,
and together sought help of foreigners. They placed
themselves under the leadership of the Spartan Thibron,
formerly Alexander's chancellor of the exchequer.
Begged by the exiled Cyrenians to help them, he now
directed his forces against Libya, fought a fierce battle,
and took possession of the harbour of Apollonia, two
miles distant from the town. He then besieged the town
of Cyrene, and forced the Cyrenians at last to sue for
peace. They were obliged to make a payment of five
hundred talents and to take back the exiles. Messengers
were sent by Thibron to incite the other towns in Cyrenaica to join him and to help him conquer their
neighbour, Libya. Thibron's followers were allowed to
plunder, and this led to quarrels, desertions, treacherous
acts, and the recruiting of his army from the Peloponne-
sus. After varying fortunes of war, in the spring of 322
B. C., some of the Cyrenians fled to Egypt, and related
to Ptolemy what had occurred in Cyrenaica, begging
him to help them back to their homes. The suggestion
was welcome to him, for victory would be easy over these
struggling factions. He sent a strong military and naval
force, under Ophelas, the Macedonian, to Cyrenaica in
the summer. When these were seen approaching, those

exiles who had found refuge with Thibron decided to join them. Their plan, however, was discovered, and they were put to death. The leader of the rabble in Cyrene (fearful for his own safety, now that the exiles who had fled to Egypt were returning) made overtures of peace to Thibron, and joined with him to repulse Ophelas. The latter worked with the utmost caution,

THE DÔM PALM.

sent an army under Epicides of Olynth against Tancheira, whilst he himself marched against Cyrene. He met Thibron in a fierce fight. The latter was completely defeated and fled towards Tancheira, where he hoped to find help, but instead fell into Epicides' hands. Thibron was given over to the people of Tancheira for punishment. He was cruelly scourged, and then dragged to Apollonia, where he was crucified. Ophelas, however, was not able to conquer the Cyrenians until Ptolemy himself arrived with fresh troops, overpowered the town and joined the province to his own satrapy.

The conquest of this Greek province was a gain equally for himself and for the Greeks. He put an end to the horrible anarchy that prevailed there, and proved himself their saviour as well as their conqueror. His name was now an honoured one among all the Greeks. When it was rumoured that war was likely to break out between Ptolemy and the royal party, the Macedonians flocked to Alexandria, " every man ready to give all and to sacrifice himself in order to help his friend." A popular belief of the day was that, although Ptolemy was known as the son of Lagos, he was in reality the son of Philip, and indeed much in his manner resembled the great founder of the Macedonian power. Amongst the successors of Alexander, not one understood as well as he how to retain and increase the power which he had won. He recognised, also, from the first, the tendency of the age: the tendency to split up the kingdom into different states; and he had made this the basis of his policy. It was under him that the first state (in the new sense of the word) was founded. He was the leader of the new movement that soon generated disunity, and to this end he made a secret contract with Antipatros against the regent Perdiccas. About this time also misunderstandings between the regent and the rulers in the West began to take a serious aspect.

At a great meeting in Babylon in the summer of the year 323, it was decided that the body of Alexander was to be taken with great solemnity to the Temple of

Amon, and that the equipping and guidance of the funeral procession should be entrusted to Arridæus. At the end of the year 323, the necessary preparations were finished. The gigantic funeral car that was to carry the kingly bier had been decorated with unparalleled magnificence. Without waiting for orders from the regent, Arridæus started with the funeral procession from Babylon. Crowds from far and near filled the streets, some curious to see the magnificent sight, others eager to show this last token of respect to the dead king. It was firmly believed amongst the Macedonians that the country in which Alexander's body had its last resting-place would become happy and powerful above all countries. This prophecy was uttered by the old seer Telmissus soon after the king's death. Did Ptolemy have this belief, or did he wish to make use of it? There were probably other reasons which had caused him to enter into an understanding with Arridæus, and to arrange with him that he was to start without orders from the regent. He was afraid that Perdiccas, in order to add to the solemnity of the procession, would himself accompany the body with the imperial army to Egypt. Ptolemy felt that his position in the lands entrusted to his care would be greatly weakened if a higher authority than himself could appear there with a military force. Arridæus led the funeral train to Damascus, as had been arranged before with Ptolemy. It was in vain that Polemon (one of Perdiccas' generals), who was in the neighbourhood, went to meet him. He was able to obtain no respect for the express order of the regent. The

funeral procession passed Damascus on its way to Egypt.
Ptolemy accompanied the body with his army as far as
Syria. It was then taken on to Memphis to rest there
until it could be sheltered by that beautiful sepulchre
of the kings at Alexandria.

Arridæus' action, in starting without permission,
and the defiance of Polemon's order, were acts of open
revolt against the higher authority of the kingdom.
Perdiccas called all loyal followers to the council of
war. Ptolemy, he said, had defied the order of the kings
in his behaviour concerning the funeral procession; and
he had also given shelter to the exiled satraps of Phrygia.
He was prepared for war, which he hoped to bring about.
It was for them (the loyal ones) to uphold the dignity
of the kingdom. They must try to take him unawares,
and to overcome them individually. The question was,
if the Egyptians or the Macedonians ought to be first
attacked. In the end, plans were carefully concerted
for an attack on Egypt and the protection of Europe.
In the early spring of B. c. 321, Perdiccas and his col-
leagues set out for Egypt with the imperial army, ordering the fleet to follow, and leaving Eumenes with
skilled officers and troops in general command of Asia
Minor for the purpose of guarding the Hellespont.

At the Egyptian frontier, Perdiccas summoned the
army together, that the men themselves should give
judgment in the case of the satrap of Egypt, in the same
way as in the preceding autumn they had given judgment in the case of Antigones. He expected a decision
which would enable him to finish what he had already

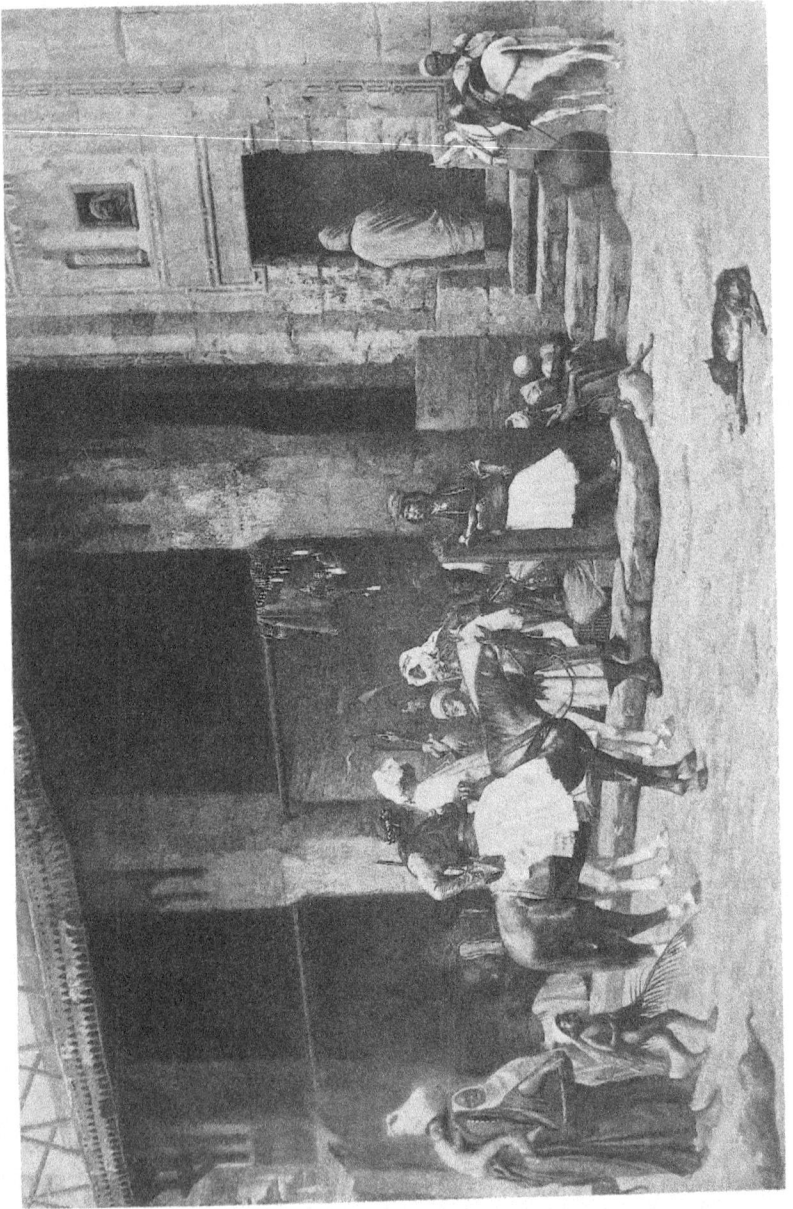

begun. The accusations were that he had refused obedience to the kings, that he had fought against and overcome the Greeks of Cyrenaica (who had received freedom from Alexander), and that he had taken possession
of the king's body, and carried it to Memphis.

According to the single account, which tells us of
these proceedings, Ptolemy himself appeared to conduct
his own defence before the assembled warriors. He had
good reason for reckoning on the impression his confi-
dence in them would make upon them, and on the love
that he knew the Macedonians bore towards him. He
knew, too, of the increasing dislike of the imperial
regent. His defence was heard with growing approval,
and the army's judgment was "freedom."

In spite of this the regent kept to the war. The
decision of the troops alienated him still more from
them. The war with Egypt was contrary to their wishes,
and they murmured openly. Perdiccas sought to put
down the refractory spirit with a stern military hand,
but the remonstrances of his officers were in vain. He
treated the first in the land in an inconsiderate and
despotic manner, removed the most deserving from their
command, and trusted himself alone. This same man,
who had climbed the path to greatness with so much
foresight, self-command, energy, and statesmanship,
seemed now, the nearer he grew to the summit of his
ambition, to lose all clearness of sight and moderation,
which traits alone could help him to take this last and
dangerous step. He had the advantage of tried troops,
the elephants of Alexander, and the fleet under the

command of his brother-in-law was near the mouth of the Nile; but he had overstepped the mark.

Just at this time, the news reached him from Asia Minor that Eumenes had conquered Neoptolemas, the governor of Armenia, who had taken the side of Ptolemy. With all the more hope, Perdiccas went to meet the enemy. He reached Pelusium undisturbed. It was highly necessary that the army should cross to the Pelusaic side of the Nile, for there were several secure places there, which, if allowed to remain in the hands of the enemy, would endan-

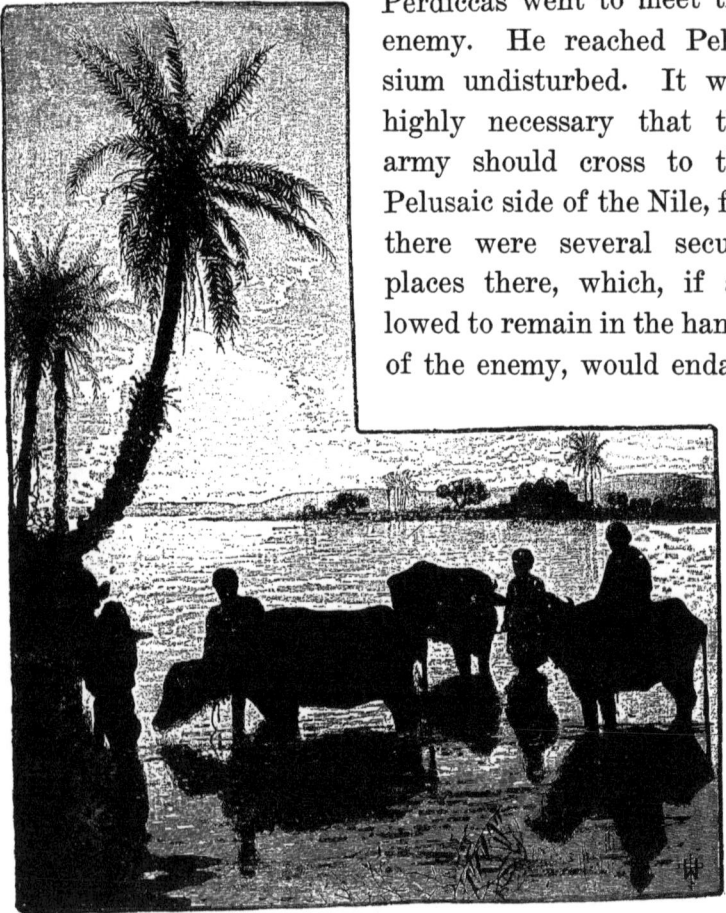

ger the forward movement. There were also plentiful supplies of provisions within the Delta, whilst the way through the so-called Arabia was sparsely inhabited.

If he did not find the Egyptians there, Perdiccas would install himself within one of the fortresses on that side, and thence conduct operations against them, and, at the same time, remain in connection with his fleet, on which he could fall back in case of need. To enable the crossing to be accomplished as easily as possible, Perdiccas ordered the cleaning out of an old and filled-in canal, that led up from the Nile. The work was evidently begun without much thought, for the fact had not been considered that, at the rising of the Nile, the canal would want a much deeper bed than the present stream required. The canal had only just been opened up, when the water rose with unusual force and rapidity; the dam was completely destroyed, and many workers lost their lives. During the disturbance, many officers and men left the camp and hurried to Ptolemy. This was the beginning of the Egyptian war. The desertion of so many important men made Perdiccas think seriously. He summoned the officers of the army, spoke to them with much condescension, gave presents to some, honoured others with promotion, and begged them, for the sake of their honour and for the cause of their kings, to fight their hardest against this rebel, and with the order to hold their men in readiness, he left them. The army was only told in the evening, at the signal for starting, where they were to march. Perdiccas feared, on account of the desertion that was taking place in his army, that his march might be discovered by the enemy. They marched with great speed through the night, and camped at last on the side of the river. At daybreak, after the troops had rested, Perdiccas gave the order to cross. First came the elephants, then the light infantry, next the storming party with ladders, and lastly, the pick of the cavalry, who, if the enemy should burst out during the storming, could easily drive them back. Perdiccas hoped, if he could only get a firm footing on that side of the river, to annihilate the Egyptian army easily with his superior force. He was right in feeling that his Macedonian troops, when face to face with the enemy, would forget their antipathy to him, and think only of their military honour. When about half the army had crossed, and just as the elephants were moving towards the fortress, the enemy were seen hurrying thither with great speed; their trumpet-calls and war-cries even were heard. They reached the fort before the Macedonians, and withdrew into the shelter of its walls. Not discouraged by this, the infantry stormed the fort. Ladders were placed against the walls, the elephants driven forward, and palisades taken from their backs to attack the ramparts.

Ptolemy, in the dress of a Macedonian soldier, stood on the wall surrounded by a few selected men. He was first in the fight. From where he stood he pierced with his lance the eyes of the leading elephant, and stabbed the Indian on its back, and he wounded many and killed numbers of the storming party. His officers and men fought with the greatest spirit; the driver of the second elephant was killed and the infantry were driven back.

ENVIRONS OF LUXOR

Perdiccas led new troops to the attack, wishing to take the fortress at all costs. By word and deed, Ptolemy urged on his men, who fought with marvellous endurance. The dreadful battle waged the whole day; many were killed and wounded; evening came on and nothing was decided. Perdiccas ordered a retreat and returned to his camp.

In the middle of the night he again started with his army, hoping that Ptolemy would stay in the fort with his troops, and that, after a trying march of some miles up-stream, he (Perdiccas) would be able to cross the river more easily. At daybreak he found himself opposite one of the many islands of the Nile; it was large enough for the camp of a great army. In spite of the difficulties of crossing, he decided to encamp his army there. The water reached up to the soldiers' knees, and it was with the greatest difficulty that they kept their footing against the force of the current. In order to break this current, Perdiccas ordered the elephants into the river to stand up-stream to the left of the fording party; he ordered the horsemen to stand at the other end to help those across that were driven down by the current. Some had, with great difficulty, managed to get across; others were still in the stream when it was noticed that the water was becoming deeper; the heavily armed men sank, and the elephants and horses stood deeper and deeper in the water. A fearful panic seized the army. They called out that the enemy had closed in the canals up-stream, and that the gods had destined bad weather in the upper provinces, on account of which

the river was swollen. Those who understood saw that
the bed of the river had become deepened by the crossing of so great a cavalcade. It was impossible for the
remainder to cross or for those on the island to return.
They were completely cut off and were at the mercy of
the enemy, who were already seen approaching. There
was nothing left but to order them to get back as well
as they could; lucky indeed were those who could swim,
and had sufficient strength to bring them across the

CROCODILES BASKING IN THE SUN.

broad expanse of water. Many saved themselves in this
way. They came without weapons, worn out and desperate, to the shore; others were drowned or eaten by
crocodiles. Some were carried down-stream, and reached
the shore where the enemy stood. Two thousand men
were missing, many officers among them. The camp of
the Egyptians was situated on the other side, and they
could be seen helping the men in the water and burning
logs of wood to show honour to the dead. On this side
of the river there was sad silence; each man sought his
comrade, or officer, and sought in vain. Food was scarce,

and there was no means of overcoming this dreadful state of affairs; night came on, and curses and complaints were heard on all sides. The lives of so many brave men had been sacrificed for nothing; it was bad enough to lose the " honour of their arms," but now, through the stupidity of their leader, their lives had been lost, and to be swallowed by crocodiles was now the distinguished death of Macedonian warriors. Many of the officers went to the tent of the regent, and told him openly that he was the cause of this calamity. Outside the tent the Macedonians yelled, beside themselves with rage. About a hundred of the officers, headed by the satrap Python, refused to share further responsibility, resigned their commissions, and left the tent. The excitement grew intense. The troops, in ungovernable rage, entered the regent's tent and threw themselves upon him. Antigonus struck the first blow, others followed, and, after a desperate but short struggle, Perdiccas fell to the ground covered with wounds.

Thus died Perdiccas, in the third year of his regency. His great idea, the unity of the kingdom entrusted to his care, should have made him worthy of more success had he given himself up to this idea with more conscientiousness. Unfortunately, with growing power, he became despotic and unjust. He was not great enough to become the successor of Alexander, to be another " ruler of the world." This last step, the one which was to lead him to his long-coveted goal, led him instead to his death.

Ptolemy soon heard the news, and the next morning he crossed the river and came to the camp. He asked

to be taken to the kings, presented them and some of
the nobles with gifts; was kind and considerate to all,
and was greeted with great joy. Then he called the
troops together and spoke to them. He told the Macedonians that it was only stern necessity that caused him
to take up arms against his old comrades. No man regretted more than he the untimely death of so many
heroes. Perdiccas was the cause of this calamity; he
had but received his just punishment. Now all enmity
was to be ended. He had saved as many as he could from
death in the water, and the corpses which the river had
brought to the shore he had buried with all honour; and
finally he told them that he had given orders for the
immediate alleviation of the want which he knew was
being felt in the camp. His speech was received with
loud cheers. He stood there unhurt and admired before
the Macedonians, who but a few hours earlier had been
his bitterest foes. Now they looked upon him as their
saviour; they all acknowledged him as the conqueror,
and for the moment he stood in unequivocal possession
of that power for which Perdiccas had worked so hard,
and which he had so much abused. Who was now to be
Perdiccas' successor, and to manage the kingdom in the
name of the kings? With one voice the people begged
Ptolemy to undertake this task. The foresight and
presence of mind of the son of Lagus were not clouded
by the allurement of such an offer gained by his sudden
change of fortune. At this supreme moment he acted
with consummate sagacity. He divined that a refusal
of the proffered honour would make him in reality more

powerful, although, at the moment, he would seem to be acting in an unselfish manner. He recommended to the army, as a favour which he had to bestow, those he thought worthy of his thanks; they were Python, the Median strategist, who had taken the first decisive step against Perdiccas; and Arridæus, who, in spite of Perdiccas' orders, had taken the body of the king to Egypt. These two were nominated regents with loud cheers.

The Macedonian army, accordingly, chose Python and Arridæus as guardians, and as rulers with unlimited power over the whole of Alexander's conquests; but, though none of the Greek generals who now held Asia Minor, Syria, Babylonia, Thrace, or Egypt dared to acknowledge it to the soldiers, yet in reality the power of the guardians was limited to the little kingdom of Macedonia. With the death of Perdiccas, and the withdrawal of his army, Phœnicia and Cœle-Syria were left unguarded, and almost without a master. In order that Egypt might take an important part in the universal policy, Ptolemy felt he must possess Syria, which would open up the way for him to the countries along the Euphrates and the Tigris, and also the island of Cyprus, where he would be near the coast of Asia Minor. He could not yet think of conquering Cyprus, which had an important fleet. He felt that, if he annexed Syria, either by diplomacy or by force, the organisation of the kingdom and the territorial division of power would be changed in a tangible manner. The Egyptian satraps already possessed some measure of authority, and he could also depend upon the satrap of Syria joining him.

Perdiccas had bestowed this satrapy upon Laomedon, the Amphysolite, who had taken no part in the great fight between Perdiccas and Ptolemy. Ptolemy now informed him that he wished to possess his satrapy, but was ready to compensate him with a sum of money. Laomedon refused this offer with scorn. Thereupon, an army under Nicanor, one of the " friends " of Ptolemy, marched into Palestine. Jerusalem was the only place that held out against the Egyptian army; but Nicanor, says the historian Agatharcides, seeing that on every seventh day the garrison withdrew from the walls, chose that day for the assault, and thus gained the city. Without further opposition the Egyptians marched onwards. At last he met Laomedon, took him prisoner, and brought him back to Egypt. Egyptian sentries now guarded the strongholds of the country; Egyptian ships took the towns along the coast. A great number of the Jews were transported to Alexandria; they received the rights of citizenship there. Without altering local conditions, Syria gradually came under the sway of the Egyptian satraps. Laomedon found means of escaping from Egypt; he fled to Alcetas in Caria, who had just withdrawn himself to the mountainous regions of Pisida, thence to begin the decisive war against Antigonus.

In the earlier times of Egyptian history, when navigation was less easy, and when seas separated kingdoms instead of joining them, the Thebaid enjoyed, under the Koptic kings, the trading wealth which followed the stream of its great river, the longest piece of inland navigation then known; but, with the improvement in

G. Richter
Theben

navigation and ship-building, countries began to feel their strength in the timber of their forests and the number of their harbours; and, as timber and sea-coast were equally unknown in the Thebaid, that country fell as Lower Egypt rose; the wealth which before centred in Thebes was then found in the ports of the Delta, where the barges of the Nile met the ships of the Mediterranean. What used to be Egypt was an inland kingdom, bounded by the desert; but Egypt under Ptolemy was a country on the sea-coast; and, on the conquest of Phœnicia and Cœle-Syria, he was master of the forests of Lebanon and Antilibanus, and stretched his coast from Cyrene to Antioch, a distance of twelve hundred miles.

The wise and mild plans which were laid down by Alexander for the government of Egypt when a province were easily followed by Ptolemy when it became his own kingdom. The Greek soldiers lived in their garrisons or in Alexandria under the Macedonian laws, while the Egyptian laws were administered by their own priests, who were upheld in all the rights of their order and in their freedom from land-tax. The temples of Phtah, of Amon-Ra, and the other gods of the country were not only kept open, but were repaired and even built at the cost of the king; the religion of the people, and not that of their rulers, was made the established religion of the state. On the death of the god Apis, the sacred bull of Memphis, the chief of the animals which were kept and fed at the cost of the several cities, and who had died of old age soon after Ptolemy came to Egypt, he spent the sum of fifty talents, or $42,500, on its funeral; and the priests, who had not forgotten that Cambyses, their former conqueror, had wounded the Apis of his day with his own sword, must have been highly pleased with this mark of his care for them. The burial-place for the bulls is an arched gallery tunnelled into the hill behind Memphis for more than two thousand feet, with a row of cells on each side of it. In every cell is a huge granite sarcophagus, within which were placed the remains of a bull that had once been the Apis of its day, which, after having for perhaps twenty years received the honours of a god, was there buried with more than kingly state. The cell was then walled up, and ornamented on the outside with various tablets in honour of the deceased animal, which were placed in these dark passages by the piety of his worshippers. The priests of Thebes were now at liberty to cut out from their monuments the names of usurping gods, and to restore those that had been before cut out. They also rebuilt the inner room, or the holy of holies, in the great temple of Karnak.

TOMBS OF THE SACRED BULLS.

It had been overthrown by the Persians in wantonness, or in hatred of the Egyptian religion; and the priests now put upon it the name of Philip Arridæus, for whom Ptolemy was nominally governing Egypt.

The Egyptians, who during the last two centuries had sometimes seen their temples plundered and their trade crushed by the grasping tyranny of the Persian satraps, and had at other times

been almost as much hurt by their own vain struggles
for freedom, now found themselves in the quiet enjoyment of good laws, with a prosperity which promised
soon to equal that of the reigns of Necho or Amasis. It
is true that they had not regained their independence
and political liberty; that, as compared with the Greeks,
they felt themselves an inferior race, and that they only
enjoyed their civil rights during the pleasure of a Greek
autocrat; but then it is to be remembered that the native rulers with whom Ptolemy was compared were the
kings of Lower Egypt, who, like himself, were surrounded by Greek mercenaries, and who never rested
their power on the broad base of national pride and love
of country; and that nobody could have hoped to see a
Theban king arise to bring back the days of Thûtmosis
and Ramses. Thebes was every day sinking in wealth
and strength; and its race of hereditary soldiers, proud
in the recollection of former glory, who had, after centuries of struggles, been forced to receive laws from
Memphis, perhaps yielded obedience to a Greek conqueror with less pain than they did formerly to their
own vassals of Lower Egypt.

Ptolemy's government was in form nearly the same
in Alexandria as in the rest of Egypt, but in reality it
was wholly different. His sway over the Egyptians was
supported by Greek force, but over the Greeks it rested
on the broad base of public opinion. Every Greek had
the privilege of bearing arms, and of meeting in the
gymnasium in public assembly, to explain a grievance,
and petition for its redress. The citizens and the soldiers

were the same body of men; they at the same time held
the force, and had the spirit to use it. But they had no
senate, no body of nobles, no political constitution which
might save their freedom in after generations from the
ambitious grasp of the sovereign, or from their own
degeneracy. While claiming to be equal among themselves they were making themselves slaves; and though
at present the government so entirely bore the stamp of
their own will that they might fancy they enjoyed a
democracy, yet history teaches us that the simple pater-
nal form of government never fails to become sooner or
later a cruel tyranny. The building of Alexandria must
be held the master-stroke of policy by which Egypt was
kept in obedience. Here, and afterwards in a few other
cities, such as Ptolemais in the Thebaid and Parembole
in Nubia, the Greeks lived without insulting or troubling
the Egyptians, and by their numbers held the country
like so many troops in garrison. It was a wise policy
to make no greater change than necessary in the kingdom, and to leave the Egyptians under their own laws
and magistrates, and in the enjoyment of their own religion; and yet it was necessary to have the country
garrisoned with Greeks, whose presence in the old cities
could not but be extremely galling to the Egyptians.
This was done by means of these new Greek cities, where
the power by which Egypt was governed was stronger
by being united, and less hateful by being out of sight.
Seldom or never was so great a monarchy founded with
so little force and so little crime.

Ptolemy, however, did not attempt the difficult task

of uniting the two races, and of treating the conquered and the conquerors as entitled to the same privileges. From the time of Necho and Psammetichus, many of the Greeks who settled in Egypt intermarried with the natives, and very much laid aside their own habits; and sometimes their offspring, after a generation or two, became wholly Egyptian. By the Greek laws the children of these mixed marriages were declared to be barbarians; not Greeks but Egyptians, and were brought up accordingly. They left the worship of Jupiter and Juno for that of Isis and Osiris, and perhaps the more readily for the greater earnestness with which the Egyptian gods were worshipped. We now trace their descendants by the form of their skulls, even into the

THE GOD SERAPIS.

priestly families; and of one hundred mummies covered with hieroglyphics, taken up from the catacombs near Thebes, about twenty show a European origin, while of those from the tombs near Memphis, seventy out of every hundred have lost their Koptic peculiarities. It is easy to foresee that an important change would have been wrought in the character of the people and in their political institutions, if the Greek laws had been humane and wise enough to grant to the children of mixed marriages the privileges, the education, and thereby the moral feelings of the more favoured parent; and it is not too much to suppose, if the Greek law of marriage had been altered by Ptolemy, that within three centuries above half the nation would have spoken the Greek language, and boasted of its Greek origin.

The stimulus given by Ptolemy Soter to the culture of the age has been already mentioned. The founding of the famous museum and library of Alexandria may be, perhaps, regarded as the rounding-off of his political plans for the consolidation of his kingdom. Alexandria became, in fact, not only a centre of commerce and government, but also the intellectual capital of the Greeks. But for this supreme importance of the city, it is doubtful whether the descendants of Ptolemy Lagus could have continued to rule the Valley of the Nile.

In return for the literature which Greece then gave to Egypt, she gained the knowledge of papyrus, a tall rush which grows wild near the sources of the Nile, and was then cultivated in the Egyptian marshes. Before that time books had been written on linen, wax, bark, or the leaves of trees; and public records on stone, brass, or lead: but the knowledge of papyrus was felt by all men of letters like the invention of printing in modern Europe. Books were then known by many for the first time, and very little else was afterwards used in Greece or Rome; for, when parchment was made about two centuries later, it was too costly to be used as long as papyrus was within reach. Copies were multiplied on frail strips of this plant, and it was found that mere thoughts, when worth preserving, were less liable to be destroyed by time than temples and palaces of the hardest stone.

While Egypt, under Ptolemy, was thus enjoying the advantages of its insulated position, and cultivating the

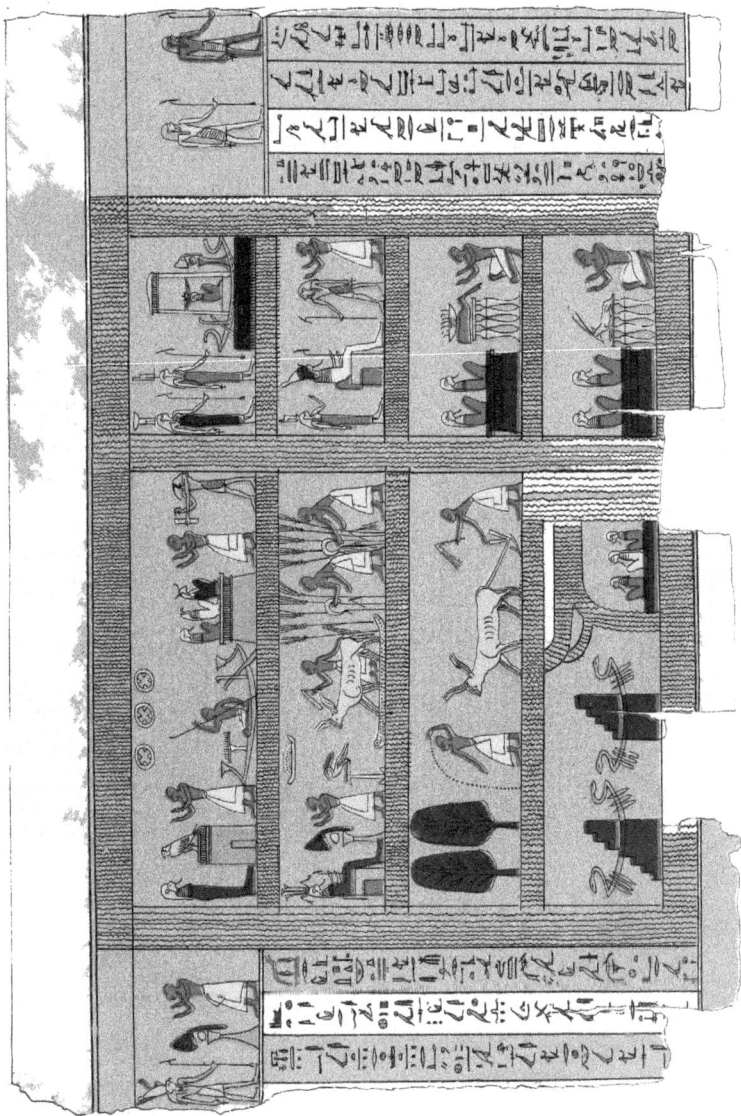

MANUSCRIPT ON PAPYRUS IN HIEROGLYPHICS, THEBES.

arts of peace, the other provinces were being harassed by the unceasing wars of Alexander's generals, who were aiming, like Ptolemy, at raising their own power. Many changes had taken place among them in the short space of eight years which had passed since the death of Alexander. Philip Arridæus, in whose name the provinces had been governed, had been put to death; Antigonus was master of Asia Minor, with a kingdom more powerful though not so easily guarded as Egypt; Cassander held Macedonia, and had the care of the young Alexander Ægus, who was then called the heir to the whole of his father's wide conquests, and whose life, like that of Arridæus, was soon to end with his minority; Lysimachus was trying to form a kingdom in Thrace; and Seleucus had for a brief period held Babylonia.

ALEXANDER ADORING HORUS.

Ptolemy bore no part in the wars which brought about these changes, beyond being once or twice called upon to send troops to guard his province of Cœle-Syria. But Antigonus, in his ambitious efforts to stretch his power over all the provinces, had by force or by treachery driven Seleucus out of Babylon, and forced him to seek Egypt for safety, where Ptolemy received him with the kindness and good policy which had before gained so many friends. No arguments of Seleucus were wanting to persuade Ptolemy that Antigonus was dreaming of universal conquest, and that his next attack would be upon Egypt. He therefore sent ambassadors to make treaties of alliance with Cassander and Lysimachus, who readily joined him against the common enemy.

The large fleet and army which Antigonus got together for the invasion of Egypt proved his opinion of the strength and skill of Ptolemy. All Syria, except one or two cities, laid down its arms before him on his approach. But he found that the whole of the fleet had been already removed to the ports of Egypt, and he ordered Phœnicia to furnish him with eight thousand ship-builders and carpenters, to build galleys from the forests of Lebanon and Antilibanus, and ordered Syria to send four hundred and fifty thousand medimni, or nearly three millions of bushels of wheat, for the use of his army within the year. By these means he raised his fleet to two hundred and forty-three long galleys or ships of war.

Ptolemy was for a short time called off from the war in Syria by a rising in Cyrene. The Cyrenians, who clung to their Doric love of freedom, and were latterly smarting at its loss, had taken arms and were besieging the Egyptian, or, as they would have called themselves, the Macedonian garrison, who had shut themselves up in the citadel. He at first sent messengers to order the Cyrenians to return to their duty; but his orders were not listened to; the rebels no doubt thought themselves safe, as his armies seemed more wanted on the eastern frontier; his messengers were put to death, and the siege of the citadel pushed forward with all possible speed. On this he sent a large land force, followed by a fleet, in order to crush the revolt at a single blow; and the ringleaders were brought to Alexandria in chains. Magas, a son of Queen Berenicê and stepson of Ptolemy, was then made governor of Cyrene.

When this trouble at home was put an end to, Ptolemy crossed over to Cyprus to punish the kings of the little states on that island for having joined Antigonus. For now that the fate of empires was to be settled by naval battles the friendship of Cyprus became very important to the neighbouring states. The large and safe harbours gave to this island a great value in the naval warfare between Egypt, Phœnicia, and Asia Minor. Alexander had given it as his opinion that the command of the sea went with the island of Cyprus. When he held Asia Minor he called Cyprus the key to Egypt; and with still greater reason might Ptolemy, looking from Egypt, think that island the key to Phœnicia. Accordingly he landed there with so large a force that he met with no resistance. He added Cyprus to the rest of his dominions: he banished the kings, and made Nicocreon governor of the whole island.

From Cyprus, Ptolemy landed with his army in Upper Syria, as the northern part of that country was called, while the part nearer to Palestine was called Cœle-Syria. Here he took the towns of Posideion and Potami-Caron, and then marching hastily into Asia Minor he took Mallus, a city of Cilicia. Having rewarded his soldiers with the booty there seized, he again embarked and returned to Alexandria. This inroad seems to have been meant to draw off the enemy from Cœle-Syria; and it had the wished-for effect, for Demetrius, who commanded the forces of his father Antigonus in that quarter, marched northward to the relief of Cilicia, but he did not arrive there till Ptolemy's fleet was already under sail for its return journey to Egypt.

Ptolemy, on reaching Alexandria, set his army in motion towards Pelusium, on its way to Palestine. His forces were eighteen thousand foot and four thousand horse, part Macedonians, as the Greeks living in Egypt were always called, and part mercenaries, followed by a crowd of Egyptians, of whom some were armed for battle, and some were to take care of the baggage. He had twenty-two thousand Greeks, and was met at Gaza by the young Demetrius with an army of eleven thousand foot and twenty-three hundred horse, followed by forty-three elephants and a body of light-armed barbarians, who, like the Egyptians in the army of Ptolemy, were not counted. But the youthful courage of Demetrius was no match for the cool skill and larger army of Ptolemy; the elephants were easily stopped by iron hurdles, and the Egyptian army, after gaining a complete victory, entered Gaza, while Demetrius fled to Azotus. Ptolemy, in his victory, showed a generosity unknown in modern warfare; he not only gave leave to the conquered army to bury their dead, but sent back the whole of the royal baggage which had fallen into his hands, and also those personal friends of Demetrius who were found among the prisoners; that is to say, all those who wished to depart, as the larger part of these Greek armies were equally ready to fight on cither side.

By this victory the whole of Phœnicia was again joined to Egypt, and Seleucus regained Babylonia. There, by following the example of Ptolemy in his good treatment of the people, and in leaving them their own laws and religion, he founded a monarchy, and gave his name to a race of kings which rivalled even the Lagidæ. He raised up again for a short time the throne of Nebuchadnezzar. But it was only for a short time. The Chaldees and Assyrians now yielded the first rank to the Greeks who had settled among them; and the Greeks were more numerous in the Syrian portion of his empire. Accordingly Seleucus built a new capital on the river Orontes, and named it Antioch after his father. Babylon then yielded the same obedience to this new Greek city that Memphis paid to Alexandria. Assyria and Babylonia became subject provinces; and the successors of Seleucus, who came to be known as Selucids, styled themselves not kings of Babylon but of Syria.

When Antigonus, who was in Phrygia on the other side of his kingdom, heard that his son Demetrius had been beaten at Gaza, he marched with all his forces to give battle to Ptolemy. He soon crossed Mount Taurus, the lofty range which divides Asia Minor from Syria and Mesopotamia, and joined his camp to that of his son in Upper Syria. But Ptolemy had gone through life without ever making a hazardous move; not indeed without ever suffering a loss, but without ever fighting a battle when its loss would have ruined him, and he did not choose to risk his kingdom against the far larger forces of Antigonus. Therefore, with the advice of his council of generals, he levelled the fortifications of Acre, Joppa, Samaria, and Gaza, and withdrew his forces and treasure into Egypt, leaving the desert between himself and the army of Antigonus.

Antigonus could not safely attempt to march through the desert in the face of Ptolemy's army. He had, therefore, first, either to conquer or gain the friendship of the Nabatæans, a warlike race of Arabs, who held the north of Arabia; and then he might march by Petra, Mount Sinai, and the coast of the Red Sea, without being in want of water for his army. The Nabatæans were the tribe at an earlier time called Edomites. But they lost that name when they carried it to the southern portion of Judæa, then called Idumæa; for when the Jews regained Idumæa, they called these Edomites of the desert Nebaoth or Nabatæans. The Nabatæans professed neutrality between Antigonus and Ptolemy, the two contending powers; but the mild temper of Ptolemy had so far gained their friendship that the haughty Antigonus, though he did not refuse their pledges of peace, secretly made up his mind to conquer them.

Petra, the city of the Nabatæans, is in a narrow valley between steep overhanging rocks, so difficult of approach that a handful of men could guard it against the largest army. Not more than two horsemen can ride abreast through the chasm in the rock by which it is entered from the east, while the other entrance from the west is down a hillside too steep for a loaded camel. The Eastern proverb reminds us that " Water is the chief thing; " and a large stream within the valley, in addition

ON THE COAST OF THE RED SEA.

to the strength of the fortress, made it a favourite resting-place for caravans, which, whether they were coming from Tyre or Jerusalem, were forced to pass by this
city in their way to the Incense Country of Arabia Felix,
or to the Elanitic Gulf of the Red Sea, and for other caravans from Egypt to Dedam on the Persian Gulf. These
warlike Arabs seem to have received a toll from the
caravans, and they held their rocky fastness uncon-
quered by the great nations which surrounded them.
Their temples and tombs were cut out of the live rock,
and hence the city was by the Jews named Selah, (the
rock), and by the Greeks named Petra, from which last
the country was sometimes called Arabia Petræa.

Antigonus heard that the Nabatæans had left Petra
less guarded than usual, and had gone to a neighbouring fair, probably to meet a caravan from the south, and
to receive spices in exchange for the woollen goods from
Tyre. He therefore sent forward four thousand light-
armed foot and six hundred horse, who overpowered the
guard and seized the city. The Arabs, when they heard
of what had happened, returned in the night, surrounded
the place, came upon the Greeks from above, by paths
known only to themselves, and overcame them with such
slaughter that, out of the four thousand six hundred
men, only fifty returned to Antigonus to tell the tale.

The Nabatæans then sent to Antigonus to complain
of this crafty attack being made upon Petra after they
had received from him a promise of friendship. He
endeavoured to put them off their guard by disowning
the acts of his general; he sent them home with

promises of peace, but at the same time sent forward his son Demetrius, with four thousand horse and four thousand foot, to take revenge upon them, and again seize their city. But the Arabs were this time upon their guard; the nature of the place was as unfavourable to the Greek arms and warfare as it was favourable to the Arabs; and these eight thousand men, the flower of the army, under brave Demetrius, were unable to force their way through the narrow pass into this remarkable city.

Had Antigonus been master of the sea, he might perhaps have marched through the desert along the coast of the Mediterranean to Pelusium, with his fleet to wait upon his army, as Perdiccas had done. But without this, the only way that he could enter Egypt was through the neighbourhood of Petra, and then along the same path which the Jews are supposed to have followed; and the stop thus put upon the invasion of Egypt by this little city shows us the strength of Ptolemy's eastern frontier. Antigonus then led his army northward, leaving the kingdom of Egypt unattacked.

This retreat was followed by a treaty of peace between these generals, by which it was agreed that each should keep the country that he then held; that Cassander should govern Macedonia until Alexander Ægus, the son of Alexander the Great, should be of age; that Lysimachus should keep Thrace, Ptolemy Egypt, and Antigonus Asia Minor and Palestine; and each wishing to be looked upon as the friend of the soldiers by whom his power was upheld, and the whole of these wide conquests kept in awe, added the very unnecessary article, that the Greeks living in each of these countries should be governed according to their own laws.

All the provinces held by these generals became more or less Greek kingdoms, yet in no one did so many Greeks settle as in Lower Egypt. Though the rest of Egypt was governed by Egyptian laws and judges, the city of Alexandria was under Macedonian law. It did not form part of the nome of Hermopolites in which it was built. It scarcely formed a part of Egypt, but was a Greek state in its neighbourhood, holding the Egyptians in a state of slavery. In that city no Egyptian could live without feeling himself of a conquered race. He was not admitted to the privileges of Macedonian citizenship, while they were at once granted to every Greek, and soon to every Jew, who would settle there.

By the treaty just spoken of, Ptolemy, in the thirteenth year after the death of Alexander, was left undisputed master of Egypt. During these years he had not only gained the love of the Egyptians and Alexandrians by his wise and just government, but had won their respect as a general by the skill with which he had kept the war at a distance. He had lost and won battles in Syria, in Asia Minor, in the island of Cyprus, and at sea; but since Perdiccas marched against him, before he had a force to defend himself with, no foreign army had drunk the sacred waters of the Nile.

It was under the government of Ptolemy that the wonders of Upper Egypt were first seen by any Greeks who had leisure, a love of knowledge, and enough of literature, to examine carefully and to describe what they saw. Loose and highly coloured accounts of the wealth of Thebes had reached Greece even before the time of Homer, and again through Herodotus and other travellers in the Delta; but nothing was certainly known of it till it was visited by Hecatæus of Abdera, who, among other works, wrote a history of the Hyperborean or northern nations, and also a history, or rather a description of Egypt, part of which we now read in the pages of Diodorus Siculus. When he travelled in Upper Egypt, Thebes, though still a populous city, was more thought of by the antiquary than by the statesman. Its wealth, however, was still great; and when, under the just government of Ptolemy, it was no longer necessary for the priests to hide their treasures, it was found that the temples still held the very large sum of three hundred talents of gold, and two thousand three hundred talents of silver, or above five million dollars, which had escaped the plundering hands of the Persian satraps. Many of the Theban tombs, which are sets of rooms tunnelled into the hills on the Libyan side of the Nile, had even then been opened to gratify the curiosity of the learned or the greediness of the conqueror. Forty-seven royal tombs were mentioned in the records of the priests, of which the entrances had been covered up with earth, and hidden in the sloping sides of the hills, in the hope that they might remain undisturbed and unplundered, and might keep safe the embalmed bodies of the kings till they should rise again at the end of the world; and seventeen of these had already been found out and broken open. Hecatæus was told that the other tombs

FACADE OF THE PALACE OF DARIUS, PERSEPOLIS.

had been before destroyed; and we owe it, perhaps, to this mistake that they remained unopened for more than two thousand years longer, to reward the searches of modern travellers, and to unfold to us the history of their builders.

The Memnonium, the great palace of Ramses II., was then standing; and though it had been plundered by the Persians, the building itself was unhurt. Its massive walls had scarcely felt the wear of the centuries which had rolled over them. Hecatæus measured its rooms, its courtyards, and its avenue of sphinxes; and by his measurements we can now distinguish its ruins from those of the other palaces of Thebes. One of its rooms, perhaps after the days of its builder, had been fitted up as a library, and held the histories and records of the priests; but the golden zodiac, or circle, on which were engraved the days of the year, with the celestial bodies seen to rise at sunrise and set at sunset, by which each day was known, had been taken away by Cambyses. Hecatæus also saw the three other palace-temples of Thebes, which we now call by the names of the villages in which they stand, namely, of Luxor, of Karnak, and of Medinet-Habu. But the Greeks, in their accounts of Egypt, have sadly puzzled us by their careless alteration of names from similarity of sound. To Miamun Ramses, they gave the common Greek name Memnon; and the city of Hahiroth they called Heroopolis, as if it meant the *city of heroes*. The capital of Upper Egypt, which was called The City, as a capital is often called, or in Koptic, *Tape* or *Thabou*, they named Thebes, and in their mythology they confounded it with Thebes in Bœotia. The city of the god Kneph they called Canopus, and said it was so named after the pilot of Menelaus. The hill of Toorah opposite Memphis they called the Trojan mountain. One of the oldest cities in Egypt, This, or with the prefix for city, Abouthis, they called Abydos, and then said that it was colonised by Milesians from Abydos in Asia. In the same careless way have the Greeks given us an account of the Egyptian gods. They thought them the same as their own, though with new faces; and, instead of describing their qualities, they have in the main contented themselves with translating their names.

If Ptolemy did not make his government as much feared by the half-armed Ethiopians as it was by the well-disciplined Europeans, it must have been because the Thebans wished to guard their own frontier rather than because his troops were always wanted against a more powerful enemy; but the inroads of the Ethiopians were so far from being checked that the country to the south of Thebes was unsafe for travellers, and no Greek was able to reach Syênê and the lower cataracts during his reign. The trade through Ethiopia was wholly stopped, and the caravans went from Thebes to Cosseir to meet the ships which brought the goods of Arabia and India from the opposite coast of the Red Sea.

In the wars between Egypt and Asia Minor, in which Palestine had the misfortune to be the prize struggled for and the debatable land on which the battles were fought, the Jews were often made to smart under the stern pride of Antigonus, and to rejoice at the milder temper of Ptolemy. The Egyptians of the Delta and the Jews had always been friends; and hence, when Ptolemy promised to treat the Jews with the same kindness as the Greeks, and more than the Egyptians, and held out all the rights of Macedonian citizenship to those who would settle in his rising city of Alexandria, he was followed by crowds of industrious traders, manufacturers, and men of letters. They chose to live in Egypt in peace and wealth, rather than to stay in Palestine in the daily fear of having their houses sacked and burnt at every fresh quarrel between Ptolemy and Antigonus. In Alexandria, a suburb by the sea, on the east side of the city, was allotted for their use, which was afterwards included within the fortifications, and thus made a fifth ward of the Lagid metropolis.

No sooner was the peace agreed upon between the four generals, who were the most powerful kings in the known world, than Cassander, who held Macedonia, put to death both the Queen Roxana and her son, the young Alexander Ægus, then thirteen years old, in whose name these generals had each governed his kingdom with unlimited sway, and who was then of an age that the soldiers, the givers of all power, were already planning to make him the real King of Macedonia and of his father's wide conquests.

The Macedonian phalanx, which formed the pride and sinews of every army, were equally held by their deep-rooted loyalty to the memory of Alexander, whether they were fighting for Ptolemy or for Antigonus, and equally thought that they were guarding a province for his heir;

and it was through fear of loosening their hold upon the
faithfulness of these their best troops that Ptolemy and
his rivals alike chose to govern their kingdoms under the
unpretending title of lieutenants of the King of Macedonia. Hence, upon the death of Alexander Ægus, there
was a throne, or at least a state prison, left empty for
a new claimant. Polysperchon, an old general of Alexander's army, then thought that he saw a way to turn
Cassander out of Macedonia, by the help of Hercules,
the natural son of Alexander by Barce; and, having proclaimed him king, he led him with a strong army against
Cassander. But Polysperchon wanted either courage or
means for what he had undertaken, and he soon yielded
to the bribes of Cassander and put Hercules to death.

The cities on the southern coast of Asia Minor yielded
to Antigonus obedience as slight as the ties which held
them to one another. The cities of Pamphylia and Cilicia,
in their habits as in their situation, were nearer the Syrians, and famous for their shipping. They all enjoyed
a full share of the trade and piracy of those seas, and were
a tempting prize to Ptolemy. The treaty of peace between the generals never lessened their jealousy nor
wholly stopped the warfare, and the next year Ptolemy,
finding that his troops could hardly keep their possessions in Cilicia, carried over an army in person to attack
the forces of Antigonus in Lycia. He landed at Phaselis,
the frontier town of Pamphylia, and, having carried that
by storm, he moved westward along the coast of Lycia.
He made himself master of Xanthus, the capital, which
was garrisoned by the troops of Antigonus; and then

of Caunus, a strong place on the coast of Caria, with two citadels, one of which he gained by force and the other by surrender. He then sailed to the island of Cos, which he gained by the treachery of Ptolemy, the nephew of Antigonus, who held it for his uncle, but who went over to the Egyptian king with all his forces. By this success he gained the whole southern coast of Asia Minor.

The brother and two children of Alexander having been in their turns, as we have seen, murdered by their guardians, Cleopatra, his sister, and Thessalonica, his niece, were alone left alive of the royal family of Macedonia. Almost every one of the generals had already courted a marriage with Cleopatra, which had either been refused by herself or hindered by his rivals; and lastly Ptolemy, now that by the death of her nephews she brought kingdoms, or the love of the Macedonian mercenaries, which was worth more than kingdoms, as her dower, sent to ask her hand in marriage. This offer was accepted by Cleopatra; but, on her journey from Sardis, the capital of Lydia, to Egypt, on her way to join her future husband, she was put to death by Antigonus. The niece was put to death a few years later. Thus every one who was of the family of Alexander paid the forfeit of life for that honour, and these two deaths ended the Macedonian dynasty with a double tragedy.

While Ptolemy was busy in helping the Greek cities of Asia to gain their liberty, Menelaus, his brother and admiral, was almost driven out of Cyprus by Demetrius. On this Ptolemy got together his fleet, to the number of one hundred and forty long galleys and two hundred transports, manned with not less than ten thousand men, and sailed with them to the help of his brother. This fleet, under the command of Menelaus, was met by Demetrius with the fleet of Antigonus, consisting of one hundred and twelve long galleys and a number of transports; and the Egyptian fleet, which had hitherto been master of the sea, was beaten near the city of Salamis in Cyprus by the smaller fleet of Demetrius. This was the heaviest loss that had ever befallen Ptolemy. Eighty long galleys were sunk, and forty long galleys, with one hundred transports and eight thousand men, were taken prisoners. He could no longer hope to keep Cyprus, and he sailed hastily back to Egypt, leaving to Demetrius the garrisons of the island as his prisoners, all of whom were enrolled in the army of Antigonus, to the number of sixteen thousand foot and six hundred horse.

This naval victory gave Demetrius the means of unburdening his proud mind of a debt of gratitude to his enemy; and accordingly, remembering what Ptolemy had done after the battle of Gaza, he sent back to Egypt, unasked for and unransomed, those prisoners who were of high rank, that is to say, all those who had any choice about which side they fought for; and among them were Leontiscus, the son, and Menelaus, the brother, of Ptolemy.

Antigonus was overjoyed with the news of his son's victory. By lessening the power of Ptolemy, it had done much to smooth his own path to the sovereignty of Alexander's empire, which was then left without an heir; and he immediately took the title of king, and gave the same

PALM AND SYCAMORE: AN EGYPTIAN CONTRAST.

title to his son Demetrius. In this he was followed by Ptolemy and the other generals, but with this difference, that while Antigonus called himself king of all the provinces, Ptolemy called himself King of Egypt; and while Antigonus gained Syria and Cyprus, Ptolemy gained the friendship of every other kingdom and of every free city in Greece; they all looked upon him as their best ally against Antigonus, the common enemy.

The next year Antigonus mustered his forces in Cœle-Syria, and got ready for a second attack upon Egypt. He had more than eighty thousand foot, accompanied with what was then the usual proportion of cavalry, namely, eight thousand horse and eighty-three elephants. Demetrius brought with him from Cyprus the fleet of one hundred and fifty long galleys, and one hundred transports laden with stores and engines of war. With this fleet, to which Ptolemy, after his late loss, had no ships that he could oppose, Antigonus had no need to ask leave of the Arabs of the little city of Petra to march through their passes; but he led his army straight through the desert to Pelusium, while the ships of burden kept close to the shore with the stores. The pride of Antigonus would not let him follow the advice of the sailors, and wait eight days till the north winds of the spring equinox had passed; and by this haste many of his ships were wrecked on the coast, while others were driven into the Nile and fell into the hands of Ptolemy. Antigonus himself, marching with the land forces, found all the strong places well guarded by the Egyptian army; and, being driven back at every point, discouraged by the loss of his ships and by seeing whole bodies of his troops go over to Ptolemy, he at last took the advice of his officers and led back his army to Syria, while Ptolemy returned to Alexandria, to employ those powers of mind in the works of peace which he had so successfully used in his various wars.

Antigonus then turned the weight of his mighty kingdom against the little island of Rhodes, which, though in sight of the coast of Asia Minor, held itself independent of him, and in close friendship with Ptolemy. The Dorian island of Rhodes had from the earliest dawn of history held a high place among the states of Greece; and in all the arts of civilised life, in painting, sculpture, letters, and commerce, it had been lately rising in rank while the other free states had been falling. Its maritime laws were so highly thought of that they were copied by most other states, and, being afterwards adopted into the Pandects of Justinian, they have in part become the law of modern Europe. It was the only state in which Greek liberty then kept its ground against the great empires of Alexander's successors.

Against this little state Demetrius led two hundred long galleys and one hundred and seventy transports, with more than forty thousand men. The Greek world looked on with deep interest while the veterans of Antigonus were again and again driven back from the walls of the blockaded city by its brave and virtuous citizens; who, while their houses were burning and their walls crumbling under the battering-ram, left the statues of Antigonus and Demetrius standing unhurt in the marketplace, saved by their love of art and the remembrance of former kindness, which, with a true greatness of mind, they would not let the cruelties of the siege outweigh. The galleys of Ptolemy, though unable to keep at sea against the larger fleet of Demetrius, often forced their way into the harbour with the welcome supplies of grain. Month after month every stratagem and machine which the ingenuity of Demetrius could invent were tried and failed; and, after the siege had lasted more than a year, he was glad to find an excuse for withdrawing his troops; and the Rhodians in their joy hailed Ptolemy with the title of Soter or *saviour*. This name he ever afterwards kept, though by the Greek writers he is more often called Ptolemy the son of Lagus. If we search the history of the world for a second instance of so small a state daring to withstand the armies of so mighty an empire, we shall perhaps not find any one more remarkable than that of the same island, when, seventeen hundred years afterwards, it again drew upon itself the eyes of the world, while it beat off the forces of the Ottoman empire under Mahomet II.; and, standing like a rock in front of Christendom, it rolled back for years the tide of war, till its walls were at last crumbled to a heap of ruins by Suleiman the Great, after a siege of many months.

The next of Ptolemy's conquests was Cœle-Syria; and soon after this the wars between these successors of Alexander were put an end to by the death of Antigonus, whose overtowering ambition was among the chief causes of quarrel. This happened at the great battle of Ipsus in Phrygia, where they all met, with more than eighty

thousand men in each army. Antigonus, King of Asia
Minor, was accompanied by his son Demetrius, and by
Pyrrhus, King of Epirus; and he was defeated by Ptolemy, King of Egypt, Seleucus, King of Babylon, Lysimachus, King of Thrace, and Cassander, King of Macedonia; and the old man lost his life fighting bravely.
After the battle Demetrius fled to Cyprus, and yielded
to the terms of peace which were imposed on him by
the four allied sovereigns. He sent his friend Pyrrhus
as a hostage to Alexandria; and there this young King
of Epirus soon gained the friendship of Ptolemy and
afterwards his stepdaughter in marriage. Ptolemy was
thus left master of the whole of the southern coast of
Asia Minor and Syria, indeed of the whole coast of the
eastern end of the Mediterranean, from the island of
Cos on the north to Cyrene on the south.

During these formidable wars with Antigonus, Ptolemy had never been troubled with any serious rising of
the conquered Egyptians; and perhaps the wars may
not have been without their use in strengthening his
throne. The first danger to a successful conqueror is
from the avarice and disappointment of his followers,
who usually claim the kingdom as their booty, and who
think themselves wronged and their past services forgotten if any limit is placed to their tyranny over the
conquered. But these foreign wars may have taught
the Alexandrians that Ptolemy was not strong enough
to ill-treat the Egyptians, and may thus have saved him
from the indiscretion of his friends and from their reproaches for ingratitude.

In the late war, the little Dorian island of Cos on the coast of Asia Minor fell, as we have seen, under the power of Ptolemy. This island was remarkable as being the first spot in Europe into which the manufacture of silk was introduced, which it probably gained when under the power of Persia before the overthrow of Darius. The luxury of the Egyptian ladies, who affected to be overheated by any clothing that could conceal their limbs, had long ago introduced a tight, thin dress which neither our climate nor notions of modesty would allow, and for this dress, silk, when it could be obtained, was much valued; and Pamphila of Cos had the glory of having woven webs so transparent that the Egyptian women were enabled to display their fair forms yet more openly by means of this clothing. Cos continued always in the power of the Ptolemies, who used it as a royal fortress, occasionally sending their treasures and their children there as to a place of safety from Alexandrian rebellion; and there the silk manufacture flourished in secret for two or three centuries. When it ceased is unknown, as it was part of the merchants' craft to endeavour to keep each branch of trade to themselves, by concealing the

ALEXANDRIAN LADY, ATTIRED
IN BOMBYX SILK.

channel through which they obtained their supply of
goods, and many of the dresses which were sold in Rome
under the emperors by the name of Coan robes may have
been brought from the East through Alexandria.

One of the most valuable gifts which Egypt owed to
Ptolemy was its coinage. Even Thebes, "where treasures were largest in the houses," never was able to pass
gold and silver from hand to hand without the trouble
of weighing, and the doubt as to the fineness of the metal.
The Greek merchants who crowded the markets of Canopus and Alexandria must have filled Lower Egypt with
the coins of the cities from whence they came, all unlike
one another in stamp and weight; but, while every little
city or even colony of Greece had its own coinage, Egypt
had as yet very few coins
of its own. We are even
doubtful whether we
know by sight those
coined by the Persians
In the early years of Ptol-
emy's government Ptolemy had issued a very few coins
bearing the names of the young kings in whose name
he held the country, but he seems not to have coined any
quantity of money till after he had himself taken the
title of king. His coins are of gold, silver, and bronze,
and are in a fine style of Greek workmanship. Those
of gold and silver bear on one side the portrait of the
king, without a beard, having the head bound with the
royal diadem, which, unlike the high priestly crown of
the native Egyptian kings, or the modern crown of gold

COIN OF PTOLEMY SOTER, B. C. 302.

and precious stones, is a plain riband tied in a bow behind. On the other side they have the name of Ptolemy Soter, or King Ptolemy, with an eagle standing upon a thunderbolt, which was only another way of drawing the eagle and sun, the hieroglyphical characters for the title Pharaoh. The gold coins of Egypt were probably made in Alexandria. The coins are not of the same weight as those of Greece; but Ptolemy followed the Egyptian standard of weight, which was that to which the Jewish shekel was adjusted, and which was in use

COIN OF SOTER, WITH JUPITER.

in the wealthy cities of Tyre and Sidon and Beryttus. The drachma weighs fifty-five grains, making the talent of silver worth about seven hundred and fifty dollars. Ptolemy's bronze coins have the head of Serapis or Jupiter in the place of that of the king, as is also the case with those of his successors; but few of these bronze pieces bear any marks from which we can learn the reign in which they were coined. They are of better metal than those of other countries, as the bronze is free from lead and has more tin in it. The historian, in his very agreeable labours, should never lose sight of the coins. They teach us by their workmanship the state of the

arts, and by their weight, number, and purity of metal,
the wealth of the country. They also teach dates, titles,
and the places where they were struck; and even in
those cases where they seem to add little to what we
learn from other sources, they are still the living witnesses to which we appeal, to prove the truth of the
authors who have told us more.

The art of engraving coins did not flourish alone in
Alexandria; painters and sculptors flocked to Egypt
to enjoy the favours of Ptolemy. Apelles, indeed, whose
paintings were thought by those who had seen them to
surpass any that had been before painted, or were likely
to be painted, had quarrelled with Ptolemy, who had
known him well when he was the friend and painter of
Alexander. Once when he was at Alexandria, somebody wickedly told him that he was invited to dine at
the royal table, and when Ptolemy asked who it was
that had sent his unwelcome guest, Apelles drew the
face of the mischief-maker on the wall, and he was
known to all the court by the likeness. It was, perhaps,
at one of these dinners, at which Ptolemy enjoyed the
society of the men of letters, or perhaps when visiting
the philosophers in their schools, that he asked Euclid
if he could not show him a shorter and easier way to
the higher truths of mathematics than that by which
he led the pupils in the Museum; and Euclid, as if to
remind him of the royal roads of Persia, which ran by
the side of the highroads, but were kept clear and free
for the king's own use, made him the well-known answer,
that there was no royal road to geometry.

Ptolemy lived in easy familiarity with the learned men of Alexandria; and at another of these literary dinners, when Diodorus, the rhetorician, who was thought to have been the inventor of the Dilemma, was puzzled by a question put to him by Stilpo, the king in joke said that his name should be Cronus, a god who had been laughed at in the comedies. Indeed, he was so teased by Ptolemy for not being able to answer it, that he got up and left the room. He afterwards wrote a book upon the subject; but the ridicule was said to have embittered the rest of his life. This was the person against whom Callimachus, some years later, wrote a bitter epigram, beginning " Cronus is a wise man." Diodorus was of the sceptical school of philosophy, which, though not far removed from the Cyrenaic school, was never popular in Alexandria. Among other paradoxes he used to deny the existence of motion. He argued that the motion was not in the place where the body moved from, nor in the place that the body moved to, and that accordingly it did not exist at all. Once he met with a violent fall which put his shoulder out of joint, and he applied to Herophilus, the surgeon, to set it. Herophilus began by asking him where the fall took place, whether in the place where the shoulder was, or in the place where it fell to; but the smarting philosopher begged him to begin by setting his limb, and they would talk about the existence of motion after the operation.

Stilpo was at this time only on a visit to Ptolemy, for he had refused his offer of money and a professorship in the Museum, and had chosen to remain at Megara where he was the ornament of his birthplace. He had been banished from Athens for speaking against their gods, and for saying that the colossal Minerva was not the daughter of Jupiter, but of Phidias, the sculptor. His name as a philosopher stood so high that when Demetrius, in his late wars with Ptolemy, took the city of Megara by storm, the conqueror " bid spare the house of Stilpo, when temple and tower went to the ground; " and when Demetrius gave orders that Stilpo should be repaid for what he had lost in the siege, the philosopher proudly answered that he had lost nothing, and that he had no wealth but his learning.

The historian Theopompus of Chios then came to Alexandria, and wrote an account of the wars between the Egyptians and the Persians. It is now lost, but it contained at least the events from the successful invasion by Artaxerxes Longimanus till the unsuccessful invasion by Artaxerxes Mnemon.

No men of learning in Alexandria were more famous than the physicians. Erasistratus of Cos had the credit of having once cured Antiochus, afterwards King of Syria. He was the grandson of Aristotle, and may be called the father of the science of anatomy: his writings are often quoted by Dioscorides. Antiochus in his youth had fallen deeply in love with his young stepmother, and was pining away in silence and despair. Erasistratus found out the cause of his illness, which was straightway cured by Seleucus giving up his wife to his own son. This act strongly points out the changed opinions of the world as to the matrimonial relation; for it was then thought the father's best title to the name of Nicator; he had before conquered his enemies, but he then conquered himself.

Erasistratus was the first who thought that a knowledge of anatomy should be made a part of the healing art. Before his time surgery and medicine had been deemed one and the same; they had both been studied by the slow and uncertain steps of experience, unguided by theory. Many a man who had been ill, whether through disease or wound, and had regained his health, thought it his duty to Esculapius and to his neighbours to write up in the temple of the god the nature of his ailings, and the simples to which he fancied that he owed his cure. By copying these loose but well-meant inscriptions of medical cases, Hippocrates had, a century earlier, laid the foundations of the science; but nothing further was added to it till Erasistratus, setting at nought the prejudices in which he was born, began dissecting the human body in the schools of Alexandria. There the mixing together of Greeks and Egyptians had weakened those religious feelings of respect for the dead which are usually shocked by anatomy; and this study flourished from the low tone of the morality as much as from the encouragement which good sense should grant to every search for knowledge.

Herophilus lived about the same time with Erasistratus, and was, like him, famous for his knowledge of the anatomy of man. But so hateful was this study in the eyes of many, that these anatomists were charged, by writers who ought to have known better, with the cruelty of cutting men open when alive. They had few followers in the hated use of the dissecting-knife. It was from their writings that Galen borrowed the anatomical parts of his work; and thus it was to the dissections of these two great men, helped indeed by opening the bodies of animals, that the world owed almost the whole of its knowledge of the anatomy of man, till the fifteenth century, when surgeons were again bold enough to face the outcry of the mob, and to study the human body with the knife.

Hegesias of Cyrene was an early lecturer on philosophy at Alexandria. His short and broken sentences are laughed at by Cicero, yet he was so much listened to, when lecturing against the fear of death, and showing that in quitting life we leave behind us more pains than pleasures, that he was stopped by Ptolemy Soter through fear of his causing self-murder among his hearers. He then wrote a book upon the same subject, for though the state watched over the public teaching, it took no notice of books; writing had not yet become the mightiest power on earth. The miseries, however, of this world, which he so eloquently and feelingly described in his lectures and writings, did not drive him to put an end to his own life.

Philostephanus of Cyrene, the friend of Callimachus, was a naturalist who wrote upon fishes, and is the first investigator that we hear of who thought it desirable to limit his studies to one branch of the science of natural history.

But Cyrene did not send all its great men to Alexandria. Plato had studied mathematics there under Theodorus, and it had a school of its own which gave its name to the Cyrenaic sect. The founder of this sect was Aristippus, the pupil of Socrates who had missed the high honour of being present at his death. He was the first philosopher who took money from his pupils, and used to say that they valued their lessons more for having to pay for them; but he was blamed by his brethren for thus lowering the dignity of the teacher. He died several years before Ptolemy Soter came into Egypt. The Cyrenaic sect thought happiness, not goodness, was the end to be aimed at through life, and selfishness, rather than kindness to others, the right spring of men's actions. It would hardly be fair to take their opinions from the mouths of their enemies; and the dialogues of Socrates, with their founder, as told to us by Xenophon, would prove a lower tone of morality than he is likely to have held. The wish for happiness and the philosophical love of self, which should lead to goodness, though a far worse rule of life than the love of goodness for its own sake, which is the groundwork of religion, was certainly far better than unguided passion and the love of to-day's pleasure. But often as this unsafe rule has been set up for our guidance, there have always been found many to make use of it in a way not meant by the teacher. The Cyrenaic sect soon fell into the disrepute to which these principles were likely to lead it, and wholly ceased when Epicurus taught the same opinions more philosophically.

Anniceris of Cyrene, though a follower of Aristippus, somewhat improved upon the low-toned philosophy of his master. He granted that there were many things worth our aim, which could not be brought within the narrow bounds of what is useful. He did not overlook friendship, kindness, honouring our parents, and serving our country; and he thought that a wise man would undertake many labours which would bring him no return in the things which were alone thought happiness.

The chair of philosophy at Cyrene was afterwards filled by Arete, the daughter of Aristippus; for such were the hindrances in the way of gaining knowledge, that few could be so well qualified to teach as the philosopher's daughter. Books were costly, and reading by no means a cheap amusement. She was followed, after her death, by her son Aristippus, who, having been brought up in his mother's lecture-room, was called, in order to distinguish him from his grandfather of the same name, Metrodidactus, or *mother-taught*. History has not told us whether he took the name himself in gratitude for the debt which he owed to this learned lady, or whether it was given him by his pupils; but in either case it was a sure way of giving to the mother the fame which was due to her for the education of her son; for no one could fail to ask who was the mother of Metrodidactus.

Theodorus, one of the pupils of Metrodidactus, though at one time banished from Cyrene, rose to honour under Soter, and was sent by him as ambassador to Lysimachus. He was called the Atheist by his enemies,

and the Divine by his friends, but we cannot now determine which title he best deserved. It was then usual
to call those atheists who questioned the existence of
the pagan gods; and we must not suppose that all who
suffered under that reproach denied that the world was
governed by a ruling providence. The disbeliever in
the false religion of the many is often the only real
believer in a God. Theodorus was of the cold school of
philosophy, which was chiefly followed in Alexandria.
It was earthly, lifeless, and unpoetical, arising from
the successful cultivation of the physical sciences, not
enough counteracted by the more ennobling pursuits of
poetry and the fine arts. Hence, while commerce and
the arts of production were carried to higher perfection
than at any former time, and science was made greatly
to assist in the supply of our bodily wants, the arts of
civilisation, though by no means neglected, were cultivated without any lofty aim, or any true knowledge
of their dignity.

Antiphilus, who was born in Egypt and had studied
painting under Ctesidemus, rose to high rank as a painter
in Alexandria. Among his best-known pictures were
the bearded Bacchus, the young Alexander, and Hip-
polytus, or rather his chariot-horses, frightened by the
bull. His boy, blowing up a fire with his mouth, was
much praised for the mouth of the boy, and for the light
and shade of the room. His Ptolemy hunting was also
highly thought of. Antiphilus showed a mean jealousy
of Apelles, and accused him of joining in a plot against
the king, for which the painter narrowly escaped

punishment; but Ptolemy, finding that the charge was
not true, sent Apelles a gift of one hundred talents
to make amends. The angry feelings of Apelles were
by no means cooled by this gift, but they boiled over
in his great picture of Calumny. On the right of the
picture sat Ptolemy, holding out his hand to Calumny,
who was coming up to him. On each side of the king
stood a woman who seemed meant for Ignorance and

THE CHARIOT OF ANTIPHILUS.

Suspicion. Calumny was a beautiful maiden, but with
angry and deep-rooted malice in her face: in her left
hand was a lighted torch, and with her right she was
dragging along by the hair a young man, who was
stretching forth his hands to heaven, and calling upon
the gods to bear witness that he was guiltless. Before
her walked Envy, a pale, hollow-eyed, diseased man,
perhaps a portrait of the accuser; and behind were two
women, Craft and Deceit, who were encouraging and
supporting her. At a distance stood Repentancë, in the

ragged, black garb of mourning, who was turning away her face for shame as Truth came up to her.

Ptolemy Soter was plain in his manners, and scarcely surpassed his own generals in the costliness of his way of life. He often dined and slept at the houses of his friends; and his own house had so little of the palace, that he borrowed dishes and tables of his friends when he asked any number of them to dine with him in return, saying that it was the part of a king to enrich others rather than to be rich himself. Before he took the title of king, he styled himself, and was styled by friendly states, by the simple name of Ptolemy the Macedonian; and during the whole of his reign he was as far from being overbearing in his behaviour as from being king-like in his dress and household. Once when he wished to laugh at a boasting antiquary, he asked him, what he knew could not be answered, who was the father of Peleus; and the other let his wit so far get the better of his prudence as in return to ask the king, who had perhaps never heard the name of his own grandfather, if he knew who was the father of Lagus. But Ptolemy took no further notice of this than to remark that if a king cannot bear rude answers he ought not to ask rude questions.

An answer which Ptolemy once made to a soothsayer might almost be taken as the proverb which had guided him through life. When his soldiers met with an anchor in one of their marches, and were disheartened on being told by the soothsayer that it was a proof that they ought to stop where they then were, the king restored their courage by remarking, that an anchor was an omen of safety, not of delay.

Ptolemy's first children were by Thais, the noted courtesan, but they were not thought legitimate. Leontiscus, the eldest, we afterwards hear of fighting bravely against Demetrius; of the second, named Lagus after his grandfather, we hear nothing.

He then married Eurydice, the daughter of Antipater, by whom he had several children. The eldest son, Ptolemy, was named Ceraunus, *the Thunderer*, and was banished by his father from Alexandria. In his distress he fled to Seleucus, by whom he was kindly received; but after the death of Ptolemy Soter he basely plotted against Seleucus and put him to death. He then defeated in battle Antigonus, the son of Demetrius, and got possession of Macedonia for a short time. He married his half-sister Arsinoë, and put her children to death; and was soon afterwards put to death himself by the Gauls, who were either fighting against him or were mercenaries in his own army. Another son of Ptolemy and Eurydice was put to death by Ptolemy Philadelphus, for plotting against his throne, to which, as the elder brother, he might have thought himself the best entitled. Their daughter Lysander married Agathocles, the son of Lysimachus; but when Agathocles was put to death by his father, she fled to Egypt with her children, and put herself under Ptolemy's care.

Ptolemy then, as we have seen, asked in marriage the hand of Cleopatra, the sister of Alexander; but on her death he married Berenicê, a lady who had come into

Egypt with Eurydice, and had formed part of her household. She was the widow of a man named Philip; and
she had by her first husband a son named Magas, whom
Ptolemy made governor of Cyrene, and a daughter, An-
tigone, whom Ptolemy gave in marriage to Pyrrhus _{when}
that young king was living in Alexandria as hostage
for Demetrius.

Berenicê's mildness and goodness of heart were useful in softening her husband's severity. Once, when
Ptolemy was unbending his mind at a game of dice with
her, one of his officers came up to his side, and began
to read over to him a list of
criminals who had been condemned to death, with their
crimes, and to ask his pleasure
on each. Ptolemy continued
playing, and gave very little
attention to the unhappy tale;
but Berenicê's feelings overcame the softness of her character, and she took the paper
out of the officer's hand, and
would not let him finish read-

BERENICÊ SOTER

ing it; saying it was very unbecoming in the king to
treat the matter so lightly, as if he thought no more
of the loss of a life than the loss of a throw.

With Berenicê Ptolemy spent the rest of his years
without anything to trouble the happiness of his family.
He saw their elder son, Ptolemy, whom we must call
by the name which he took late in life, Philadelphus,

grow up everything that he could wish him to be; and, moved alike by his love for the mother and by the good qualities of the son, he chose him as his successor on the throne, instead of his eldest son, Ptolemy Ceraunus, who had shown, by every act in his life, his unfitness for the royal position.

His daughter Arsinoë married Lysimachus in his old age, and urged him against his son, Agathocles, the husband of her own sister. She afterwards married her half-brother, Ptolemy Ceraunus; and lastly became the wife of her brother Philadelphus. Argæus, the youngest son of Ptolemy, was put to death by Philadelphus on a charge of treason. Of his youngest daughter Philotera we know nothing, except that her brother Philadelphus afterwards named a city on the coast of the Red Sea after her.

After the last battle with Demetrius, Ptolemy had regained the island of Cyprus and Cœle-Syria, including Judæa; and his throne became stronger as his life drew to an end. With a wisdom rare in kings and conquerors, he had never let his ambition pass his means; he never aimed at universal power; and he was led, both by his kind feelings and wise policy, to befriend all those states which, like his own, were threatened by that mad ambition in others.

His history of Alexander's wars is lost, and we therefore cannot judge of his merits as an author; but we may still point out with pleasure how much his people gained from his love of letters; though indeed we do not need the example of Ptolemy to show that learning

and philosophy are as much in place, and find as wide a
field of usefulness, in governing a kingdom as in the
employments of the teacher, the lawyer, or the physician,
who so often claim them as their own.

His last public act, in the thirty-eighth year of his
reign, was ordered by the same forbearance which had
governed every part of his life. Feeling the weight of
years press heavily upon him, that he was less able than
formerly to bear the duties of his office, and wishing to
see his son firmly seated on the throne, he laid aside his
diadem and his title, and, without consulting either the
army or the capital, proclaimed Ptolemy, his son by
Berenicê, king, and contented himself with the modest
rank of somatophylax, or satrap, to his successor. He
had used his power so justly that he was not afraid to
lay it down; and he has taught us how little of true greatness there is in rank by showing how much more there
is in resigning it. This is perhaps the most successful
instance known of a king, who had been used to be
obeyed by armies and by nations, willingly giving up his
power when he found his bodily strength no longer equal
to it. Ptolemy Soter had the happiness of having a son
willing to follow in the track which he had laid down
for him, and of living to see the wisdom of his own laws
proved by the well-being of the kingdom under his son
and successor.

But while we are watching the success of Ptolemy's
plans, and the rise of this Greek monarchy at Alexandria,
we cannot help being pained with the thought that the
Kopts of Upper Egypt are forgotten, and asking whether

it would not have been still better to have raised Thebes
to the place which it once held, and to have recalled the
days of Ramses, instead of trying what might seem the
hopeless task of planting Greek arts in Africa. But a re-
view of this history will show that, as far as human fore-
thought can judge, this could not have been done. A
people whose religious opinions were fixed against all
change, like the pillars upon which they were carved,
and whose philosophy had not noticed that men's minds
were made to move forward, had no choice but to be left
behind and trampled on, as their more
active neighbours marched onwards in
the path of improvement. If Thebes had
fallen only on the conquest by Cambyses,
if the rebellions against the Persians had
been those of Kopts throwing off their
chains and struggling for freedom, we
might have hoped to have seen Egypt,
on the fall of Darius, again rise under
kings of the blood and language of the
people; and we should have thought the
gilded and half-hid chains of the Ptolemies were little better than the heavy
yoke of the Persians. This, however, is
very far from having been the case. We
first see the kings of Lower Egypt guarding their thrones
at Saïs by Greek soldiers; and then, that every struggle
of Inarus, of Nectanebo, and of Tachos, against the Persians, was only made by the courage and arms of Greeks
hired in the Delta by Egyptian gold. During the three

NIT, GODDESS
OF SAÏS.

hundred years before Alexander was hailed by Egypt as its deliverer, scarcely once had the Kopts, trusting to their own courage, stood up in arms against either Persians or Greeks; and the country was only then con- quered without a battle because the power and arms were already in the hands of the Greeks; because in the mixed races of the Delta the Greeks were so far the strongest, though not the most numerous, that a Greek king- dom rose there with the same ease, and for the same reasons, that an Arab kingdom rose in the same place nine centuries later.

Moral worth, national pride, love of country, and the better feelings of clanship are the chief grounds upon which a great people can be raised. These feelings are closely allied to self-denial, or a willingness on the part of each man to give up much for the good of the whole. By this, chiefly, public monuments are built, and citi- zens stand by one another in battle; and these feelings were certainly A CAT MUMMY. strong in Upper Egypt in the days of its greatness. But, when the throne was moved to Lower Egypt, when the kingdom was governed by the kings of Saïs, and even afterwards, when it was strug- gling against the Persians, these virtues were wanting,

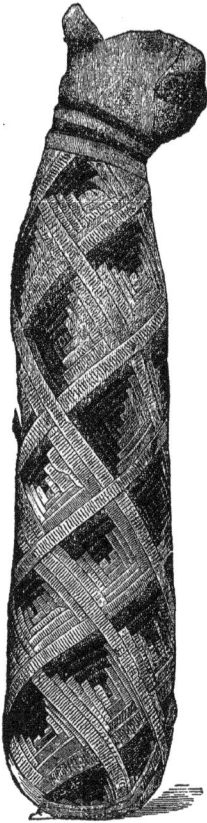

and they trusted to foreign hirelings in their struggle
for freedom. The Delta was peopled by three races of
men, Kopts, Greeks, and Phœnicians, or Arabs; and
even before the sceptre was given to the Greeks by
Alexander's conquests, we have seen that the Kopts had
lost the virtues needed to hold it.

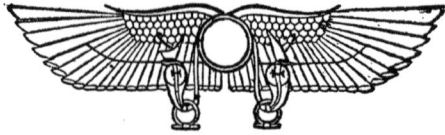

PTOLEMY II. AND HIS FIRST WIFE.

CHAPTER III

PTOLEMY PHILADELPHUS. B. C. 284-246

WE know of few princes who ever mounted a throne with such fair prospects before them as the second Ptolemy. He was born in Cos, an island on the coast of Caria, which the Ptolemies kept as a family fortress, safe from Egyptian rebellion and Alexandrian rudeness, and, while their fleets were masters of the sea, safe from foreign armies. He had been brought up with great care, and, being a younger son, was not spoilt by that flattery which in all courts is so freely offered to the heir. He first studied letters and philosophy under Philetas of Cos, an author of some elegies and epigrams now lost; and as he grew up, he found himself surrounded by all the philosophers and writers with whom his father mixed on

the easiest terms of friendship. During the long reign
of Ptolemy Soter the people had been made happy by

PHAROS IN OLD
ALEXANDRIA.

wise regulations and good laws, trade
had been flourishing, the cities had
greatly prospered, and the fortresses
had been everywhere strengthened.
The Grecian troops were well trained,
their loyalty undoubted, and the
Egyptians were enrolled in a phalanx, armed and disciplined like the
Macedonians. The population of the
country was counted at seven millions. Alexandria, the capital of
the kingdom, was not only the largest trading city in the world, but
was one of the most favoured seats
of learning. It surely must have been
easy to foresee that the prince, then
mounting the throne, even if but slightly gifted with
virtues, would give his name to a reign which could not
be otherwise than remarkable in the history of Egypt.
But Philadelphus, though like his father he was not free
from the vices of his times and of his rank, had more of
wisdom than is usually the lot of kings; and, though we
cannot but see that he was only watering the plants and
gathering the fruit where his father had planted, yet
we must at the same time acknowledge that Philadelphus
was a successor worthy of Ptolemy Soter. He may have
been in the twenty-third year of his age when his father
gave up to him the cares and honours of royalty.

The first act of his reign, or rather the last of his father's reign, was the proclamation, or the ceremony, of showing the new king to the troops and people. All that was dazzling, all that was costly or curious, all that the wealth of Egypt could buy or the gratitude of the provinces could give, was brought forth to grace this religious show, which, as we learn from the sculptures in the old tombs, was copied rather from the triumphs of Ramses and Thûtmosis than from anything that had been seen in Greece.

The procession began with the pomp of Osiris, at the head of which were the Sileni in scarlet and purple cloaks, who opened the way through the crowd. Twenty satyrs followed on each side of the road, bearing torches; and then Victories with golden wings, clothed in skins, each with a golden staff six cubits long, twined round with ivy. An altar was carried next, covered with golden ivy-leaves, with a garland of golden vine-leaves tied with white ribands; and this was followed by a hundred and twenty boys in scarlet frocks, carrying bowls of crocus, myrrh, and frankincense, which made the air fragrant with the scent. Then came forty dancing satyrs crowned with golden ivy-leaves, with their naked bodies stained with gay colours, each carrying a crown of vine leaves and gold; then two Sileni in scarlet cloaks and white boots, one having the hat and wand of Mercury and the other a trumpet; and between them walked a man, six feet high, in tragic dress and mask, meant for the Year, carrying a golden cornucopia. He was followed by a tall and beautiful woman, meant for the Lustrum of five

years, carrying in one hand a crown and in the other
a palm-branch. Then came an altar, and a troop of satyrs
in gold and scarlet, carrying golden drinking-cups.

Then came Philiscus the poet, the priest of Osiris,
with all the servants of the god; then the Delphic tri-
pods, the prizes which were to be given in the wrestling
matches; that for the boys was nine cubits high, and that
for the men twelve cubits high. Next came a four-
wheeled car, fourteen cubits long and eight wide, drawn
along by one hundred and eighty men, on which was the
statue of Osiris, fifteen feet high, pouring wine out of a
golden vase, and having a scarlet frock down to his feet,
with a yellow transparent robe over it, and over all a
scarlet cloak. Before the statue was a large golden bowl,
and a tripod with bowls of incense on it. Over the whole
was an awning of ivy and vine leaves; and in the same
chariot were the priests and priestesses of the god.

This was followed by a smaller chariot drawn by
sixty men, in which was the statue of Isis in a robe of
yellow and gold. Then came a chariot full of grapes,
and another with a large cask of wine, which was poured
out on the road, as the procession moved on, and at which
the eager crowd filled their jugs and drinking-cups.
Then came another band of satyrs and Sileni, and more
chariots of wine; then eighty Delphic vases of silver,
and Panathenaic and other vases; and sixteen hundred
dancing boys in white frocks and golden crowns: then
a number of beautiful pictures; and a chariot carrying
a grove of trees, out of which flew pigeons and doves, so
tied that they might be easily caught by the crowd.

On another chariot, drawn by an elephant, came Osiris, as he returned from his Indian conquests. He was followed by twenty-four chariots drawn by elephants, sixty drawn by goats, twelve by some kind of stags, seven by gazelles, four by wild asses, fifteen by buffaloes, eight by ostriches, and seven by stags of some other kind. Then came chariots loaded with the tributes of the conquered nations; men of Ethiopia carrying six hundred elephants' teeth; sixty huntsmen leading two thousand four hundred dogs; and one hundred and fifty men carrying trees, in the branches of which were tied parrots and other beautiful birds. Next walked the foreign animals, Ethiopian and Arabian sheep, Brahmin bulls, a white bear, leopards, panthers, bears, a camelopard, and a rhinoceros; proving to the wondering crowd the variety and strangeness of the countries that owned their monarch's sway.

In another chariot was seen Bacchus running away from Juno, and flying to the altar of Rhea. After that came the statues of Alexander and Ptolemy Soter crowned with gold and ivy: by the side of Ptolemy stood the statues of Virtue, of the god Chem, and of the city of Corinth; and he was followed by female statues of the conquered cities of Ionia, Greece, Asia Minor, and Persia; and the statues of other gods. Then came crowds of singers and cymbal-players, and two thousand bulls with gilt horns, crowns, and breast-plates.

Then came Amon-Ra and other gods; and the statue of Alexander between Victory and the goddess Neith, in a chariot drawn by elephants: then a number of thrones of ivory and gold; on one was a golden crown, on another a golden cornucopia, and on the throne of Ptolemy Soter was a crown worth ten thousand *aurei*, or nearly thirty thousand dollars; then three thousand two hundred golden crowns, twenty golden shields, sixty-four suits of golden armour; and the whole was closed with forty waggons of silver vessels, twenty of golden vessels, eighty of costly Eastern scents, and fifty-seven thousand six hundred foot soldiers, and twenty-three thousand two hundred horse. The procession

BRONZE COSMETIC HOLDER.

began moving by torchlight before day broke in the morning, and the sun set in the evening before it had all passed on its way.

It went through the streets of Alexandria to the royal tents on the outside of the city, where, as in the procession, everything that was costly in art, or scarce in nature, was brought together in honour of the day. At the public games, as a kind of tax or coronation money, twenty golden crowns were given to Ptolemy Soter, twenty-three to Berenicê, and twenty to their son, the new king, beside other costly gifts; and two thousand two hundred and thirty-nine talents, or one million seven hundred and fifty thousand dollars, were spent on the amusements of the day. For the account of this curious procession we are indebted to Callixenes of Rhodes, who was then travelling in Egypt, and who wrote a history of Alexandria.

Ptolemy Soter lived two years after he had withdrawn himself from the cares of government; and the weight of his name was not without its use in adding steadiness to the throne of his successor. Instead of parcelling out his wide provinces among his sons as so many kingdoms, he had given them all to one son, and that not the eldest; and on his death the jealousy of those who had been disinherited and disappointed broke out in rebellion.

It is with peculiar interest that we hear in this reign for the first time that the bravery and rising power of the Romans had forced themselves into the notice of Philadelphus. Pyrrhus, the King of Epirus, had been beaten by the Romans, and driven out of Italy; and the King of Egypt thought it not beneath him to send an ambassador to the senate, to wish them joy of their success, and to make a treaty of peace with the republic. The embassy, as we might suppose, was received in Rome with great joy; and three ambassadors, two of the proud name of Fabius, with Quintus Ogulnius, were sent back to seal the treaty. Philadelphus gave them some costly gifts, probably those usually given to ambassadors; but Rome was then young, her citizens had not yet made gold the end for which they lived, and the ambassadors returned the gifts, for they could receive nothing beyond the thanks of the senate for having done their duty. This treaty was never broken; and in the war which broke out in the middle of this reign between Rome and Carthage, usually called the first Punic war, when the Carthaginians sent to Alexandria to beg for a loan of two thousand talents, Philadelphus refused it, saying that he would help them against his enemies, but not against his friends.

From that time forward we find Egypt in alliance with Rome. But we also find that they were day by day changing place with one another: Egypt soon began to sink, while Rome was rising in power; Egypt soon received help from her stronger ally, and at last became a province of the Roman empire.

At the time of this embassy, when Greek arts were nearly unknown to the Romans, the ambassadors must have seen much that was new to them, and much that was worth copying; and three years afterwards, when one of them, Quintus Ogulnius, together with Caius Fabius Pictor, were chosen consuls, they coined silver for the first time in Rome. With them begins the series of consular denarii, which throws such light on Roman life and history.

About the middle of this reign, Berenicê, the mother of the king, died, and it was most likely then that Philadelphus began to date from the beginning of his own reign: he had before gone on like his father, dating from the beginning of his father's reign. In the year after her death, the great feast of Osiris, in the month of Mesore, was celebrated at Alexandria with more than usual pomp by the Queen Arsinoë. Venus, or Isis, had

OSIRIS AND ISIS AND THE FOUR CHILDREN OF HORUS
WITHIN A SHRINE.

just raised Berenicê to heaven; and Arsinoë, in return, showed her gratitude by the sums of money spent on the feast of Osiris, or Adonis as he was sometimes called by the Greeks. Theocritus, who was there, wrote a poem on the day, and tells us of the crowds in the streets, of the queen's gifts to the temple, and of the beautiful tapestries, on which were woven the figures of the god and goddess breathing as if alive; and he has given a free translation of the Maneros, the national poem in which the priests each year consoled the goddess Isis for the death of Osiris, which was sung through the streets of Alexandria by a Greek girl in the procession.

One of the chief troubles in the reign of Philadelphus was the revolt of Cyrene. The government of that part of Africa had been entrusted to Magas, the half-brother of the king, a son of Berenicê by her former husband. Berenicê, who had been successful in setting aside Ceraunus to make room for her son Philadelphus on the throne of Egypt, has even been said to have favoured the rebellious and ungrateful efforts of her elder son Magas to make himself King of Cyrene. Magas, without waiting till the large armies of Egypt were drawn together to crush his little state, marched hastily towards Alexandria, in the hopes of being joined by some of the restless thousands of that crowded city. But he was quickly recalled to Cyrene by the news of the rising of the Marmaridæ, the race of Libyan herdsmen that had been driven back from the coast by the Greek settlers who founded Cyrene. Philadelphus then led his army along the coast against the rebels; but he was, in the same way, stopped by the fear of treachery among his own Gallic mercenaries. With a measured cruelty which the use of foreign mercenaries could alone have taught him, he led back his army to the marshes of the Delta, and, entrapping the four thousand distrusted Gauls[1] on one of the small islands, he hemmed them in between the water and the spears of the phalanx, and they all died miserably, by famine, by drowning, or by the sword.

Magas had married Apime, the daughter of Antiochus Soter, King of Syria; and he sent to his father-in-law to beg him to march upon Cœle-Syria and Palestine, to call off the army of Philadelphus from Cyrene. But Philadelphus did not wait for this attack: his armies moved before Antiochus was ready, and, by a successful inroad upon Syria, he prevented any relief being sent to Magas.

After the war between the brothers had lasted some years, Magas made an offer of peace, which was to be sealed by betrothing his only child, Berenicê, to the son of Philadelphus. To this offer Philadelphus yielded; as by the death of Magas, who was already worn out by luxury and disease, Cyrene would then fall to his own son. Magas, indeed, died before the marriage took place; but, notwithstanding the efforts made by his widow to break the agreement, the treaty was kept, and on this marriage Cyrene again formed part of the Ptolemaic kingdom of Egypt.

---

[1] It is not known for certain from what part of the world these Gauls were recruited. The race known as Gallic was at one time spread over a wide district from Gallicia in the East to Gallia in the West.

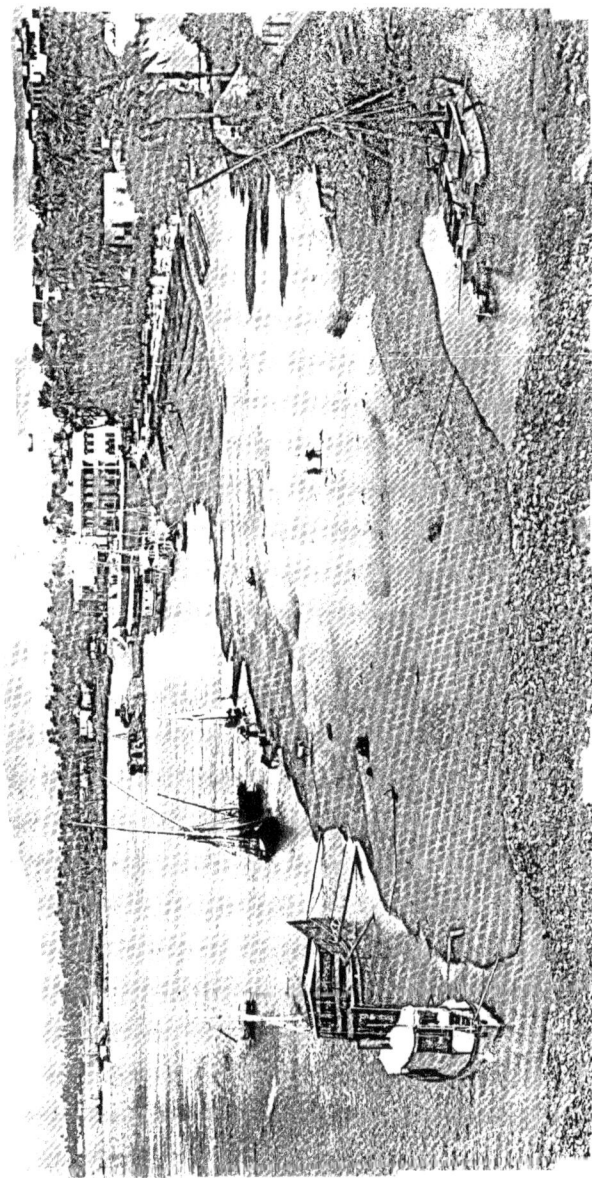

VIEW OF ASSOWAN

The black spot upon the character of Philadelphus, which all the blaze of science and letters by which he was surrounded can not make us overlook, is the death of two of his brothers: a son of Eurydice, who might, perhaps, have thought that he was robbed of the throne of Egypt by his younger brother, and who was unsuccessful in raising the island of Cyprus in rebellion; and a younger brother, Argæus, who was also charged with joining in a plot; both lost their lives by his orders.

It was only in the beginning of this reign, after Egypt had been for more than fifty years under the rule of the Macedonians, that the evils which often follow conquest were brought to an end. Before this reign no Greek was ever known to have reached Elephantine and Syênê or Aswan since Herodotus made his hasty tour in the Thebaid; and during much of the last reign no part of Upper Egypt was safe for a Greek traveller, if he were alone, or if he quitted the highroad. The peasants, whose feelings of hatred we can hardly wonder at, waylaid the stragglers, and Egyptian-like as the Greeks said, or slave-like as it would be wiser to say, often put them to death in cold blood. But a long course of good government had at last quieted the whole country, and left room for further improvements by Philadelphus.

Among other buildings, Philadelphus raised a temple in Alexandria to the honour of his father and mother, and placed in it their statues, made of ivory and gold, and ordered that they should be worshipped like the gods and other kings of the country. He also built a temple to Ceres and Proserpine, and then the Eleusinian

mysteries were taught in Alexandria to the few who
were willing and worthy to be admitted. The south-
east quarter of the city in which this temple stood was
called the Eleusinis; and here the troop of maidens were
to be seen carrying the sacred basket through the streets,
and singing hymns in
honour of the goddess;
while they charged all
profane persons, who
met the procession, to
keep their eyes upon the
ground, lest they should
see the basket and the
priestesses, who were
too pure for them to
look upon.

In this reign was
finished the lighthouse
on the island of Pharos,
as a guide to ships when
entering the harbour of
Alexandria by night.
The navigation of the
waters of the Red Sea,

ROSETTA BRANCH OF THE NILE.

along which the wind blows hard from the north for nine
months in the year, was found so dangerous by the little
vessels from the south of Arabia, that they always chose
the most southerly port in which they could meet the
Egyptian buyers. The merchants with their bales of
goods found a journey on camels through the desert,

where the path is marked only by the skeletons of the animals that have died upon the route, less costly than a coasting voyage. Hence, when Philadelphus had made the whole of Upper Egypt to the cataracts at Aswan (Syênê) as quiet and safe as the Delta, he made a new port on the rocky coast of the Red Sea, nearly two hundred miles to the south of Cosseir, and named it Berenicê after his mother. He also built four public inns, or watering-houses, where the caravans might find water for the camels, and shelter from the noonday sun, on their twelve days' journey through the desert from Koptos on the Nile to this new port. He rebuilt, and at the same time renamed, the old port of Cosseir, or Ænnum as it was before called, and named it Philotera after his younger sister. The trade which thus passed down the Nile from Syênê, from Berenicê, and from Philotera, paid a toll or duty at the custom-house station of Phylake a little below Lycopolis on the west bank of the river, where a guard of soldiers was encamped; and this station gradually grew into a town.

Philadelphus also built a city on the sands at the head of the Red Sea, near where Suez now stands, and named it Arsinoë, after his sister; and he again opened the canal which Necho II. and Darius had begun, by which ships were to pass from the Nile to this city on the Red Sea. This canal began in the Pelusiac branch of the river, a little above Bubastis, and was carried to the Lower Bitter Lakes in the reign of Darius. From thence Philadelphus wished to carry it forward to the Red Sea, near the town of Arsinoë, and moreover cleared it from the

sands which soon overwhelmed it and choked it up whenever it was neglected by the government. But his undertaking was stopped by the engineers finding the waters
of the canal several feet lower than the level of the Red
Sea; and that, if finished, it would become a salt-water
canal, which could neither water the fields nor give drink
to the cities in the valley. He also built a second city of
the name of Berenicê, called the Berenicê Epidires, at
the very mouth of the Red Sea on a point of land where
Abyssinia is hardly more than fifteen miles from the
opposite coast of Arábia. This naming of cities after his
mother and sisters was no idle compliment; they probably received the crown revenues of those cities for their
personal maintenance.

With a view further to increase the trade with the
East, Philadelphus sent Dionysius on an expedition over-
land to India, to gain a knowledge of the country and
of its means and wants. He went by the way of the
Caspian Sea through Bactria, in the line of Alexander's
march. He dwelt there, at the court of the sovereign,
soon after the time that Megasthenes was there; and he
wrote a report of what he saw and learned. But it is
sad to find, in our search for what is valuable in the history of past times, that the information gained on this
interesting journey of discovery is wholly lost.

In the number of ports which were then growing into
the rank of cities, we see full proof of the great trade of
Egypt at that time; and we may form some opinion of
the profit which was gained from the trade of the Red
Sea from the report of Clitarchus to Alexander, that the

people of one of the islands would give a talent of gold for a horse, so plentiful with them was gold, and so scarce the useful animals of Europe; and one of the three towns named after the late queen, on that coast, was known by the name of the Nubian or Golden Berenicê, from the large supply of gold which was dug from the mines in the neighbourhood. In latitude 17°, separated from the Golden Berenicê by one of the forests of Ethiopia, was the new city of Ptolemais, which, however, was little more than a post from which the hunting parties went out to catch elephants for the armies of Egypt. Philadelphus tried to command, to persuade, and to bribe the neighbouring tribes not to kill these elephants for food, but they refused all treaty with him; these zealous huntsmen answered that, if he offered them the kingdom of Egypt with all its wealth, they would not give up the pleasure of catching and eating elephants. The Ethiopian forests, however, were able to supply the Egyptian armies with about one elephant for every thousand men, which was the number then thought best in the Greek military tactics. Asia had been the only country from which the armies had been supplied with elephants before Philadelphus brought them from Ethiopia.

The temple of Isis among the palm groves in Philæ, a rocky island in the Nile near the cataracts of Syênê, was begun in this reign, though not finished till some reigns later. It is still the wonder of travellers, and by its size and style proves the wealth and good taste of the priests. But its ornaments are not so simple as those of the older temples; and the capitals of its columns are varied by the full-blown papyrus flower of several sizes, its half-opened buds, its closed buds, and its leaves, and by palm-branches. It seems to have been built on the site of an older temple which may have been overthrown by the Persians. This island of Philæ is the most beautiful spot in Egypt; where the bend of the river just above the cataracts forms a quiet lake surrounded on all sides by fantastic cliffs of red granite. Its name is a corruption from Abu-lakh, the city of the frontier. This temple was one of the places in which Osiris was said to be buried. None but priests ever set foot on this sacred

TEMPLE OF PHILÆ.

island, and no oath was so binding as that sworn in the name of Him that lies buried in Philæ. The statues of the goddess in the temple were all meant for portraits of the queen Arsinoë. The priests who dwelt in the cells within the courtyards of the temples of which we see the remains in this temple at Philæ, were there confined for life to the service of the altar by the double force of religion and the stone walls. They showed their zeal for their gods by the amount of want which they were able to endure, and they thought that sitting upon the ground in idleness, with the knees up to the chin, was one of the first of religious duties.

The Museum of Alexandria held at this time the highest rank among the Greek schools, whether for poetry, mathematics, astronomy, or medicine, the four branches into which it was divided. Its library soon held two hundred thousand rolls of papyrus; which, however, could hardly have been equal to ten thousand printed volumes. Many of these were bought by Philadelphus in Athens and Rhodes; and his copy of Aristotle's works was bought of the philosopher Nileus, who had been a hearer of that great man, and afterwards inherited his books through Theophrastus, to whom they had been left by Aristotle. The books in the museum were of course all Greek; the Greeks did not study foreign languages, and thought the Egyptian writings barbarous.

At the head of this library had been Demetrius Phalereus, who, after ruling Athens with great praise, was banished from his country, and fled to Ptolemy Soter, under whom he consoled himself for the loss of power in the enjoyment of literary leisure. He was at the same time the most learned and the most polished of orators. He brought learning from the closet into the forum; and, by the soft turn which he gave to public speaking, made that sweet and lovely which had before been grave and severe. Cicero thought him the great master in the art of speaking, and seems to have taken him as the model upon which he wished to form his own style. He wrote upon philosophy, history, government, and poetry; but the only one of his works which has reached our time is his treatise on elocution; and the careful thought which he there gives to the choice of words and to the form of a sentence, and even the parts of a sentence, shows the value then set upon style. Indeed he seems rather to have charmed his hearers by the softness of his words than to have roused them to noble deeds by the strength of his thoughts. He not only advised Ptolemy Soter what books he should buy, but which he should read, and he chiefly recommended those on government and policy; and it is alike to the credit of the king and of the librarian, that he put before him books which, from their praise of freedom and hatred of tyrants, few persons would even speak of in the presence of a king. But Demetrius had also been consulted by Soter about the choice of a successor, and had given his opinion that the crown ought to be left to his eldest son, and that wars would arise between his children if it were not so left; hence we can hardly wonder that, on the death of Soter, Demetrius should have lost his place at the head of the museum, and been ordered to leave

ANUBIS, GOD OF THE LOWER WORLD.

Alexandria. He died, as courtiers say, in disgrace; and he was buried near Diospolis in the Busirite nome of the Delta. According to one account he was put to death by the bite of an asp, in obedience to the new king's orders, but this story is not generally credited; although this was not an uncommon way of inflicting death.

Soon after this we find Zenodotus of Ephesus filling the office of librarian to the museum. He was a poet, who, with others, had been employed by Soter in the education of his children. He is also known as the first of those Alexandrian critics who turned their thoughts towards mending the text of Homer, and to whom we are indebted for the tolerably correct state of the great poet's works, which had become faulty through the carelessness of the copiers. Zenodotus was soon followed by other critics in this task of editing Homer. But their labours were not approved of by all; and when Aratus asked Timon which he thought the best edition of the poet, the philosopher shrewdly answered, " That which has been least corrected."

At the head of the mathematical school was Euclid; who is, however, less known to us by what his pupils have said of him than by his own invaluable work on geometry. This is one of the few of the scientific writings of the ancients that are still in use. The discoveries of the man of science are made use of by his successor, and the discoverer perhaps loses part of his reward when his writings are passed by, after they have served us as a stepping-stone to mount by. If he wishes his works to live with those of the poet and orator, he must, like them, cultivate those beauties of style which are fitted to his matter. Euclid did so; and his Elements have been for more than two thousand years the model for all writers on geometry. He begins at the beginning, and leads the learner, step by step, from the simplest propositions, called axioms, which rest upon metaphysical rather than mathematical proof, to high geometrical truths. The mind is indeed sometimes wearied by being made to stop at every single step in the path, and wishes, with Ptolemy Soter, for a shorter road; but, upon the whole, Euclid's clearness has never been equalled.

Ctesibus wrote on the theory of hydrostatics, and was the inventor of several water-engines; an application of mathematics which was much called for by the artificial

AT THE HEAD OF THE RED SEA.

irrigation of Egypt. He also invented that useful instrument, the water-clock, to tell the time after sunset.

Among the best known of the men of letters who came to Alexandria to enjoy the patronage of Philadelphus was Theocritus. Many of his poems are lost; but his pastoral poems, though too rough for the polished taste of Quintilian, and perhaps more like nature than we wish any works of imitative art to be, have always been looked upon as the model of that kind of poetry. If his shepherds do not speak the language of courtiers, they have at least a rustic propriety which makes us admire the manners and thoughts of the peasant. He repaid the bounty of the king in the way most agreeable to him; he speaks of him as one

> to freemen kind,
> Wise, fond of books and love, of generous mind;
> Knows well his friend, but better knows his foe;
> Scatters his wealth; when asked he ne'er says No,
> But gives as kings should give.
>
> IDYLL, xiv. 60.

Theocritus boasted that he would in an undying poem place him in the rank of the demigods; and, writing with the pyramids and the Memnonium before his eyes, assured him that generosity towards the poets would do more to make his name live for ever than any building that he could raise.

In a back street of Alexandria, in the part of the city named Eleusinis, near the temple of Ceres and Proserpine, lived the poet Callimachus, earning his livelihood by teaching. But the writer of the Hymns could not long dwell so near the court of Philadelphus unknown and unhonoured. He was made professor of poetry in the museum, and even now repays the king and patron for what he then received. He was a man of great industry, and wrote in prose and in all kinds of verse; but of these only a few hymns and epigrams have come down to our time. Egypt seems to have been the birthplace of the mournful elegy, and Callimachus was the chief of the elegiac poets. He was born at Cyrene; and though, from the language in which he wrote, his thoughts are mostly Greek, yet he did not forget the place of his birth. He calls upon Apollo by the name of Carneus, because, after Sparta and Thera, Cyrene was his chosen seat. He paints Latona, weary and in pain in the island of Delos, as leaning against a palm-tree, by the side of the river Inopus, which, sinking into the ground, was to rise again in Egypt, near the cataracts of Syênê; and, prettily pointing to Philadelphus, he makes Apollo, yet unborn, ask his mother not to give birth to him in the island of Cos, because that island was already chosen as the birthplace of another god, the child of the gods Soteres, who would be the copy of his father, and under whose diadem both Egypt and the islands would be proud to be governed by a Macedonian.

The poet Philætas, who had been the first tutor of Philadelphus, was in elegy second only to Callimachus; but Quintilian (while advising us about books, to read much but not many) does not rank him among the few first-rate poets by whom the student should form his taste; and his works are now lost. He was small and thin in person, and it was jokingly said of him that he wore leaden soles to his shoes lest he should be blown away by the wind. But in losing his poetry, we have perhaps lost the point of the joke. While these three, Theocritus, Callimachus, and Philætas, were writing in Alexandria, the museum was certainly the chief seat of the muses. Athens itself could boast of no such poet but Menander, with whom Attic literature ended; and him Philadelphus earnestly invited to his court. He sent a ship to Greece on purpose to fetch him; but neither

DAHABIEH DESCENDING THE NILE

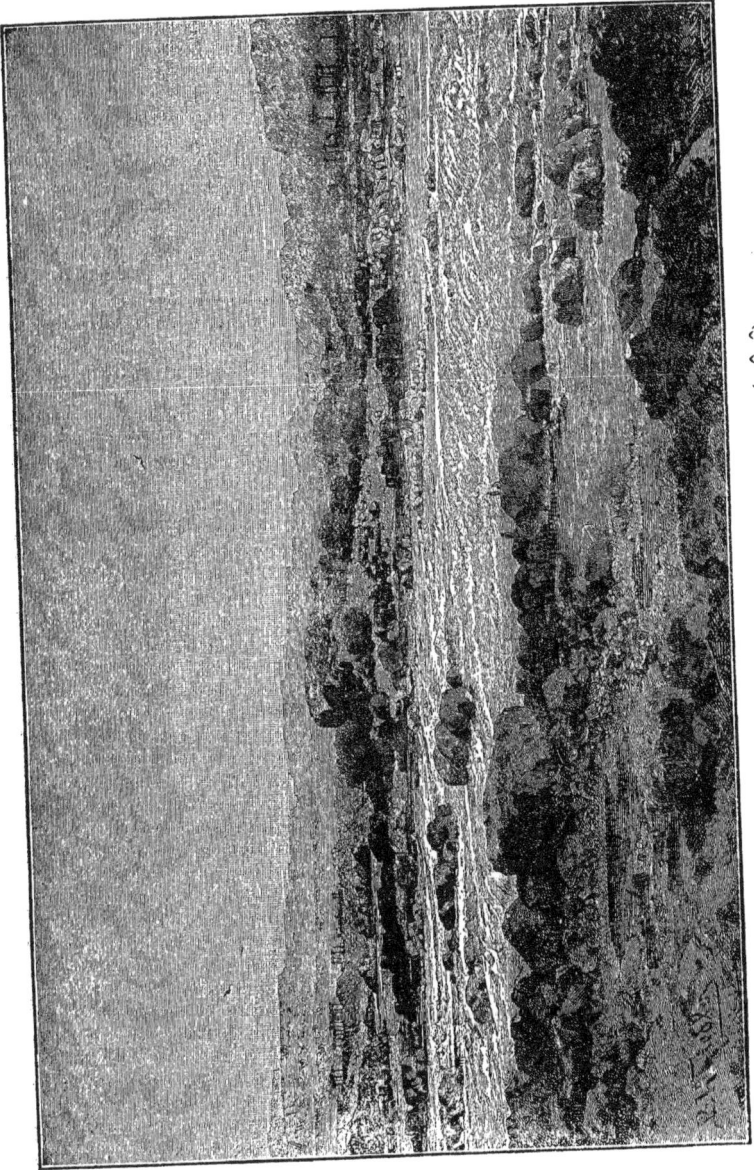

THE FIRST CATARACT ON THE NILE AT ASWAN (SYÊNÊ).

this honour nor the promised salary could make him quit his mother country and the schools of Athens; and, in the time of Pausanias, his tomb was still visited by the scholar on the road to the Piræus, and his statue was still seen in the theatre.

Strato, the pupil of Theophrastus, though chiefly known for his writings on physics, was also a writer on many branches of knowledge. He was one of the men of learning who had taken part in the education of Philadelphus; and the king showed his gratitude to his teacher by making him a present of eighty talents, or sixty thousand dollars. He was for eighteen years at the head of one of the Alexandrian schools.

Timocharis, the astronomer, made some of his observations at Alexandria in the last reign, and continued them through half of this reign. He began a catalogue of the fixed stars, with their latitudes and their longitudes measured from the equinoctial point; by the help of which Hipparchus, one hundred and fifty years afterwards, made the great discovery that the equinoctial point had moved. He has left an observation of the place of Venus, on the seventeenth day of the month of Mesore, in the thirteenth year of this reign, which by the modern tables of the planets is known to have been on the eighth day of October, B. C. 272; from which we learn that the first year of Philadelphus ended in October, B. C. 284, and the first year of Ptolemy Soter ended in October, B. C. 322; thus fixing the chronology of these reigns with a certainty which leaves nothing to be wished for. Aristillus also made some observations of the same kind at

Alexandria. Few of them have been handed down to us, but they were made use of by Hipparchus.

Aristarchus, the astronomer of Samos, most likely came to Alexandria in the last reign, as some of his observations were made in the very beginning of the reign of Philadelphus. He is the first astronomer who is known to have taken the true view of the solar system. He said that the sun was the centre round which the earth moved in a circle; and, as if he had foreseen that even in after ages we should hardly be able to measure the distance of the fixed stars, he said that the earth's yearly path bore no greater proportion to the hollow globe of the heavens in which the stars were set, than the point without size in the centre of a circle does to its circumference. But the work in which he proved these great truths, or perhaps threw out these happy guesses, is lost; and the astronomers who followed him clung to the old belief that the earth was the centre round which the sun moved. The only writings of Aristarchus which now remain are his short work on the distances and magnitude of the sun and moon, in which the error in his results arises from the want of good observations, rather than from any mistake in his mathematical principles.

Aratus, who was born in Cilicia, is sometimes counted among the pleiades, or seven stars of Alexandria. His *Phenomena* is a short astronomical poem, without life or feeling, which scarcely aims at any of the grace or flow of poetry. It describes the planets and the constellations one by one, and tells us what stars are seen in

the head, feet, and other parts of each figure; and then
the seasons, and the stars seen at night at each time
of the year. When maps were little known, it must have
been of great use, to learners; and its being in verse
made it the more easy to remember. The value which
the ancients set upon this poem is curiously shown by
the number of Latin translations which were made from
it. Cicero in his early youth, before he was known as
an orator or philosopher, perhaps before he himself knew
in which path of letters he was soon to take the lead,
translated this poem. The next translation is by Ger-
manicus Cæsar, whose early death and many good qualities have thrown such a bright light upon his name.
He shone as a general, as an orator, and as an author;
but his Greek comedies, his Latin orations, and his poem
on Augustus are lost, while his translation of Aratus
is all that is left to prove that this high name in literature was not given to him for his political virtues alone.
Lastly Avienus, a writer in the reign of Diocletian, or
perhaps of Theodosius, has left a rugged, unpolished
translation of this much-valued poem. Aratus, the poet
of the heavens, will be read, said Ovid, as long as the
sun and moon shall shine.

Sosibius was one of the rhetoricians of the museum
who lived upon the bounty of Philadelphus. The king,
wishing to laugh at his habit of verbal criticism, once
told his treasurer to refuse his salary, and say that it
had been already paid. Sosibius complained to the king,
and the book of receipts was sent for, in which Philadelphus found the names of Soter, Sosigines, Bion, and

Apollonius, and showing to the critic one syllable of his name in each of those words, said that putting them together, they must be taken as the receipt for his salary.

Other authors wrote on lighter matters. Apollodorus Gelöus, the physician, addressed to Philadelphus a volume of advice as to which Greek wines were best fitted for his royal palate. The Italian and Sicilian were then unknown in Egypt, and those of the Thebaid were wholly beneath his notice, while the vine had as yet hardly been planted in the neighbourhood of Alexandria. He particularly praised the Naspercenite wine from the southern banks of the Black Sea, the Oretic from the island of Euboea; the Œneatic from Locris; the Leucadian from the island of Leucas; and the Ambraciote from the kingdom of Epirus. But above all these he placed the Peparethian wine from the island of Peparethus, a wine which of course did not please the many, as this experienced taster acknowledges that nobody is likely to have a true relish for it till after six years' acquaintance.

Such were the Greek authors who basked in the sunshine of royal favour at Alexandria; who could have told us, if they had thought it worth their while, all that we now wish to know of the trade, religion, language, and early history of Egypt. But they thought that the barbarbians were not worth the notice of men who called themselves Macedonians. Philadelphus, however, thought otherwise; and by his

AN ATHLETE DISPORT-
ING ON A CROCODILE.

command Manetho, an Egyptian, wrote in Greek a history of Egypt, copied from the hieroglyphical writing on the temples, and he dedicated it to the king. We know it only in the quotations of Josephus and Julius Africanus, and what we have is little more than a list of kings' names. He was a priest of Heliopolis, the great seat of Egyptian learning. The general correctness of Manetho's history, which runs back for nearly two thousand years, is shown by our finding the kings' names agree with many Egyptian inscriptions. Manetho owes his reputation to the merit of being the first who distinguished himself as a writer and critic upon religion and philosophy, as well as chronology and history, using the Greek language, but drawing his materials from native sources, especially the Sacred Books. That he was "skilled in Greek letters" we learn from Josephus, who also declares that he contradicted many of Herodotus' erroneous statements. Manetho was better suited for the task of writing a history of Egypt than any of his contemporaries. As an Egyptian he could search out and make use of all the native Egyptian sources, and, thanks to his knowledge of Greek, he could present them in a form intelligible to the Hellenes. It must be confessed that he has occasionally fallen into the error of allowing Greek thoughts and traditions to slip into his work. The great worth in Manetho's work lies in the fact that he relates the history of Egypt based on monumental sources and charters preserved in the temples. Moreover, he treats quite impartially the times of the

foreign rulers, which the form of the Egyptian history
employed by Diodorus does not mention; but above all,
Manetho gives us a list of Egyptian rulers arranged
according to a regular system. But however important
in this respect Manetho's work may be, it must not be
forgotten what difficulties he had to contend with in the
writing of it, and what unreliable sources lay in these
difficulties. He could not use the sources in the form
in which he found them. He was obliged to re-write
them, and he added to them synchronisms and relations
to other peoples which necessarily exposed him to the
dangers of colouring his report correspondingly.

But a much greater difficulty consisted in the fact
that the chronological reports of the earlier history were
all arranged according to the reigning years of the rulers,
so that Manetho was obliged to construct an era for his
work. Boeckh was the first to discover with certainty
the existence and form of this era. According to his
researches, the whole work of Manetho is based upon
Sothicycles of 1460 Julianic years. The Egyptian year
was movable, and did not need the extra day every
few years, but the consequence was that every year remained a quarter of a day behind the real year. When
1460—1 years had elapsed this chronological error had
mounted to a whole year, and so the movable year and
the fixed year fell together again. It is this Sothic period
which Manetho has employed in his account of Egyptian
history. Besides his history, Manetho has left us a work
on astrology, called *Apotelesmatica*, or Events, a work
of which there seems no reason to doubt the genuineness.

It is a poem in hexameter verse, in good Greek, addressed to King Ptolemy, in which he calls, not only upon Apollo and the Muse, but, like a true Egyptian, upon Hermes, from whose darkly worded writings he had gained his knowledge. He says that the king's greatness might have been foretold from the places of Mars and the Sun at the time of his birth, and that his marriage with his sister Arsinoë arose from the places of Venus and Saturn at the same time. But while we smile at this being said as the result of astronomical calculations, we must remember that for centuries afterwards, almost in our own time, the science of judicial astrology was made a branch of astronomy, and that the fault lay rather in the age than in the man; and we have the pain of thinking that, while many of the valuable writings by Manetho are lost, the copiers and readers of manuscripts have carefully saved for us this nearly worthless poem on astrology.

Petosiris was another writer on astrology and astronomy who was highly praised by his friend Manetho; and his calculations on the distances of the sun and planets are quoted by Pliny. His works are lost; but his name calls for our notice, as he must have been a native Egyptian, and a priest. Like Manetho, he also wrote on the calculation of nativities; and the later Greek astrologers, when what they had foretold did not come to pass, were wont to lay the blame on Petosiris. The priests were believed to possess these and other supernatural powers; and to help their claims to be believed many of them practised ventriloquism.

Timosthenes, the admiral under Philadelphus, must

not be forgotten in this list of authors; for though his verses to Apollo were little worth notice, his voyages of discovery, and his work in ten books on harbours, placed him in the first rank among geographers. Colotes, a pupil and follower of Epicurus, dedicated to Philadelphus a work of which the very title proves the nature of his philosophy, and how soon the rules of his master had fitted themselves to the habits of the sensualist. Its title was " That it is impossible even to support life according to the philosophical rules of any but the Epicureans." It was a good deal read and talked about; and three hundred years afterwards Plutarch thought it not a waste of time to write against it at some length.

At a time when books were few, and far too dear to be within reach of the many, and indeed when the number of those who could read must have been small, other means were of course taken to meet the thirst after knowledge; and the chief of these were the public readings in the theatre. This was not overlooked by Philadelphus, who employed Hegesias to read Herodotus, and Hermophantus to read Homer, the earliest historian and the earliest poet, the two authors who had taken deepest root in the minds of the Greeks. These public readings, which were common throughout Greece and its colonies, had not a little effect on the authors. They then wrote for the ear rather than the eye, to be listened to rather than to be read, which was one among the causes of Greek elegance and simplicity of style.

Among others who were brought to Alexandria by the fame of Philadelphus' bounty was Zoilus, the grammarian, whose ill-natured criticism on Homer's poems had earned for him the name of Homeromastix, or the scourge of Homer. He read his criticisms to Philadelphus, who was so much displeased with his carping and unfair manner of finding fault, that he even refused to relieve him when in distress. The king told him, that while hundreds had earned a livelihood by pointing out the beauties of the Iliad and Odyssey in their public readings, surely one person who was so much wiser might be able to live by pointing out the faults.

Timon, a tragic poet, was also one of the visitors to this court; but, as he was more fond of eating and drinking than of philosophy, we need not wonder at our knowing nothing of his tragedies, or at his not being made a professor by Philadelphus. But he took his revenge on the better-fed philosophers of the court, in a poem in which he calls them literary fighting-cocks, who were being fattened by the king, and were always quarrelling in the coops of the museum.

The Alexandrian men of science and letters maintained themselves, some few by fees received from their pupils, others as professors holding salaries in the museum, and others by civil employments under the government. There was little to encourage in them the feelings of noble pride or independence. The first rank in Alexandria was held by the civil and military servants of the crown, who enjoyed the lucrative employments of receiving the taxes, hearing the lawsuits by appeal, and repressing rebellions. With these men the philosophers mixed, not as equals, but partaking of their wealth and luxuries, and paying their score with wit and conversation. There were no landholders in the city, as the soil of the country was owned by Egyptians; and the wealthy trading classes, of all nations and languages, could bestow little patronage on Greek learning, and therefore little independence on its professors.

Philadelphus was not less fond of paintings and statues than of books; and he seems to have joined the Achaian league as much for the sake of the pictures which Aratus, its general, was in the habit of sending to him, as for political reasons. Aratus, the chief of Sicyon, was an acknowledged judge of paintings, and Sicyon was then the first school of Greece. The pieces which he sent to Philadelphus were mostly those of Pamphilus, the master, and of Melanthius, the fellow-pupil, of Apelles. Pamphilus was famed for his perspective; and he is said to have received from every pupil the large sum of ten talents, or seven thousand five hundred dollars, a year. His best known pieces were, Ulysses in his ship, and the victory of the Athenians near the town of Phlius. It was through Pamphilus that, at first in Sicyon, and afterwards throughout all Greece, drawing was taught to boys as part of a liberal education. Neacles also painted for Aratus; and we might almost suppose that it was as a gift to the King of Egypt that he painted his Sea-fight between the Egyptians and the Persians, in which the painter shows us that it was fought within the mouth of the Nile by making a crocodile bite at an ass drinking on the shore.

Helena, the daughter of Timon, was a painter of some

note at this time, at Alexandria; but the only piece of
hers known to us by name is the Battle of Issus, which
three hundred years afterwards was hung up by Ves-
pasian in the Temple of Peace at Rome. We must wonder
at a woman choosing to paint the horrors and pains of
a battle-piece; but, as we are not told what point of time
was chosen, we may hope that it was after the battle,

METHOD OF EGYPTIAN DRAFTSMANSHIP.

when Alexander, in his tent, raised up from their knees
the wife and lovely daughter of Darius, who had been
found among the prisoners. As for the Egyptians, they
showed no taste in painting. Their method of drawing
the human figure mathematically by means of squares,
which was not unsuitable in working a statue sixty feet
high, checked all flights of genius; and it afterwards destroyed Greek art, when the Greek painters were idle
enough to use it. We hear but little of the statues and
sculptures made for Philadelphus; but we cannot help

remarking that, while the public places of Athens were filled with the statues of the great and good men who had deserved well of their country, the statues which were most common in Alexandria were those of Cline, a favourite damsel, who filled the office of cup-bearer to the king of Egypt.

The favour shown to the Jews by Ptolemy Soter was not withdrawn by his son. He even bought from his own soldiers and freed from slavery one hundred and twenty thousand men of that nation, who were scattered over Egypt. He paid for each, out of the royal treasury, one hundred and twenty drachmas, or about fifteen dollars, to those of his subjects who held them either by right of war or by purchase. In fixing the amount of the ransom, the king would seem to have been guided by his Jewish advisers, as this is exactly equal to thirty shekels, the sum fixed by the Jewish law as the price of a slave. The Jews who lived in Lower Egypt, in the enjoyment of civil and religious liberty, looked upon that country as their home. They had already a Greek translation of either the whole or some part of their sacred writings, which had been made for those whose families had been for so many generations in Egypt that they could not read the language of their forefathers. But they now hoped, by means of the king's friendship and the weight which his wishes must carry with them, to have a Greek translation of the Bible which should bear the stamp of official authority.

Accordingly, to please them, Philadelphus sent Aristæus, a man whose wisdom had gained his friendship, and Andræus, a captain of the guard, both of them Greek Jews, with costly gifts to Eleazer, the high priest of Jerusalem; and asked him to employ learned and fit men to make a Greek translation of the Bible for the library at Alexandria. Eleazer, so runs the tradition, named seventy elders to undertake the task, who held their first sitting on the business at the king's dinner-table; when Menedemus, the Socratic philosopher, the pupil of Plato, was also present, who had been sent to Philadelphus as ambassador from Eubœa. The translators then divided the work among themselves; and when each had finished his task it was laid before a meeting of the seventy, and then published by authority. Thus was said to have been made the Greek translation of the Old Testament, which, from the number of the translators, we now call the Septuagint; but a doubt is thrown upon the whole story by the fables which have been mingled with it to give authority to the translation. By this translation the Bible became known for the first time to the Greek philosophers. We do not indeed hear that they immediately read it or noticed it, we do not find it quoted till after the spread of Christianity; but it had a silent effect on their opinions, which we trace in the new school of Platonists soon afterwards rising in Alexandria.

When Aratus of Sicyon first laid a plot to free his country from its tyrant, who reigned by the help of the King of Macedonia, he sent to Philadelphus to beg for money. He naturally looked to the King of Egypt for help when entering upon a struggle against their common rival; but the king seems to have thought the plans of this young man too wild to be countenanced. Aratus, however, soon raised Sicyon to a level with the first states of Greece, and made himself leader of the Achaian league, under which band and name the Greeks were then struggling for freedom against Macedonia; and when, by his courage and success, he had shown himself worthy of the proud name which was afterwards given him, of the " Last of the Greeks," Philadelphus, like other patrons, gave him the help which he less needed. Aratus, as we have seen, bought his friendship with pictures, the gifts of all others the most welcome; and, when he went to Egypt, Philadelphus gave him one hundred and fifty talents, or forty-five thousand dollars, and joined the Achaian league, on the agreement that in carrying on the war by sea and land they should obey the orders from Alexandria.

The friendship of Philadelphus, indeed, was courted by all the neighbouring states; the little island of Delos set up its statue to him; and the cities of Greece vied with one another in doing him honour. The Athenians named one of the tribes of their city and also one of their public lecture-rooms by his name; and two hundred years afterwards, when Cicero and his friend Atticus were learning wisdom and eloquence from the lips of Antiochus in Athens, it was in the gymnasium of Ptolemy.

Philadelphus, when young, had married Arsinoë, the daughter of Lysimachus of Thrace, by whom he had three children, Ptolemy, who succeeded him, Lysimachus, and Berenicê; but, having found that his wife was intriguing with Amyntas, and with his physician Chrysippus of Rhodes, he put these two to death and banished the Queen Arsinoë to Koptos in the Thebaid.

He then took Arsinoë, his own sister, as the partner of his throne. She had married first the old Lysimachus, King of Thrace, and then Ceraunus, her half-brother, when he was King of Macedonia. As they were not children of the same mother, this second marriage was neither illegal nor improper in Macedonia; but her third marriage with Philadelphus could only be justified by the laws of Egypt, their adopted country. They were both past the middle age, and whether Philadelphus looked upon her as his wife or not, at any rate they had no children. Her own children by Lysimachus had been put to death by Ceraunus, and she readily adopted those of her brother with all the kindness of a mother. She was a woman of an enlarged mind; her husband and her stepchildren alike valued her; and Eratosthenes showed his opinion of her learning and strong sense by giving the name of Arsinoë to one of his works, which perhaps a modern writer would have named Table-talk. This seeming marriage, however, between brother and sister did not escape blame with the Greeks of Alexandria. The poet Sotades, whose verses were as licentious as his life, wrote some coarse lines against the queen, for which he was forced to fly from Egypt, and, being overtaken at sea, he was wrapped up in lead and thrown overboard.

COIN WITH HEADS OF SOTER AND BERENICE ; AND PHILADELPHUS AND ARSINOE.

In the Egyptian inscriptions Ptolemy and Arsinoë are always called the brother-gods; on the coins they are called Adelphi, the brothers; and afterwards the king took the name of Philadelphus, or sister-loving, by which he is now usually known. In the first half of his reign Philadelphus dated his coins from the year that his father came to the throne; and it was not till the nineteenth year of his reign, soon after the death of his mother, that he made an era of his own, and dated his coins by the year of his own reign. The wealth of the country is well shown by the great size of those most in use, which were, in gold the tetra-stater or piece of eight drachms, and in silver the tetra-drachma, or piece of four drachms, while Greece had hardly seen a piece of gold larger than the single stater. In Alexandrian accounts also the unit of money was the silver didrachm, and thus double that

COIN WITH HEADS OF SOTER, PHILA-
DELPHUS, AND BERENICE.

in use among the merchants of Greece. Among the coins is one with the heads of Soter and Philadelphus on the one side, and the head of Berenicë, the wife of the one and mother of the other, on the other side. This we may suppose to have been struck during the first two years of his reign, in the lifetime of his father. Another bears on one side the heads of Ptolemy Soter and Berenicë, with the title of " the gods," and on the other side the heads of Philadelphus and his wife Arsinoë, with the title of " the brothers." This was struck after the death of his parents. A third was struck by the king in honour of his queen and sister. On the one side is the head of the queen, and on the other is the name of " Arsinoë, the brother-loving," with the cornucopia, or horn of Amalthea, an emblem borrowed by the queens of Egypt from the goddess Amalthea, the wife of the Libyan Amon. This was struck after his second marriage.

On the death of Arsinoë, Philadelphus built a tomb for her in Alexandria, called the Arsinoëum, and set up in it an obelisk eighty cubits high, which had been made by King Nectanebo, but had been left plain, without carving. Satyrus, the architect, had the charge of moving it. He dug a canal to it as it lay upon the ground, and moved two heavily laden barges under it. The burdens were then taken out of the barges, and as they floated higher they raised the obelisk off the ground. He then found it a task as great or greater to set it up in its place; and this Greek engineer must surely have looked back with wonder on the labour and knowledge of mechanics which must have been used in setting up the obelisks, colossal statues, and pyramids, which he saw scattered over the country. This obelisk now ornaments the cathedral of the Popes on the Vatican hill at Rome.

COIN OF ARSINOË, SISTER OF PTOLEMY II.

Satyrus wrote a treatise on precious stones, and he also carved on them with great skill; but his works are known only in the following lines, which were written by Diodorus on his portrait of Arsinoë cut in crystal:

E'en Zeuxis had been proud to trace
      The lines within this pebble seen;
Satyrus here hath carved the face
      Of fair Arsinoë, Egypt's queen;
But such her beauty, sweetness, grace,
      The copy falls far short, I ween.

Two beautiful cameos cut on sardonyx are extant, one with the heads of Philadelphus and his first wife, Arsinoë, and the other with the heads of the same king and his second wife, Arsinoë. It is not impossible that one or both of them may be the work of Satyrus.

Philadelphus is also said to have listened to the whimsical proposal of Dinochares, the architect, to build a room of loadstone in Arsinoë's tomb, so that an iron statue of the queen should hang in the air between the floor and the roof. But the death of the king and of the architect took place before this was tried. He set up there, however, her statue six feet high, carved out of a most remarkable block of topaz, which had been presented to his mother by Philemon, the prefect of the Troglodytic coast in the last reign.

Philadelphus lived in peace with Ergamenes, King of Meroë or Upper Ethiopia, who, while seeking for a knowledge of philosophy and the arts of life from his Greek neighbours, seems also to have gained a love of despotism, and a dislike of that control with which the priests of Ethiopia and Egypt had always limited the power of their kings. The King of Meroë had hitherto reigned like Amenôthes or Thûtmosis of old, as the head of the priesthood, supported and controlled by the priestly aristocracy by which he was surrounded. But he longed for the absolute power of Philadelphus. Accordingly he surrounded the golden temple with a chosen body of troops, and put the whole of the priests to death; and from that time he governed Ethiopia as an autocrat. But, with the loss of their liberties, the Ethiopians lost the wish to guard the throne; by grasping at more power, their sovereign lost what he already possessed; and in the next reign their country was conquered by Egypt.

The wars between Philadelphus and his great neighbour, Antiochus Theos, seem not to have been carried on very actively, though they did not wholly cease till Philadelphus offered as a bribe his daughter Berenicê, with a large sum of money under the name of a dower. Antiochus was already married to Laodice, whom he loved dearly, and by whom he had two children, Seleucus and Antiochus; but political ambition had deadened the feelings of his heart, and he agreed to declare this first marriage void and his two sons illegitimate, and that his children, if any should be born to him by Berenicê, should inherit the throne of Babylon and the East. Philadelphus, with an equal want of feeling, and disregarding the consequences of such a marriage, led his daughter to Pelusium on her journey to her betrothed husband, and sent with her so large a sum of gold and silver that he was nicknamed the "dower-giver."

The peace between the two countries lasted as long as Philadelphus lived, and was strengthened by kindnesses which each did to the other. Ptolemy, when in Syria, was much struck by the beauty of a statue of Diana, and begged it of Antiochus as an ornament for Alexandria. But as soon as the statue reached Egypt, Arsinoë fell dangerously ill, and she dreamed that the goddess came by night, and told her that the illness was sent to her for the wrong done to the statue by her husband; and accordingly it was sent back with many gifts to the temple from which it had been brought.

While Berenicë and her husband lived at Antioch, Philadelphus kindly sent there from time to time water from the sacred Nile for her use, as the Egyptians believed that none other was so wholesome. Antiochus, when ill, sent to Alexandria for a physician; and Cleombrotus of Cos accordingly went, by command of Ptolemy, to Syria. He was successful in curing the king, and on his return he received from Philadelphus a present of one hundred talents, or seventy-five thousand dollars, as a fee for his journey.

Philadelphus was a weak frame of body, and had delicate health; and, though a lover of learning beyond other kings of his time, he also surpassed them in his unmeasured luxury and love of pleasure. He had many mistresses, Egyptian as well as Greek, and the names of some of them have been handed down to us. He often boasted that he had found out the way to live for ever; but, like other free-livers, he was sometimes, by the gout in his feet, made to acknowledge that he was only a man, and indeed to wish that he could change places with the beggar whom he saw from his palace windows, eating the garbage on the banks of the Nile with an appetite which he had long wanted. It was during illness that he found most time for reading, and his mind most open to the truths of philosophy; and he chiefly wooed the Muses when ill health left him at leisure from his other courtships. He had a fleet of eight hundred state barges with gilt prows and poops and scarlet awnings upon the decks, which were used in the royal processions and religious shows, and which usually lay in dock at Schedia, on the Canopic River, five and twenty miles from Alexandria. He was no doubt in part withheld from war by this luxurious love of ease; but his reign taught the world the new lesson, that an ambitious monarch may gratify his wish for praise and gain the admiration of surrounding nations, as much by cultivating the blessed arts of peace as by plunging his people into the miseries of war.

He reigned over Egypt, with the neighbouring parts of Arabia; also over Libya, Phœnicia, Cœle-Syria, part of Ethiopia, Pamphylia, Cilicia, Lycia, Caria, Cyprus, and the isles of the Cyclades. The island of Rhodes and many of the cities of Greece were bound to him by the closest ties of friendship, for past help and for the hope of future. The wealthy cities of Tyre and Sidon did homage to him, as before to his father, by putting his crowned head upon their coins. The forces of Egypt reached the very large number of two hundred thousand foot and twenty thousand horse, two thousand chariots, four hundred Ethiopian elephants, fifteen hundred ships of war and one thousand transports. Of this large force, it is not likely that even one-fourth should have been Greeks; the rest must have been Egyptians and Syrians, with some Gauls. The body of chariots, though still forming part of the force furnished for military service by the Theban tenants of the crown, was of no use against modern science; and the other Egyptian troops, though now chiefly armed and disciplined like Greeks, were very much below the Macedonian phalanx in real strength. The galleys also, though no doubt under the guidance and skill of Greeks and Phœnicians, were in part manned by Egyptians, whose inland habits wholly unfitted them for the sea, and whose religious prejudices made them feel the conscription for the navy as a heavy grievance.

These large forces were maintained by a yearly income equally large, of fourteen thousand eight hundred talents, or twelve million two hundred and fifty thousand dollars, beside the tax on grain, which was taken in kind, of a million and a half of artabas, or about five millions of bushels. To this we may add a mass of gold, silver, and other valuable stores in the treasury, which were boastfully reckoned at the unheard-of sum of seven hundred and forty thousand talents, or above five hundred million dollars.

The trade down the Nile was larger than it had ever been before; the coasting trade on the Mediterranean was new; the people were rich and happy; justice was administered to the Egyptians according to their own laws, and to the Greeks of Alexandria according to the Macedonian laws: the navy commanded the whole of the eastern half of the Mediterranean; the schools and library had risen to a great height upon the wise plans of Ptolemy Soter; in every point of view Alexandria was the

chief city in the world. Athens had no poets or other writers during this century equal in merit to those who ennobled the museum. Philadelphus, by joining to the greatness and good government of his father the costly splendour and pomp of an eastern monarch, so drew the eyes of after ages upon his reign that his name passed into a proverb: if any work of art was remarkable for its good taste or costliness, it was called Philadelphian; even history and chronology were set at nought, and we sometimes find poets of a century later counted among the Pleiades of Alexandria in the reign of Philadelphus.

It is true that many of these advantages were forced in the hotbed of royal patronage; that the navy was built in the harbours of Phœnicia and Asia Minor; and that the men of letters who then drew upon themselves the eyes of the world were only Greek settlers, whose writings could have done little to raise the character of the native Kopts. But the Ptolemies, in raising this building of their own, were not at the same time crushing another. Their splendid monarchy had not been built on the ruins of freedom; and even if the Greek settlers in the Delta had formed themselves into a free state, we can hardly believe that the Egyptians would have been so well treated as they were by this military despotism. From the temples which were built or enlarged in Upper Egypt, and from the beauty of the hieroglyphical inscriptions, we find that even the native arts were more flourishing than they had ever been since the fall of the kings of Thebes; and we may almost look upon the Greek conquest as a blessing to Upper Egypt.

Philadelphus, though weak in body, was well suited
by his keen-sightedness and intelligence for the tasks
which the state of affairs at that time demanded from an
Egyptian king. He was a diplomat rather than a warrior,
and that was exactly what Egypt needed.

A curious anecdote about Ptolemy Philadelphus is
related by Niebuhr. He had reached the zenith of his
glory, when suddenly he was attacked by a species of
insanity, consisting of an indescribable fear of death.
Chemical artifices were practised in Egypt from the
earliest times; and hence Ptolemy took every imagina-
ble pains to find the elixir of life; but it was all in vain,
for his strength was rapidly decreasing. Once, like Louis
XI., he was looking from a window of his palace upon
the seacoast, and seriously meditated upon the subject
of his longing; it must have been in winter-time, when
the sand, exposed to the rays of the sun, becomes very
warm. He saw some poor boys burying themselves in
the warm sand and screaming with delight, and the aged
king began bitterly to cry, seeing the ragged urchins
enjoying their life without any apprehension of losing
it; for he felt that with all his riches he could not purchase that happiness, and that his end was very near
at hand. He died in the thirty-eighth year of his reign,
and perhaps the sixty-first of his age. He left the kingdom as powerful and more wealthy than when it came
to him from his father; and he had the happiness of having a son who would carry on, even for the third generation, the wise plans of the first Ptolemy.

PTOLEMAIC TEMPLE AT KOM OMBO.

CHAPTER IV

PTOLEMY EUERGETES, PTOLEMY PHILOPATOR, AND PTOLEMY EPIPHANES.

The struggle for Syria — Decline of the dynasty — Advent of Roman control.

PTOLEMY, the eldest son of Philadelphus, succeeded his father on the throne of Egypt, and after a short time was accorded the name of Euergetes. The new reign was clouded by dark occurrences, which again involved Egypt and Syria in war. It has been already related that when peace was concluded between Antiochus and Philadelphus, the latter gave to the former his daughter Berenicë in marriage, stipulating that the offspring of that union should succeed

STATUE OF NEITH.

153

to the Syrian throne, though Antiochus had, by his wife Laodice, a son, already arrived at the age of manhood. The repudiated queen murdered her husband, and placed Seleucus on the vacant throne; who, in order to remove all competition on the part of Berenicë and her child, made no scruple to deprive them both of life. Euergetes could not behold such proceedings unmoved. Advancing into Syria at the head of a powerful army, he took possession of the greater part of the country, which seems not to have been defended, the majority of the cities opening their gates at his approach. The important town of Seleucia Pieria, the seaport of the capital, fell into his hands, in the neighbourhood of which he was still further gratified with the apprehension of the cruel Laodice, at whose instigation his sister and nephew lost their lives. The punishment of this unprincipled woman seems, however, to have completely satiated his resentment; for, instead of securing his conquests in Syria, and achieving the entire humiliation of Seleucus, he led his army on a plundering expedition into the remote provinces of Asia, whence, on the news of domestic troubles, he returned to the shores of Africa in triumph, laden with an immense booty, comprising among other objects all the statues of the Egyptian deities which had been carried off by Cambyses to Persia or Babylon. These he restored to their respective temples, an act by which he earned the greatest popularity among his native Egyptian subjects, who bestowed upon him, in consequence, the title of Euergetes (Benefactor), by which he is generally known. He brought back also from this expedition a vast number of other works of art, for the museums were a passion with the Ptolemies. The Asiatics might, indeed, have got over these things, but he levied, in addition, immense contributions from the Asiatics, and is said to have raised over forty thousand talents. On his march homeward, he laid his gifts upon the altar in the Temple of Jerusalem, and there returned thanks to Heaven for his victories. He had been taught to bow the knee to the crowds of Greek and Egyptian gods; and, as Palestine was part of his kingdom, it seemed quite natural to add the God of the Jews to the list.

Of the insurrection in Egypt, which obliged him to return, we know no particulars, but Euergetes seems to have become convinced that Egypt was too small a basis for such an empire. "If he had wished to retain all his conquests," relates the chronicler, "he would have been obliged to make Antioch his residence, and this would weaken the ground of his strength. He, moreover, appears to have been well aware that the conquests had been made too quickly." He accordingly divided them, retaining for himself Syria as far as Euphrates, and the coast districts of Asia Minor and Thrace, so that he had a complete maritime empire. The remaining territories he divided into two states: the country beyond the Euphrates was given, according to St. Jerome, to one Xantippus, who is otherwise unknown, and Western Asia was left to Antiochus Hierax. It would seem that after this he never visited those countries again.

One of the notable incidents of the war against Syria was an offer of help to Egypt from the Romans. From

the middle of the reign-of Philadelphus till the fifth year
of this reign, for twenty-two years, the Romans had been
struggling with the Carthaginians for their very being,
in the first Punic war, which they had just brought to a
close, and on hearing of Ptolemy's war in Syria, they sent
to Egypt with friendly offers of help. But their ambassadors did not reach Alexandria before peace was made,
and they were sent home with many thanks. The event
serves to show the trend of the aspirations of this now
important nation, which was afterwards destined to en-
gulf the kingdoms of Egypt and Syria alike.

After Euergetes had, as he thought, established his
authority in Asia, a party hostile to him came forward
to oppose him. The Rhodians, with their wise policy,
who had hitherto given no decided support to either empire, now stepped forward, setting to other maritime
cities the example of joining that hostile party. The
confederates formed a fleet, with the assistance of which,
and supported by a general insurrection of the Asiatics,
who were exasperated against the Egyptians on account
of their rapacity, Seleucus Callinicus rallied again. He
recovered the whole of upper Asia, and for a time he was
united with his brother, Antiochus Hierax. The insurrection in Egypt must have been of a very serious nature,
and Ptolemy, being pressed on all sides, concluded a truce
of ten years with Seleucus on basis of *uti possidetis*.
Both parties seem to have retained the places which they
possessed at the time, so that all the disadvantage was
on the side of the Seleucidæ, for the fortified town of
Seleucia, for example, remained in the hands of the

Egyptians, whereby the capital was placed in a dangerous position. A part of Cilicia, the whole of Caria, the Ionian cities, the Thracian Chersonesus, and several Macedonian towns likewise continued to belong to Egypt.

Soon after his re-appearance in Egypt, Euergetes was solicited by Cleomenes, the King of Sparta, to grant the assistance of his arms in the struggle which that republic was then supporting with Antigonus, the ruler of Macedon, and with the members of the Achaian league. But the battle of Sellasia proved that the aid offered was inadequate. Cleomenes fled to the banks of the Nile, where he found his august ally reposing under the successful banners of a numerous army, which he had just led home from the savage mountains of Ethiopia, whither his love of romantic conquest had conducted them. He appears to have penetrated into the interior provinces of Abyssinia, and to have subdued the rude tribes which dwelt on the shores of the Red Sea, levying on the unfortunate natives the most oppressive contributions in cattle, gold, perfumes, and other articles belonging to that valuable merchandise which the Ethiopians and Arabs had long carried on with their Egyptian neighbours. At Adule, the principal seaport of Abyssinia, he collected his victorious troops, and made them a speech on the wonderful exploits which they had achieved under his auspices, and on the numerous benefits which they had thereby secured to their native country. The throne on which he sat, composed of white marble and supported by a slab of porphyry, was consecrated to the god of war, whom he chose to claim for his father and patron, and

that the descendants of the vanquished Ethiopians might
not be ignorant of their obligations to Ptolemy Euergetes,
King of Egypt, he gave orders that his name and principal triumphs should be inscribed on the votive chair.
But not content with his real conquests, which reached
from the Hellespont to the Euphrates, he added, like
Ramses, that he had conquered Thrace, Persia, Media,
and Bactria. He thus teaches us that monumental inscriptions, though read with difficulty, do not always tell
the truth. This was the most southerly spot to which
the kings of Egypt ever sent an army. But they kept
no hold on the country. Distance had placed it not only
beyond their power, but almost beyond their knowledge;
and two hundred years afterwards, when the geographer
Strabo was making inquiries about that part of Arabia,
as it was called, he was told of this monument as set up
by the hero Sesostris, to whom it was usual to give the
credit of so many wonderful works. These inscriptions,
it is worthy of remark, are still preserved, and constitute
the only historical account that has reached these times
of the Ethiopian warfare of this Egyptian monarch.
About seven hundred years after the reign of Euergetes,
they were first published in the *Topography* of Cosmas
Indicopleustes, a Grecian monk, by whom they were copied on the spot. The traveller Bruce, moreover, informs
us that the stone containing the name of Ptolemy Euergetes serves as a footstool to the throne on which the
kings of Abyssinia are crowned to this day. Amid the
ruins of Ascum, also, the ancient capital of that country,
various fragments of marble have been found bearing

the name and title of the same Egyptian sovereign. This empty fame, however, is the only return that ever re- compensed the toils of Euergetes among the fierce bar- barians of the south.

Euergetes, as part of his general policy of conciliating the Egyptians, enlarged the great temple at Thebes, which is now called the temple of Karnak, on the walls of which we see him handing an offering to his father and mother, the brother-gods. In one place he is in a Greek dress, which is not common on the Ptolemaic build- ings, as most of the Greek kings are carved upon the walls in the dress of the country. The early kings had often shown their piety to a temple by enlarging the sacred area and adding a new wall and gateway in front of the former; and this custom Euergetes followed at Karnak. As these grand stone sculptured gateways belonged to a wall of unbaked bricks which has long since crumbled to pieces, they

GATE AT KARNAK.

now stand apart like so many triumphal arches. He also added to the temple at Hibe in the Great Oasis, and began a small temple at Esne, or Latopolis, where he is drawn upon the walls in the act of striking down the chiefs of the conquered nations, and is followed by a tame lion. He built a temple to Osiris at Canopus, on the mouth of the Nile; for, notwithstanding the large number of Greeks and strangers who had settled there, the ancient religion was not yet driven out of the Delta; and he dedicated it to the god in a Greek inscription on a plate of gold, in the names of himself and Berenicë, whom he called his wife and sister. She is also called the king's sister in many of the hieroglyphical inscriptions, as are many of the other queens of the Ptolemies who were not so related to their husbands. This custom, though it took its rise in the Egyptian mythology, must have been strengthened by the marriages of Philadelphus and some of his successors with their sisters. In the hieroglyphical inscriptions he is usually called " beloved by Phtah," the god of Memphis, an addition to his name which was used by most of his successors.

During this century the Greek artists in Egypt, as indeed elsewhere, adopted in their style an affectation of antiquity, which, unless seen through, would make us think their statues older than they really are. They sometimes set a stiff beard upon a face without expression, or arranged the hair of the head in an old-fashioned manner, and, while making the drapery fly out in a direction opposed to that of the figure, gave to it formal zigzag lines, which could only be proper if it were hanging down in quiet. At other times, while they gave to the human figure all the truth to which their art had then reached, they yet gave to the drapery these stiff zigzag forms. No habit of mind would have been more improving to the Alexandrian character than a respect for antiquity; but this respect ought to be shown in a noble rivalry, in trying to surpass those who have gone before them, and not as in this manner by copying their faults. Hieroglyphics seem to have flourished in their

RUINS OF SAÏS.

more ancient style and forms under the generous patronage of the Ptolemies. In the time of the Egyptian
kings of Lower Egypt, we find new grammatical endings
to the nouns, and more letters used to spell each word
than under the kings of Thebes; but, on comparing the
hieroglyphics of the Ptolemies with the others, we find
that in these and some other points they are more like
the older writings, under the kings of Thebes, than the
newer, under the kings of Saïs.

But, while the Egyptians were flattered, and no doubt
raised in moral worth, by their monarch's taking up the
religious feelings of the country, and throwing aside
some of the Greek habits of his father and grandfather,
Euergetes was sowing the seeds of a greater change than
he could himself have been aware of. It was by Greek
arms and arts of war that Egypt then held its place
among nations, and we shall see in the coming reigns
that, while the court became more Asiatic and less European, the army and government did not retain their
former characteristics.

Since Cœle-Syria and Judæa were by the first Ptolemy made a province of Egypt, the Jews had lived in
unbroken tranquillity, and with very little loss of freedom. The kings of Egypt had allowed them to govern
themselves, to live under their own laws, and choose
their own high priest; but they required of them the
payment to Alexandria of a yearly tribute. Part of this
was the sacred poll-tax of half a shekel, or about sixteen
cents for every male above the age of twenty, which by
the Mosaic law they had previously paid for the service

of the Temple. This is called in the Gospels the Didrachms; though the Alexandrian translators of the Bible, altering the sum, either through mistake or on purpose, have made it in the Greek Pentateuch only half a didrachm, or about eight cents. This yearly tribute from the Temple the high priest of Jerusalem had been usually allowed to collect and farm; but in the latter end of this reign, the high priest Onias, a weak and covetous old man, refused to send to Alexandria the twenty talents, or fifteen thousand dollars, at which it was then valued. When Euergetes sent Athenion as ambassador to claim it, and even threatened to send a body of troops to fetch it, still the tribute was not paid; notwithstanding the fright of the Jews, the priest would not part with his money.

On this, Joseph, the nephew of Onias, set out for Egypt, to try and turn away the king's anger. He went to Memphis, and met Euergetes riding in his chariot with the queen and Athenion, the ambassador. The king, when he knew him, begged him to get into the chariot and sit with him; and Joseph made himself so agreeable that he was lodged in the palace at Memphis, and dined every day at the royal table. While he was at Memphis, the revenues of the provinces for the coming year were put up to auction; and the farmers bid eight thousand talents, or six million dollars, for the taxes of Cœle-Syria, Phœnicia, and Samaria. Joseph then bid double that sum, and, when he was asked what security he could give, he playfully said that he was sure that Euergetes and the queen would willingly become bound for his honesty;

and the king was so much pleased with him that the office was at once given to him, and he held it for twenty-two years.

Among the men of letters who at this time taught in the Alexandrian schools was Aristophanes, the grammarian, who afterwards held the office of head of the museum. At one of the public sittings at which the king was to hear the poems and other writings of the pupils read, and, by the help of seven men of letters who sat with him as judges, was to give away honours and rewards to the best authors, one of the chairs was empty, one of the judges happened not to be there. The king asked who should be called up to fill his place; and, after thinking over the matter, the six judges fixed upon Aristophanes, who had made himself known to them by being seen daily studying in the public library. When the reading was over, the king, the public, and the six other judges were agreed upon which was the best piece of writing; but Aristophanes was bold enough to think otherwise, and he was able, by means of his great reading, to find the book in the library from which the pupil had copied the greater part of his work. The king was much struck with this proof of his learning, and soon afterwards made him keeper of the library which he had already so well used. Aristophanes followed Zenodotus in his critical efforts to mend the text of Homer's poems. He also invented the several marks by which grammarians now distinguish the length and tone of a syllable and the breathing of a vowel, that is, the marks for long and short, and the accents and aspirate. The last two, after his time, were always placed over Greek words, and are still used in printed books.

Eratosthenes of Cyrene, the inventor of astronomical geography, was at this time the head of the mathematical school. He has the credit for being the first to calculate the circumference of the earth by means of his Theory of Shadows. As a poet he wrote a description of the constellations. He also wrote a history of Egypt, to correct the errors of Manetho. What most strikes us with wonder and regret is, that of these two writers, Manetho, an Egyptian priest who wrote in Greek, Eratosthenes, a Greek who understood something of Egyptian, neither of them took the trouble to lay open to their readers the peculiarities of the hieroglyphics. Through all these reigns, the titles and praises of the Ptolemies were carved upon the temples in the sacred characters. These two histories were translated from the same inscriptions. We even now read the names of the kings which they mention carved on the statues and temples; and yet the language of the hieroglyphics still remained unknown beyond the class of priests; such was the want of curiosity on the part of the Greek grammarians of Alexandria. Such, we may add, was their want of respect for the philosophy of the Egyptians; and we need no stronger proof that the philosophers of the museum had hitherto borrowed none of the doctrines of the priests.

Lycon of Troas was another settler in Alexandria. He followed Strato at the head of one of the schools in the museum. He was very successful in bringing up

GATEWAY OF PTOLEMY EUERGETES AT KARNAK.

the young men, who needed, he used to say, modesty and the love of praise, as a horse needs bridle and spur. His eloquence was so pleasing that he was wittily called Glycon, or the sweet. Carneades of Cyrene at the same time held a high place among philosophers; but as he had removed to Athens, where he was at the head of a school, and was even sent to Rome as the ambassador of the Athenians, we must not claim the whole honour of him for the Ptolemies under whom he was born. It is therefore enough to say of him that, though a follower of Plato, he made such changes in the opinions of the Academy, by not wholly throwing off the evidence of the senses, that his school was called the New Academy.

Apollonius, who was born at Alexandria, but is commonly called Apollonius Rhodius because he passed many years of his life at Rhodes, had been, like Eratosthenes, a hearer of Callimachus. His only work which we now know is his *Argonautics*, a poem on the voyage of Jason to Colchis in search of the golden fleece. It is a regular epic poem, in imitation of Homer; and, like other imitations, it wants the interest which hangs upon reality of manners and story in the Iliad.

Callimachus showed his dislike of his young rival by hurling against him a reproachful poem, in which he speaks of him under the name of an Ibis. This is now lost, but it was copied by Ovid in his poem of the same name; and from the Roman we can gather something of the dark and learned style in which Callimachus threw out his biting reproaches. We do not know from what this quarrel arose, but it seems to have been the cause

of Apollonius leaving Alexandria. He removed to
Rhodes, where he taught in the schools during all the
reign of Philopator, till he was recalled by Epiphanes,
and made librarian of the museum in his old age, on
the death of Eratosthenes.

Lycophron, the tragic writer, lived about this time
at Alexandria, and was one of the seven men of letters
sometimes called the Alexandrian Pleiades, though writers are not agreed upon the names which fill up the list.
His tragedies are all lost, and the only work of his which
we now have is the dark and muddy poem of Alcandra,
or Cassandra, of which the lines most striking to the
historian are those in which the prophetess foretells
the coming greatness of Rome; that the children of
Æneas will raise the crown upon their spears, and seize
the sceptres of sea and land. Lycophron was the friend
of Menedemus and Aratus; and it is not easy to believe
that these lines were written before the overthrow of
Hannibal in Italy, and of the Greek phalanx at Cynocephalæ, or that one who was a man in the reign of Philadelphus should have foreseen the triumph of the Roman
arms. These words must have been a later addition to
the poem, to improve the prophecy.

Conon, one of the greatest of the Alexandrian astronomers, has left no writings for us to judge of his
merits, though they were thought highly of, and made
great use of, by his successors. He worked both as an
observer and an inquirer, mapping out the heavens by
his observations, and collecting the accounts of the
eclipses which had been before observed in Egypt. He

was the friend of Archimedes of Syracuse, to whom he
sent his problems, and from whom he received that great
geometrician's writings in return.

Apollonius of Perga came to Alexandria in this reign,
to study mathematics under the pupils of Euclid. He
is well known for his work on conic sections, and he may
be called the founder of this study. The Greek mathematicians sought after knowledge for its own sake, and
followed up those branches of their studies which led
to no end that could in the narrow sense be called useful,
with the same zeal that they did other branches out of
which sprung the great practical truths of mechanics,
astronomy, and geography. They found reward enough
in the enlargement of their minds and in the beauty of
the truth learnt. Alexandrian science gained in loftiness
of tone what its poetry and philosophy wanted. Thus
the properties of the ellipse, the hyperbola, and the par-
abola, continued to be studied by after mathematicians;
but no use was made of this knowledge till nearly two
thousand years later, when Kepler crowned the labours
of Apollonius with the great discovery that the paths
of the planets round the sun were conic sections. The
Egyptians, however, made great use of mathematical
knowledge, particularly in the irrigation of their fields;
and Archimedes of Syracuse, who came to Alexandria
about this time to study under Conon, did the country
a real service by his invention of the cochlea, or screw-
pump. The more distant fields of the valley of the Nile,
rising above the level of the inundation, have to be
watered artificially by pumping out of the canals into

ditches at a higher level. For this work Archimedes proposed a spiral tube, twisting round an axis, which was to be put in motion either by the hand or by the force of the stream out of which it was to pump; and this was found so convenient that it soon became the machine most in use throughout Egypt for irrigation.

But while we are dazzled by the brilliancy of these clusters of men of letters and science who graced the court of Alexandria, we must not shut our eyes to those faults which are always found in works called forth rather by the fostering warmth of royal pensions than by a love of knowledge in the people. The well-fed and well-paid philosophers of the museum were not likely to overtake the mighty men of Athens in its best days, who had studied and taught without any pension from the government, without taking any fee from their pupils; who were urged forward towards excellence by the love of knowledge and of honour; who had no other aim than that of being useful to their hearers, and looked for no reward beyond their love and esteem.

In oratory Alexandria made no attempts whatever; it is a branch of literature not likely to flourish under a despotic monarchy. In Athens it fell with the loss of liberty, and Demetrius Phalereus was the last of the real Athenian orators. After his time the orations were declamations written carefully in the study, and coldly spoken in the school for the instruction of the pupils, and wholly wanting in fire and genius; and the Alexandrian men of letters forbore to copy Greece in its lifeless harangues. For the same reasons the Alexandrians were

not successful in history. A species of writing, which
a despot requires to be false and flattering, is little likely
to flourish; and hence the only historians of the museum
were chronologists, antiquaries, and writers of travels.

The coins of Euergetes bear the name of "Ptolemy
the king," round the head on the one side, with no title
by which they can be known from the other kings of the
same name. But his portrait is known from his Phœnician coins. In the same
way the coins of his
queen have only the
name of "Berenicë the
queen," but they are
known from those of the
later queens by the

COIN OF PTOLEMY III.

beauty of the workmanship, which soon fell far below
that of the first Ptolemies.

Euergetes had married his cousin Berenicë, who like
the other queens of Egypt is sometimes called Cleopatra;
by her he left two sons, Ptolemy and Magas, to the eldest
of whom he left his kingdom, after a reign of twenty-five
years of unclouded prosperity. Egypt was during this
reign at the very height of its power and wealth. It had
seen three kings, who, though not equally great men,
not equally fit to found a monarchy or to raise the literature of a people, were equally successful in the parts
which they had undertaken. Euergetes left to his son
a kingdom perhaps as large as the world had ever seen
under one sceptre; and though many of his boasted victories were like letters written in the sand, of which the

traces were soon lost, yet he was by far the greatest, and possibly the wisest, monarch of his day.

We may be sure that in these prosperous reigns life and property were safe, and justice was administered fairly by judges who were independent of the crown; as even centuries afterwards we find that it was part of a judge's oath on taking office, that, if he were ordered by the king to do what was wrong, he would not obey him. But here the bright pages in the history of the Ptolemies end. Though trade and agriculture still enriched the country, though arts and letters did not quit Alexandria, we have from this time forward to mark the

COIN OF BERENICÊ, WIFE OF PTOLEMY III.

growth only of vice and luxury, and to measure the wisdom of Ptolemy Soter by the length of time that his laws and institutions were able to bear up against the misrule and folly of his descendants.

Ptolemy, the eldest son of Euergetes, inherited the crown of his forefathers, but none of the great qualities by which they had won and guarded it. He was then about thirty-four years old. His first act was to call together his council, and to ask their advice about putting to death his mother Berenicë and his brother Magas. Their crime was the being too much liked by the army; and the council was called upon to say whether it would be safe to have them killed. Cleomenes, the banished King of Sparta, who was one of the council, alone raised

his voice against their murder, and wisely said that the
throne would be still safer if there were more brothers
to stand between the king and the daring hopes of a
traitor. The minister Sosibius, on the other hand, said
that the mercenaries could not be trusted while Magas
was alive; but Cleomenes remarked to him, that more
than three thousand of them were Peloponnesians, and
that they would follow him sooner than they would
follow Magas.

Berenicë and Magas were, however, put to death, but
the speech of Cleomenes was not forgotten. If his popularity with the mercenaries could secure their allegiance,
he could, when he chose, make them rebel; from that
time he was treated rather as a prisoner than as a friend,
and by his well-meaning but incautious observation he
lost all chance of being helped to regain his kingdom.

Nothing is known of the death of Euergetes, the late
king, and there is no proof that it was by unfair means.
But when his son began a cruel and wicked reign by putting to death his mother and brother, and by taking the
name of Philopator, or father-loving, the world seems
to have thought that he was the murderer of his father,
and had taken this name to throw a cloak over the deed.

By this murder of his brother, and by the minority
both of Antiochus, King of Syria, and of Philip, King of
Macedonia, Philopator found himself safe from enemies
either at home or abroad, and he gave himself up to a life
of thoughtlessness and pleasure. The army and fleet
were left to go to ruin, and the foreign provinces, which
had hitherto been looked upon as the bulwarks of Egypt,

were only half-guarded; but the throne rested on the virtues of his forefathers, and it was not till his death that it was found to have been undermined by his own follies and vice.

Egypt had been governed by kings of more than usual wisdom for above one hundred years, and was at the very height of its power when Philopator came to the throne. He found himself master of Ethiopia, Cyrene, Phœnicia, Cœle-Syria, part of Upper Syria, Cyprus, Rhodes, the cities along the coast of Asia Minor from Pamphilia to Lysimachia, and the cities of Ænos and Maronea in Thrace. The unwilling obedience of distant provinces usually costs more than it is worth; but many of these possessions across the Mediterranean had put themselves willingly into the power of his predecessors for the sake of their protection, and they cost little more than a message to warn off invaders. Egypt was the greatest naval power in the world, having the command of the sea and the whole of the coast at the eastern end of the Mediterranean.

On the death of Euergetes, the happiness of the people came to an end. The first trouble arose from the loose and vicious habits of the new king, and was an attempt made upon his life by Cleomenes, who found the palace in Alexandria had now become a prison. The Spartan took advantage of the king's being at Canopus to escape from his guards, and to raise a riot in Alexandria; but not being able to gain the citadel, and seeing that disgrace and death must follow upon his failure, he stabbëd himself with his own dagger.

The kingdom of Syria, after being humbled by Ptolemy Euergetes, had risen lately under the able rule of Antiochus, son of Seleucus Callinicus. He was a man possessed of abilities of a high order. His energy and courage soon recovered from Egypt the provinces that Syria had before lost, and afterwards gained for him the name of Antiochus the Great. He made himself master of the city of Damascus by a stratagem. Soon after this, Seleucia, the capital, which had been taken by Euergetes, was retaken by Antiochus, or rather given up to him by treachery. Theodotus also, the Alexandrian governor of Cœle-Syria, delivered up to him that province; and Antiochus marched southward, and had taken Tyre and Ptolemaïs before the Egyptian army could be brought into the field. There he gained forty ships of war, of which twenty were decked vessels with four banks of oars, and the others smaller. He then marched towards Egypt, and on his way learned that Ptolemy was at Memphis. On his arrival at Pelusium he found that the place was strongly guarded, and that the garrison had opened the flood-gates from the neighbouring lake, and thereby spoiled the fresh water of all the neighbourhood; he therefore did not lay siege to that city, but seized many of the open towns on the east side of the Nile.

On this, Philopator roused himself from his idleness, and got together his forces against the coming danger. His troops consisted of Greeks, Egyptians, and mercenaries to the total of seventy-three thousand men and seventy-three elephants, or one elephant to every thousand men, which was the number usually allowed to the

armies about this time. But before this army reached
Pelusium, Antiochus had led back his forces to winter in
Seleucia. The next spring Antiochus again marched
towards Egypt with an army of seventy-two thousand
foot, six thousand horse, and one hundred and two elephants. Philopator led his whole forces to the frontier
to oppose his march, and met the Syrian army near the
village of Raphia, the border town between Egypt and
Palestine. Arsinoë, his queen and sister, rode with him
on horseback through the ranks, and called upon the
soldiers to fight for their wives and children. At first
the Egyptians seemed in danger of being beaten. As the
armies approached one another, the Ethiopian elephants
trembled at the very smell of the Indian elephants, and
shrunk from engaging with beasts so much larger than
themselves. On the charge, the left wing of each army
was routed, as was often the case among the Greeks,
when, from too great a trust in the shield, every soldier
kept moving to the right, and thus left the left wing
uncovered. But before the end of the day the invading
army was defeated; and, though some of the Egyptian
officers treacherously left their posts, and carried their
troops over to Antiochus, yet the Syrian army was
wholly routed, and Arsinoë enjoyed the knowledge and
the praise of having been the chief cause of her husband's
success. The king in gratitude sacrificed to the gods
the unusual offering of four elephants.

By this victory Philopator regained Cœle-Syria, and
there he spent three months; he then made a hasty, and,
if we judge his reasons rightly, we must add, a disgrace-

ful treaty with the enemy, that he might the sooner get back to his life of ease. Before going home he passed through Jerusalem, where he gave thanks and sacrificed to the Hebrew god in the temple of the Jews; and, being struck with the beauty of the building, asked to be shown into the inner room, in which were kept the ark of the covenant, Aaron's rod that budded, and the golden pot of manna, with the tables of the covenant. The priests told him of their law, by which every stranger, every Jew, and every priest but the high priest, was forbidden to pass beyond the second veil; but Philopator roughly answered that he was not bound by the Jewish laws, and ordered them to lead him into the holy of holies.

The city was thrown into alarm by this unheard-of wickedness; the streets were filled with men and women in despair; the air was rent with shrieks and cries, and the priests prayed to Javeh to guard his own temple from the stain. The king's mind, however, was not to be changed; the refusal of the priests only strengthened his wish, and all struggle was useless while the court of the temple was filled with Greek soldiers. But, says the Jewish historian, the prayer of the priests was heard; the king fell to the ground in a fit, like a reed broken by the wind, and was carried out speechless by his friends and generals.

On his return to Egypt, he showed his hatred of the nation by his treatment of the Jews in Alexandria. He made a law that they should lose the rank of Macedonians, and be enrolled among the class of Egyptians. He ordered them to have their bodies marked with pricks,

in the form of an ivy leaf, in honour of Bacchus; and
those who refused to have this done were outlawed, or
forbidden to enter the courts of justice. The king himself had an ivy leaf marked with pricks upon his fore-
head, from which he received the nickname of Gallus.
This custom of marking the body had been forbidden
in the Levitical law: it was not known among the Kopts,
but must always have been in use among the Lower
Egyptians. It was used by the Arab prisoners of Ramses, and is still practiced among the Egyptian Arabs
of the present day.

He also ordered the Jews to sacrifice on the pagan
altars, and many of them were sent up to Alexandria
to be punished for rebelling against his decree. Their
resolution, however, or, as their historian asserts, a mira-
cle from heaven changed the king's mind. They expected to be trampled to death in the hippodrome by
furious elephants; but after some delay they were released unhurt. The history of their escape, however, is
more melancholy than the history of their danger. No
sooner did the persecution cease than they turned with
pharisaical cruelty against their weaker brethren who
had yielded to the storm; and they put to death three
hundred of their countrymen, who in the hour of danger
had yielded to the threats of punishment, and complied
with the ceremonies required of them.

The Egyptians, who, when the Persians were conquered by Alexander, could neither help nor hinder the
Greek army, and who, when they formed part of the
troops under the first Ptolemy, were uncounted and un-

valued, had by this time been armed and disciplined like Greeks; and in the battle of Raphia the Egyptian phalanx had shown itself not an unworthy rival of the Macedonians. By this success in war, and by their hatred of their vicious and cruel king, the Egyptians were now for the first time encouraged to take arms against the Greek government. The Egyptian phalanx murmured against their Greek officers, and claimed their right to be under an Egyptian general. But history has told us nothing more of the rebellion than that it was successfully put down. The Greeks were still the better soldiers.

The ships built by Philopator were more remarkable for their unwieldy size, their luxurious and costly furniture, than for their fitness for war. One was four hundred and twenty feet long and fifty-seven feet wide, with forty banks of oars. The longest oars were fifty-seven feet long, and weighted with lead at the handles that they might be the more easily moved. This huge ship was to be rowed by four thousand rowers, its sails were to be shifted by four hundred sailors, and three thousand soldiers were to stand in ranks upon deck. There were seven beaks in front, by which it was to strike and sink the ships of the enemy. The royal barge, in which the king and court moved on the quiet waters of the Nile, was nearly as large as this ship of war. It was three hundred and thirty feet long, and forty-five feet wide; it was fitted up with staterooms and private rooms, and was nearly sixty feet high to the top of the royal awning. A third ship, which even surpassed these in its fittings and ornaments, was given to Philopator by Hiero, King of Syracuse. It was built under the care of Archimedes, and its timbers would have made sixty triremes. Beside baths, and rooms for pleasures of all kinds, it had a library, and astronomical instruments, not only for navigation, as in modern ships, but for study, as in an observatory. It was a ship of war, and had eight towers, from each of which stones were to be thrown at the enemy by six men. Its machines, like modern cannons, could throw stones of three hundred pounds weight, and arrows of eighteen feet in length. It had four anchors of wood, and eight of iron. It was called the ship of Syracuse, but after it had been given to Philopator it was known by the name of the ship of Alexandria.

In the second year of Philopator's reign the Romans began that long and doubtful war with Hannibal, called the second Punic war, and in the twelfth year of this reign they sent ambassadors to renew their treaty of peace with Egypt. They sent as their gifts robes of purple for Philopator and Arsinoë, and for Philopator a chair of ivory and gold, which was the usual gift of the republic to friendly kings. The Alexandrians kept upon good terms both with the Romans and the Carthaginians during the whole of the Punic wars.

When the city of Rhodes, which had long been joined in close friendship with Egypt, was shaken by an earthquake, that threw down the colossal statue of Apollo, together with a large part of the city walls and docks, Philopator was not behind the other friendly kings and states in his gifts and help. He sent to his brave allies a large sum of money, with grain, timber, and hemp.

On the birth of his son and heir, in B. C. 209, ambassadors crowded to Alexandria with gifts and messages of joy. But they were all thrown into the shade by Hyrcanus, the son of Joseph, who was sent from Jerusalem by his father, and who brought to the king one hundred boys and one hundred girls, each carrying a talent of silver.

Philopator, soon after the birth of this his only child, employed Philammon, at the bidding of his mistress, to put to death his queen and sister Arsinoë, or Eurydice, as she is sometimes called. He had already forgotten his rank, and his name ennobled by the virtues of three generations, and had given up his days and nights to vice and riot. He kept in his pay several fools, or laughing-stocks as they were then called, who were the chosen companions of his meals; and he was the first who brought eunuchs into the court of Alexandria. His mistress Agathoclea, her brother Agathocles, and their mother Œnanthe, held him bound by those chains which clever, worthless, and selfish favourites throw around the mind of a weak and debauched king. Agathocles, who never left his side, was his adviser in matters of business or pleasure, and governed alike the army, the courts of justice, and the women. Thus was spent a reign of seventeen years, during which the king had never but once, when he met Antiochus in battle, roused himself from his life of sloth.

The misconduct and vices of Agathocles raised such an outcry against him, that Philopator, without giving up the pleasure of his favourite's company, was forced to take away from him the charge of receiving the taxes. That high post was then given to Tlepolemus, a young man, whose strength of body and warlike courage had made him the darling of the soldiers. Another charge given to Tlepolemus was that of watching over the supply and price of corn in Alexandria. The wisest statesmen of old thought it part of a king's duty to take care that the people were fed, and seem never to have found out that it would be better done if the people were left to take care of themselves. They thought it moreover a piece of wise policy, or at any rate of clever kingcraft, to keep down the price of food in the capital at the cost of the rest of the kingdom, and even sometimes to give a monthly fixed measure of corn to each citizen. By such means as these the crowd of poor and restless citizens, who swell the mob of every capital, was larger in Alexandria than it otherwise would have been; and the danger of riot, which it was meant to lessen, was every year increased.

Sosibius had made himself more hated than Agathocles; he had been the king's ready tool in all his murders. He had been stained, or at least reproached, with the murder of Lysimachus, the son of Philadelphus; then of Magas, the son of Euergetes, and Berenicê, the widow of Euergetes; of Cleomenes, the Spartan; and lastly, of Arsinoë, the wife of Philopator. For these crimes Sosibius was forced by the soldiers to give up to Tlepolemus the king's ring, or what in modern language would be called the great seal of the kingdom, the badge of office by which Egypt was governed; but the world soon saw that a body of luxurious mercenaries were as little able to choose a wise statesman as the king had been.

With all his vices, Philopator had yet inherited the love of letters which has thrown so bright a light around the whole of the family; and to his other luxurie8 he sometimes added that of the society of the learned men

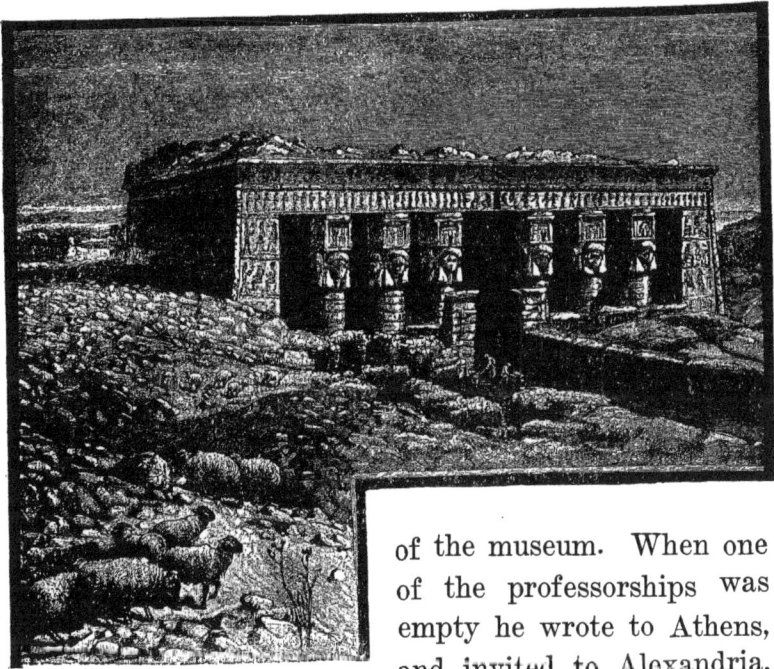

TEMPLE OF HATHOR.

of the museum. When one of the professorships was empty he wrote to Athens, and invited to Alexandria, Sphærus, who had been the pupil of Zeno. One day when Sphærus was dining with the king, he said that a wise man should never guess, but only say what he knows. Philopator, wishing to tease him, ordered some waxen pomegranates to be handed to him, and when Sphærus bit one of them he laughed at him for guessing that it was real fruit. But the stoic answered that there are many cases in which our actions must be guided by what seems probable. None of the works of Sphærus have come down to us.

Eratosthenes, of whom we have before spoken, was librarian of the museum during this reign; and Ptolemy, the son of Agesarchus, then wrote his history of Alexandria, a work now lost. The want of moral feeling in Alexandria was poorly supplied by the respect for talent. Philopator built there a shrine or temple to Homer, in which he placed a sitting figure of the poet, and round it seven worshippers, meant for the seven cities which claimed the honour of giving him birth. Had Homer himself worshipped in such temples, and had his thoughts been raised by no more lofty views, he would not have left us an Iliad or an Odyssey. In Upper Egypt there was no such want of religious earnestness; there the priests placed the name of Philopator upon a small temple near Medinet-Habu, dedicated to Amon-Ra and the goddess Hâthor; his name is also seen upon the temple at Karnak, and on the additions to the sculptures on the temple of Thot at Pselcis in Ethiopia.

COIN OF PTOLEMY PHILOPATOR.

Some of this king's coins bear the name of "Ptolemy Philopator," while those of the queen have her name, "Arsinoë Philopator," around the head. They are of a good style of art. He was also sometimes named Eupator; and it was under that name that the people of Paphos set up a monument to him in the temple of Venus.

The first three Ptolemies had been loved by their subjects and feared by their enemies; but Philopator, though his power was still acknowledged abroad, had by his vices and cruelty made himself hated at home, and had undermined the foundations of the government. He began his reign like an Eastern despot; instead of looking to his brother as a friend for help and strength, he distrusted him as a rival, and had him put to death. He employed the ministers of his vicious pleasures in the high offices of government; and instead of philosophers and men of learning, he brought eunuchs into the palace as the companions of his son. In B. C. 204 he died, worn out with disease, in the seventeenth year of his reign and about the fifty-first of his age; and very few lamented his decease.

On the death of Philopator his son was only five years old. The minister Agathocles, who had ruled over the country with unbounded power, endeavoured, by the help of his sister Agathoclea and the other mistresses of the late king, to keep his death secret; so that while the women seized the money and jewels of the palace, he might have time to take such

COIN OF ARSINOË PHILOPATOR.

steps as would secure his own power over the kingdom.

But the secret could not be long kept, and Agathocles called together the citizens of Alexandria to tell them of the death of Philopator, and to show them their young king.

He went to the meeting, followed by his sister Agathoclea and the young Ptolemy, afterwards called Epiphanes. He began his speech, " Ye men of Macedonia," as this mixed body of Greeks and Jews was always called. He wiped his eyes in well-feigned grief, and showed them the new king, who had been trusted, he said, by his father, to the motherly care of Agathoclea and to their loyalty. He then accused Tlepolemus of aiming at the throne, and brought forward a creature of his own to prove the truth of the charge. But his voice was soon drowned in the loud murmurs of the citizens; they had smarted too long under his tyranny, and were too well acquainted with his falsehoods, to listen to anything that he could say against his rival. Besides, Tlepolemus had the charge of supplying Alexandria with corn, a duty which was more likely to gain friends than the pandering to the vices of their hated tyrant. Agathocles soon saw that his life was in danger, and he left the meeting and returned to the palace, in doubt whether he should seek for safety in flight, or boldly seize the power which he was craftily aiming at, and rid himself of his enemies by their murder.

While he was wasting these precious minutes in doubt, the streets were filled with groups of men, and of boys, who always formed a part of the mobs of Alexandria. They sullenly but loudly gave vent to their

hatred of the minister; and if they had but found a
leader they would have been in rebellion. In a little
while the crowd moved off to the tents of the Macedonians, to learn their feelings on the matter, and then
to the quarters of the mercenaries, both of which were
close to the palace, and the mixed mob of armed and
unarmed men soon told the fatal news, that the soldiers
were as angry as the citizens. But they were still without a leader; they sent messengers to Tlepolemus, who
was not in Alexandria, and he promised that he would
soon be there; but perhaps he no more knew what to
do than his guilty rival.

Agathocles, in his doubt, did nothing; he sat down
to supper with his friends, perhaps hoping that the storm
might blow over of itself, perhaps trusting to chance and
to the strong walls of the palace. His mother, Œnanthe,
ran to the temple of Ceres and Proserpine, and sat down
before the altar in tears, believing that the sanctuary
of the temple would be her best safeguard; as if the
laws of heaven, which had never bound her, would bind
her enemies. It was a festal day, and the women in the
temple, who knew nothing of the storm which had risen
in the forum within these few hours, came forward to
comfort her; but she answered them with curses; she
knew that she was hated and would soon be despised,
and she added the savage prayer, that they might have
to eat their own children. The riot did not lessen at
sunset. Men, women, and boys were moving through
the streets all night with torches. The crowds were
greatest in the stadium and in the theatre of Bacchus,

but most noisy in front of the palace. Agathocles was awakened by the noise, and in his fright ran to the bedroom of the young Ptolemy; and, distrusting the palace walls, hid himself, with his own family, the king, and two or three guards, in the underground passage which led from the palace to the theatre.

The night, however, passed off without any violence; but at daybreak the murmurs became louder, and the thousands in the palace yard called for the young king. By that time the Greek soldiers joined the mob, and then the guards within were no longer to be feared. The gates were soon burst open, and the palace searched. The mob rushed through the halls and lobbies, and, learning where the king had fled, hastened to the underground passage. It was guarded by three doors of iron grating; but, when the first was beaten in, Aristomenes was sent out to offer terms of surrender. Agathocles was willing to give up the young king, his misused power, his illgotten wealth and estates; he asked only for his life. But this was sternly refused, and a shout was raised to kill the messenger; and Aristomenes, the best of the ministers, whose only fault was the being a friend of Agathocles, and the having named his little daughter Agathoclea, would certainly have been killed upon the spot if somebody had not reminded them that they wanted to send back an answer.

Agathocles, seeing that he could hold out no longer, then gave up the little king, who was set upon a horse, and led away to the stadium amid the shouts of the crowd. There they seated him on the throne, and, while he was crying at being surrounded by strange faces, the mob loudly called for revenge on the guilty ministers. Sosibius, the somatophylax, the son of the former general of that name, seeing no other way of stopping the fury of the mob and the child's sobs, asked him if the enemies of his mother and of his throne should be given up to the people. The child of course answered " yes," without understanding what was meant; and on that they let Sosibius take him to his own house to be out of the uproar. Agathocles was soon led out bound, and was stabbed by those who two days before would have felt honoured by a look from him. Agathoclea and her sister were then brought out, and lastly Œnanthe, their mother was dragged away from the altar of Ceres and Proserpine. Some bit them, some struck them with sticks, some tore their eyes out; her body was torn to pieces, and her limbs scattered among the crowd; to such lengths of madness and angry cruelty was the Alexandrian mob sometimes driven.

In the meanwhile some of the women called to mind that Philammon, who had been employed in the murder of Arsinoë, had within those three days come to Alexandria, and they made a rush at his house. The doors quickly gave way before their blows, and he was killed upon the spot by clubs and stones; his little son was strangled by these raging mothers, and his wife dragged naked into the street, and there torn to pieces. Thus died Agathocles and all his family; and the care of the young king then fell to Sosibius, and to Aristomenes, who had already gained a high character for wisdom and firmness.

While Egypt was thus without a government, Philip of Macedonia and Antiochus of Syria agreed to divide the foreign provinces between them; and Antiochus marched against Cœle-Syria and Phœnicia. The guardians of the young Ptolemy sent against him an army under Scopas, the Ætolian, who was at first successful, but was afterwards beaten by Antiochus at Paneas in the valley of the Jordan, three and twenty miles above the Lake of Tiberias, and driven back into Egypt. In these battles the Jews, who had not forgotten the ill treatment that they had received from Philopator, joined Antiochus, after having been under the government of Egypt for exactly one hundred years; and in return Antiochus released Jerusalem from all taxes for three years, and afterwards from one-third of the taxes. He also sent a large sum of money for the service of the temple, and released the elders, priests, scribes, and singing men from all taxes for the future.

The Alexandrian statesmen had latterly shown themselves in their foreign policy very unworthy pupils of Ptolemy Soter and Philadelphus, who had both ably trimmed the balance of power between the several successors of Alexander. But even had they been wiser, they could hardly, before the end of the second Punic war, have foreseen that the Romans would soon be their most dangerous enemies. The overthrow of Hannibal, however, might perhaps have opened their eyes; but it was then too late; Egypt was too weak to form an alliance with Macedonia or Syria against the Romans. About this time, also, the Romans sent to Alexandria, to inform the king that they had conquered Hannibal, and brought to a close the second Punic war, and to thank him for the friendship of the Egyptians during that long and doubtful struggle of eighteen years, when so many of their nearer neighbours had joined the enemy. They begged that if the senate felt called upon to undertake a war against Philip, who, though no friend to the Egyptians, had not yet taken arms against them, it might cause no breach in the friendship between the King of Egypt and the Romans. In answer to this embassy, the Alexandrians, rushing to their own destruction, sent to Rome a message, which was meant to place the kingdom wholly in the hands of the senate. It was to beg them to undertake the guardianship of the young Ptolemy, and the defence of the kingdom against Philip and Antiochus during his childhood.

The Romans, in return, gave the wished-for answer; they sent ambassadors to Antiochus and Philip, to order them to make no attack upon Egypt, on pain of falling under the displeasure of the senate; and they sent Marcus Lepidus to Alexandria, to accept the offered prize, and to govern the foreign affairs of the kingdom, under the modest name of tutor to the young king. This high honour was afterwards mentioned by Lepidus, with pride, upon the coins struck when he was consul, in the eighteenth year of this reign. They have the city of Alexandria on the one side, and on the other the title of "Tutor to the king," with the figure of the Roman in his toga, putting the diadem on the head of the young Ptolemy.

The haughty orders of the senate at first had very little weight with the two kings. Antiochus conquered Phœnicia and Cœle-Syria; and he was then met by a second message from the senate, who no longer spoke in the name of their ward, the young King of Egypt, but ordered him to give up to the Roman people the states which he had seized, and which belonged, they said, to the Romans by the right of war. On this, Antiochus made peace with Egypt by a treaty, in which he betrothed his daughter Cleopatra to the young Ptolemy, and added the disputed provinces of Phœnicia and Cœle-Syria as a dower, which were to be given up to Egypt when the king was old enough to be married.

ROMAN COIN, ISSUED UNDER
PTOLEMY V.

Philip marched against Athens and the other states of Greece which had heretofore held themselves independent and in alliance with Egypt; and, when the Athenian embassy came to Alexandria to beg for the usual help, Ptolemy's ministers felt themselves so much in the power of the senate that they sent to Rome to ask whether they should help their old friends, the Athenians, against Philip, the common enemy, or whether they should leave it to the Romans to help them. And these haughty republicans, who wished all their allies to forget the use of arms, who valued their friends not for their strength but for their obedience, sent them word that the senate did not wish them to help the Athenians, and that the Roman people would take care of their own allies. The Alexandrians looked upon the proud but unlettered Romans only as friends, as allies, who asked for no pay, who took no reward, who fought only for ambition and for the glory of their country.

Soon after this, the battle of Cynocephalæ in Thessaly was fought between Philip and the Romans, in which the Romans lost only seven hundred men, while as many as eight thousand Macedonians were left dead upon the field. This battle, though only between Rome and Macedonia, must not be passed unnoticed in the history of Egypt, where the troops were armed and disciplined like Macedonians; as it was the first time that the world had seen the Macedonian phalanx routed and in flight before any troops not so armed.

The phalanx was a body of spearsmen, in such close array that each man filled a space of only one square yard. The spear was seven yards long, and, when held in both hands, its point was five yards in front of the soldier's breast. There were sixteen ranks of these men, and, when the first five ranks lowered their spears, the point of the fifth spear was one yard in front of the foremost rank. The Romans, on the other hand, fought in open ranks, with one yard between each, or each man filled a space of four square yards, and in a charge would have to meet ten Macedonian spears. But then the Roman soldiers went into battle with much higher feelings than those of the Greeks. In Rome, arms were trusted only to the citizens, to those who had a country to love, a home to guard, and who had some share in making the laws which they were called upon to obey. But the Greek armies of Macedonia, Egypt, and Syria were made up either of natives who bowed their necks in slavery, or of mercenaries who made war their trade and rioted in its lawlessness; both of whom felt that they had little to gain from victory, and nothing to lose by a change of masters. Moreover, the warlike skill of the Romans was far greater than any that had yet been brought against the Greeks. It had lately been improved in their wars with Hannibal, the great master of that science. They saw that the phalanx could use its whole strength only on a plain; that a wood, a bog, a hill, or a river were difficulties which this close body of men could not always overcome. A charge or a retreat equally lessened its force; the phalanx was meant to stand the charge of others. The Romans, therefore, chose their own time and their own ground; they loosened their ranks and widened their front, avoided the charge, and attacked the Greeks at the side and in the rear; and the fatal discovery was at last made that the Macedonian phalanx was not unconquerable, and that closed ranks were only strong against barbarians. This news must have been heard by every statesman of Egypt and the East with alarm; the Romans were now their equals, and were soon to be their masters.

But to return to Egypt. It was, as we have seen, a country governed by men of a foreign race. Neither the poor who tilled the land, nor the rich who owned the estates, had any share in the government. They had no public duty except to pay taxes to their Greek masters, who walked among them as superior beings, marked out for fitness to rule by greater skill in the arts both

of war and peace. The Greeks by their arms, or rather
by their military discipline, had enforced obedience for
one hundred and fifty years; and as they had at the same
time checked lawless violence, made life and property
safe, and left industry to enjoy a large share of its own
earnings, this obedience had been for the most part
granted to them willingly. They had even trusted the
Egyptians with arms. But none are able to command
unless they are at the same time able to obey. The Alexandrians were now almost in rebellion against their
young king and his ministers; and the Greek government no longer gave the usual advantages in return for
the obedience which it tyrannically enforced. Confusion
increased each year during the childhood of the fifth
Ptolemy, to whom Alexandrian flattery gave the title
of Epiphanes, or The Illustrious. The Egyptian phalanx
had in the last reign shown signs of disobedience, and
at length it broke out in open rebellion. The discontented party strengthened themselves in the Busirite
nome, in the middle of the Delta, and fortified the city
of Lycopolis against the government; and a large supply
of arms and warlike stores which they there got together
proved the length of time that they had been preparing
for resistance. The royal troops laid siege to the city
in due form; they surrounded it with mounds and
ditches; they dammed up the bed of the river on each
side of it, and, being helped by a rise in the Nile, which
was that year greater than usual, they forced the rebels
to surrender, on the king's promise that they should
be spared. But Ptolemy was not bound by promises;

he was as false and cruel as he was weak; the rebels
were punished; and many of the troubles in his reign
arose from his discontented subjects not being able to
rely upon his word.

The rich island of Cyprus also, which had been left
by Philopator under the command of Polycrates, showed
some signs of wishing to throw off the Egyptian yoke.
But Polycrates was true to his trust; and, though the
king's ministers were almost too weak either to help
the faithful or punish the treacherous, he not only saved
the island for the minor, but, when he gave up his government to Ptolemy of Megalopolis, he brought to the
royal treasury at Alexandria a large sum from the revenues of his province. By this faithful conduct he gained
great weight in the Alexandrian councils, till, corrupted
by the poisonous habits of the place, he gave way to
luxury and vice.

About the same time Scopas, who had lately led back
to Alexandria his Ætolian mercenaries, so far showed
signs of discontent and disobedience that the minister,
Aristomenes, began to suspect him of planning resistance
to the government. Scopas was greedy of money; nothing would satisfy his avarice. The other Greek generals
of his rank received while in the Egyptian service a
mina, or ten dollars a day, under the name of mess-
money, beyond the usual military pay; and Scopas
claimed and received for his services the large sum of
ten minæ, or one hundred and twenty-five dollars, a day
for mess-money. But even this did not content him.
Aristomenes observed that he was collecting his friends

THE ROSETTA STONE (BRITISH MUSEUM).

for some secret purpose, and in frequent consultation with them. He therefore summoned him to the king's presence, and, being prepared for his refusal, he sent a large force to fetch him. Fearing that the mercenaries might support their general, Aristomenes had even ordered out the elephants and prepared for battle. But, as the blow came upon Scopas unexpectedly, no resistance was made, and he was brought prisoner to the palace. Aristomenes, however, did not immediately venture to punish him, but wisely summoned the Ætolian ambassadors and the chiefs of the mercenaries to his trial, and, as they made no objection, he then had him poisoned in prison.

No sooner was this rebellion crushed than the council took into consideration the propriety of declaring the king's minority at an end, as the best means of re-establishing the royal authority; and they thereupon determined shortly to celebrate his Anacleteria, or the grand ceremony of exhibiting him to the people as their monarch, though he wanted some years of the legal age; and accordingly, in the ninth year of his reign, the young king was crowned with great pomp at Memphis, the ancient capital of the kingdom.

On this occasion he came to Memphis by barge, in grand state, where he was met by the priests of Upper and Lower Egypt, and crowned in the temple of Phtah with the double crown, called Pschent, the crown of the two provinces. After the ceremony, the priests made the Decree in honour of the king, which is carved on the stone known by the name of the Rosetta Stone, in the

British Museum. Ptolemy is there styled King of Upper and Lower Egypt, son of the gods Philopatores, approved by Phtah, to whom Ra has given victory, a living image of Amon, son of Ra, Ptolemy immortal, beloved by Phtah, god Epiphanes most gracious. In the date of the decree we are told the names of the priests of Alexander, of the gods Soteres, of the gods Adelphi, of the gods Euergetæ, of the gods Philopatores, of the god Epiphanes himself, of Berenicë Euergetis, of Arsinoë Philadelphus, and of Arsinoë Philopator. The preamble mentions with gratitude the services of the king, or rather of his wise minister, Aristomenes; and the enactment orders that the statue of the king shall be worshipped in every temple of Egypt, and be carried out in the processions with those of the gods of the country; and lastly, that the decree is to be carved at the foot of every statue of the king, in sacred, in common, and in Greek writing. It is to this stone, with its three kinds of letters, and to the skill and industry of Dr. Thomas Young, and of the French scholar, Champollion, that we now owe our knowledge of hieroglyphics. The Greeks of Alexandria, and after them the Romans, who might have learned how to read this kind of writing if they had wished, seem never to have taken the trouble: it fell into disuse on the rise of Christianity in Egypt; and it was left for an Englishman to unravel the hidden meaning after it had been forgotten for nearly thirteen centuries.

The preamble of this decree tells us also that during the minority of the king the taxes were lessened; the

crown debtors were forgiven; those who were found in
prison charged with crimes against the state were released; the allowance from government for upholding
the splendour of the temples was continued, as was the
rent from land belonging to the priests; the first-fruits,
or rather the coronation money, a tax paid by the priests
to the king on the year of his coming to the throne, which
was by custom allowed to be less than what the law
ordered, was not increased; the priests were relieved
from the heavy burden of making a yearly voyage to do
homage at Alexandria; there was a stop put to the impressing men for the navy, which had been felt as a great
cruelty by an inland people, whose habits and religion
alike made them hate the sea, and this was a boon which
was the more easily granted, as the navy of Alexandria,
which was built in foreign dockyards and steered by
foreign pilots, had very much fallen off in the reign of
Philopator. The duties on linen cloth, which was the
chief manufacture of the kingdom, and, after grain, the
chief article exported, were lessened; the priests, who
manufactured linen for the king's own use, probably
for the clothing of the army, and the sails for the navy,
were not called upon for so large a part of what they
made as before; and the royalties on the other linen
manufactories and the duties on the samples or patterns,
both of which seem to have been unpaid for the whole of
the eight years of the minority, were wisely forgiven.
All the temples of Egypt, and that of Apis at Memphis in particular, were enriched by his gifts; in which
pious actions, in grateful remembrance of their former

benefactor, and with a marked slight to Philopator, they said that he was following the wishes of his grandfather, the god Euergetes. From this decree we gain some little insight into the means by which the taxes were raised under the Ptolemies; and we also learn that they were so new and foreign that they had no Egyptian word by which they could speak of them, and therefore borrowed the Greek word *syntaxes*.

History gives us many examples of kings who, like Epiphanes, gained great praise for the mildness and weakness of the government during their minorities. Aristomenes, the minister, who had governed Egypt for Epiphanes, fully deserved that trust. While the young king looked up to him as a father, the country was well governed, and his orders obeyed; but, as he grew older, his good feelings were weakened by the pleasures which usually beset youth and royalty. The companions of his vices gained that power over his mind which Aristomenes lost, and it was not long before this wise tutor and counsellor was got rid of. The king, weary perhaps with last night's debauchery, had one day fallen asleep when he should have been listening to the speech of a foreign ambassador. Aristomenes gently shook him and awoke him. His flatterers, when alone with him, urged him to take this as an affront. If, said they, it was right to blame the king for falling asleep when worn out with business and the cares of state, it should have been done in private, and not in the face of the whole court. So Aristomenes was put to death by being ordered to drink poison. Epiphanes then lost that love of his people which the wisdom of the minister had gained for him; and he governed the kingdom with the cruelty of a tyrant, rather than with the legal power of a king. Even Aristonicus, his favourite eunuch, who was of the same age as himself, and had been brought up as his playfellow, passed him in the manly virtues of his age, and earned

OUTSIDE ROSETTA.

the praise of the country for setting him a good example, and checking him in his career of vice.

In the thirteenth year of his reign (B.C. 192), when the young king reached the age of eighteen, Antiochus the Great sent his daughter Cleopatra into Egypt, and the marriage, which had been agreed upon six years before, was then carried into effect; and the provinces of Cœle-Syria, Phœnicia, and Judæa, which had been promised as a dower, were, in form at least, handed over to the generals of Epiphanes. Cleopatra was a woman of strong mind and enlarged understanding; and Antiochus hoped that, by means of the power which she would have over the weaker mind of Epiphanes, he should gain more than he lost by giving up Cœle-Syria and Phœnicia. But she acted the part of a wife and a queen, and, instead of betraying her husband into the hands of her father, she was throughout the reign his wisest and best counsellor.

Antiochus seems never to have given up his hold upon the provinces which had been promised as the dower; and the peace between the two countries, which had been kept during the six years after Cleopatra had been betrothed, was broken as soon as she was married. The war was still going on between Antiochus and the Romans; and Epiphanes soon sent to Rome a thousand pounds weight of gold and twenty thousand pounds of silver, to help the republic against their common enemy. But the Romans neither hired mercenaries nor fought as such, the thirst for gold had not yet become the strongest feeling in the senate, and they sent back the money to Alexandria with many thanks.

In the twentieth year of his reign Epiphanes was troubled by a second serious rebellion of the Egyptians. Polycrates marched against them at the head of the Greek troops; and, as he brought with him a superior force, and the king's promise of a free pardon to all who should return to their obedience, the rebels yielded to necessity and laid down their arms. The leaders of the rebellion, Athinis, Pausiras, Chesuphus, and Irobashtus, whose Koptic names prove that this was a struggle on the part of the Egyptians to throw off the Greek yoke, were brought before the king at Saïs. Epiphanes, in whose youthful heart were joined the cruelty and cowardice of a tyrant, who had not even shown himself to the army during the danger, was now eager to act the conqueror; and in spite of the promises of safety on which these brave Kopts had laid down their arms, he had them tied to his chariot wheels, and copying the vices of men whose virtues he could not even understand, like Achilles and Alexander, he dragged them living round the city walls, and then ordered them to be put to death. He then led the army to Naucratis, which was the port of Saïs, and there he embarked on the Nile for Alexandria, and taking with him a further body of mercenaries, which Aristonicus had just brought from Greece, he entered the city in triumph.

Ptolemy of Megalopolis, the new governor of Cyprus, copied his predecessor, Polycrates, in his wise and careful management. His chief aim was to keep the province quiet, and his next to collect the taxes. He was at first distrusted by the Alexandrian council for the large sum of money which he had got together and kept within his own power; but when he sent it all home to the empty treasury, they were as much pleased as they were surprised.

Apollonius, whom we have spoken of in the reign of Euergetes, and who had been teaching at Rhodes during the reign of Philopator, was recalled to Alexandria in the beginning of this reign, and made librarian of the museum on the death of Eratosthenes. But he did not long enjoy that honour. He was already old, and shortly afterwards died at the age of ninety.

The coins of this king are known by the glory or rays of sun which surround his head, and which agrees with his name, Epiphanes, illustrious, or as it is written in the hieroglyphics, " light bearing." On the other side is the cornucopia between two stars, with the name of

A DESERT ROAD BETWEEN EGYPT AND SYRIA.

" King Ptolemy." No temples, and few additions to temples, seem to have been built in Upper Egypt during this reign, which began and ended in rebellion. We find, however, a Greek inscription at Philæ, of " King Ptolemy and Queen Cleopatra, gods Epiphanes, and Ptolemy their son, to Asclepius," a god whom the Egyptians called Imothph the son of Pthah.

Cyprus and Cyrene were nearly all that were left to Egypt of its foreign provinces. The cities of Greece,

which had of their own wish put themselves under Egypt
for help against their nearer neighbours, now looked to
Rome for that help; part of Asia Minor was under Seleucus, the son of Antiochus the Great; Cœle-Syria and
Phœnicia, which had been given up to Epiphanes, had
been again soon lost; and the Jews, who in all former
wars had sided with the Kings of Egypt, as being not
only the stronger but the milder rulers, now joined
Seleucus. The ease with which the wide-spreading provinces of this once mighty empire fell off from their allegiance, showed how the whole had been upheld by the
warlike skill of its kings, rather than by a deep-rooted
hold in the habits of the people. Instead of wondering
that the handful of Greeks in Alexandria, on whom the
power rested, lost those wide provinces, we should rather
wonder that they were ever able to hold them.

After the death of Antiochus the Great, Ptolemy
again proposed to enforce his rights over Cœle-Syria,
which he had given up only in the weakness of his minority; and he is said to have been asked by one of his
generals, how he should be able to pay for the large forces
which he was getting together for that purpose; and he
playfully answered, that his treasure was in the number
of his friends. But his joke was taken in earnest; they
were afraid of new taxes and fresh levies on their estates; and means were easily taken to poison him. He
died in the twenty-ninth year of his age, after a reign of
twenty-four years; leaving the navy unmanned, the
army in disobedience, the treasury empty, and the whole
framework of government out of order.

Just before his death he had sent to the Achaians to offer to send ten galleys to join their fleet; and Polybius, the historian, to whom we owe so much of our knowledge of these reigns, although he had not yet reached the age called for by the Greek law, was sent by the Achaians as one of the ambassadors, with his father, to return thanks; but before they had quitted their own country they were stopped by the news of the death of Epiphanes.

Those who took away the life of the king seem to have had no thoughts of mending the form of government, nor any plan by which they might lessen the power of his successor. It was only one of those outbreaks of private vengeance which have often happened in unmixed monarchies, where men are taught that the only way to check the king's tyranny is by his murder; and the little notice that was taken of it by the people proves their want of public virtue as well as of political wisdom.

COIN OF PTOLEMY V. EPIPHANES.

CHAPTER V

PTOLEMY PHILOMETOR AND PTOLEMY EUERGETES II.

The Syrian Invasion: The Jews and the Bible: Relations with Rome:
Literature of the Age.

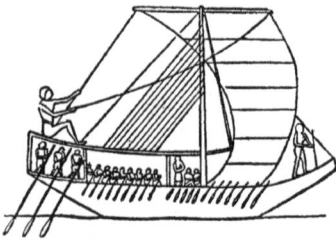

SHIP ON THE NILE.

A T the beginning of the last reign the Alexandrians had sadly felt the want of a natural guardian to the young king, and they were now glad to copy the customs of the conquered Egyptians.
Epiphanes had left behind him two sons, each named Ptolemy, and a daughter named Cleopatra; and the elder son, though still a child, mounted the throne under the able guardianship of his mother, Cleopatra, and took the very suitable name of Philometor, or *mother-loving.* The mother governed the kingdom for seven years as regent during the minority of her son. When Philometor reached his fourteenth year, the age at which his minority ceased, his coronation was celebrated with great pomp. Ambassadors from several foreign states were

213

sent to Egypt to wish the king joy, to do honour to the
day, and to renew the treaties of peace with him: Caius
Valerius and four others were sent from Rome; Apollonius, the son of Mnestheus, was sent from Judæa; and
we may regret with Polybius that he himself was not
able to form part of the embassy then sent from the
Achaians, that he might have seen the costly and curious
ceremony, and given us an account of it.

While Cleopatra lived, she had been able to keep
her son at peace with her brother, Antiochus Epiphanes,
but upon her death, Leneus and the eunuch Eulaius,
who then had the care of the young king, sought to re-
conquer Cœle-Syria; and they embroiled the country
in a war, at a time when weakness and decay might have
been seen in every part of the army and navy, and when
there was the greatest need of peace. Cœle-Syria and
Phœnicia had been given to Ptolemy Epiphanes as his
wife's dower; but, when Philometor seemed too weak
to grasp them, Antiochus denied that his father had
ever made such a treaty, and got ready to march against
Egypt, as the easiest way to guard Cœle-Syria.

By this time the statesmen of Egypt ought to have
learned the mistake in their foreign policy. By widen-
ing their frontier they always weakened it. They should
have fortified the passes between the Red Sea and the
Mediterranean, not cities in Asia. When Antiochus
entered Egypt he was met at Pelusium by the army of
Philometor, which he at once routed in a pitched battle.
The whole of Egypt was then in his power; he marched
upon Memphis with a small force, and seized it without

having to strike a blow, helped perhaps by the plea that he was acting on behalf of his nephew, Ptolemy Philometor, who then fell into his hands.

On this, the younger Ptolemy, the brother of Philometor, who was with his sister Cleopatra in Alexandria, and was about fifteen years old, declared himself king, and sent ambassadors to Rome to ask for help against Antiochus; and taking the name of the most popular of his forefathers, he called himself Euergetes. He is, however, better known in history as Ptolemy Physcon, or *bloated*, a nickname which was afterwards given to him when he had grown fat and unwieldy from the diseases of luxury.

Comanus and Cineas were the chief advisers of the young Euergetes; and in their alarm they proposed to send the foreign ambassadors to meet the invader on his march from Memphis, and to plead for peace. This task the ambassadors kindly undertook. There were then in Alexandria two embassies from the Achaians, one to renew the treaty of peace, and one to settle the terms of the coming wrestling match. There were there three embassies from Athens, one with gifts from the city, one about the Panathenaic games, and one about the celebration of the mysteries. There was also an embassy from Miletus, and one from Clazomenæ. On the day of their arrival at Memphis, Antiochus feasted these numerous ambassadors in grand state, and on the next day gave them an audience. But their arguments for peace carried no weight with him; and he denied that his father, Antiochus the Great, had ever given Cœle-

Syria as a dower with his daughter Cleopatra to Epiphanes. To gain time he promised the ambassadors that
he would give them an answer as soon as his own ambassadors returned from Alexandria; and in the meanwhile he carried his army down the Nile to Naucratis,
and thence marched to the capital to begin the siege.

Antiochus, however, was defeated in his first assault
upon Alexandria, and finding that he should not soon
be able to bring the siege to an end, he sent off an embassy to Rome with a hundred and fifty talents of gold,
fifty as a present to the senate, and the rest to be divided
among the states of Greece, whose help he might need.
At the same time, also, an embassy from the Rhodians
arrived in the port of Alexandria, to attempt to restore
peace to the country of their old allies. Antiochus received the Rhodian ambassadors in his tent, but would
not listen to the long speech with which they threatened
him, and shortly told them that he came as the friend
of his elder nephew, the young Philometor, and if the
Alexandrians wished for peace they should open the
gates to their rightful king. Antiochus was, however,
defeated in all his assaults on the city, and he at last
withdrew his army and returned to Syria. He left
Euergetes, King of the Greeks, at Alexandria, and Philometor at Memphis, King of the rest of Egypt. But he
kept Pelusium, where he placed a strong garrison that
he might be able easily to re-enter Egypt whenever he
chose.

Ptolemy Macron, the Alexandrian governor of Cyprus, added to the troubles of the country by giving

up his island to Antiochus. But he met with the usual
fate of traitors, he was badly rewarded; and when he
complained of his treatment, he was called a traitor by
the very men who had gained by his treachery, and he
poisoned himself in the bitterness of his grief. Antiochus, like most invaders, carried off whatever treasure fell into his hands. Egypt was a sponge which had
not lately been squeezed, and his court and even his own
dinner-table then shone with a blaze of silver and gold
unknown in Syria before this inroad into Egypt.

By these acts, and by the garrison left in Pelusium,
the eyes of Philometor were opened, and he saw that his
uncle had not entered Egypt for his sake, but to make
it a province of Syria, after it had been weakened by
civil war. He therefore wisely forgave his rebellious
brother and sister in Alexandria, and sent offers of peace
to them; and it was agreed that the two Ptolemies should
reign together, and turn their forces against the common
enemy. It was most likely at this time, and as a part
of this treaty, that Philometor married his sister Cleopatra. It was mainly by her advice and persuasion that
the quarrel between the two brothers was for the time
healed. On this treaty between the brothers the year
was called the twelfth of Ptolemy Philometor and the
first of Ptolemy Euergetes, and the public deeds of the
kingdom were so dated.

The next year Antiochus Epiphanes again entered
Egypt, claiming the island of Cyprus and the country
round Pelusium as the price of his forbearance; and, on
his marching forward, Memphis a second time opened its

gates to him without a battle. He came down by slow marches towards Alexandria, and crossed the canal at Leucine, four miles from the city. There he was met by the Roman ambassadors, who ordered him to quit the country. On his hesitating, Popilius, who was one of them, drew a circle round him on the sand with his stick, and told him that, if he crossed that line without promising to leave Egypt at once, it should be taken as a declaration of war against Rome. On this threat Antiochus again quitted Egypt, and the brothers sent ambassadors to Rome to thank the senate for their help, and to acknowledge that they owed more to the Roman people than they did to the gods or to their forefathers.

The treaty made on this occasion between Philometor and Antiochus was written by Heraclides Lembus, the son of Serapion, a native of Oxyrynchus, who wrote on the succession of the philosophers in the several Greek schools, and other works on philosophy, but whose chief work was a history named the Lembeutic History.

Four years afterwards, in B. C. 164, Antiochus Epiphanes died; and the Jews of Judæa, who had been for some time struggling for liberty, then gained a short rest for their unhappy country. Judas Maccabæus had raised his countrymen in rebellion against the foreigners; he had defeated the Syrian forces in several battles; and was at last able to purify the temple and re-establish the service there as of old. He therefore sent to the Jews of Egypt to ask them to join their Hebrew brethren in celebrating the feast of tabernacles on that great occasion.

The unhappy quarrels between the Egyptian kings
soon broke out again; and, as the party of Euergetes
was the stronger, Philometor was driven from his kingdom, and he fled to Rome for safety and for help. He
entered the city privately, and took up his lodgings in
the house of one of his own subjects, a painter of Alex-

TEMPLE OF HERMONTHIS.

andria. His pride led him to refuse the offers of better
entertainment which were made to him by Demetrius,
the nephew of Antiochus, who, like himself, was hoping
to regain his kingdom by the help of the Romans. The
Kings of Egypt and Syria, the two greatest kingdoms in
the world, were at the same time asking to be heard at
the bar of the Roman senate, and were claiming the

thrones of their fathers at the hands of men who could make and unmake kings at their pleasure.

As soon as the senate heard that Philometor was in Rome, they lodged him at the cost of the state in a manner becoming his high rank, and soon sent him back to Egypt, with orders that Euergetes should reign in Cyrene, and that the rest of the kingdom should belong to Philometor. This happened in the seventeenth year of Philometor and the sixth of Euergetes, which was the last year that was named after the two kings. Cassius Longinus, who was next year consul at Rome, was most likely among the ambassadors who replaced Philometor on the throne; for he put the Ptolemaic eagle and thunderbolt on his coins, as though to claim the sovereignty of Egypt for the senate.

To these orders Euergetes was forced to yield; but the next year he went himself to Rome to complain to the senate that they had made a very unfair division of the kingdom, and to beg that they would add the island of Cyprus to his share. After hearing the ambassadors from Philometor, who were sent to plead on the other side, the senate granted the prayer of Euergetes, and sent ambassadors to Cyprus, with orders to hand that island over to Euergetes, and to make use of the fleets and armies of the republic if these orders were disobeyed.

Euergetes, during his stay in Rome, if we may believe Plutarch, made an offer of marriage to Cornelia, the mother of the Gracchi; but this offer of a throne could not make the high-minded matron quit her children and her country. He left Italy with the Roman ambassadors, and, in passing through Greece, he raised a large body of mercenaries to help him to wrest Cyprus from his brother, as it would seem that the governor, faithful to his charge, would not listen to the commands of Rome. But the ambassadors had been told to conquer Cyprus, if necessary, with the arms of the republic only, and they therefore made Euergetes disband his levies. They sailed for Alexandria to enforce their orders upon Philometor, and sent Euergetes home to Cyrene. Philometor received the Roman ambassadors with all due honours; he sometimes gave them fair promises, and sometimes put them off till another day; and tried to spin out the time without saying either yes or no to the message from the senate. Euergetes sent to Alexandria to ask if they had gained their point; but though they threatened to return to Rome if they were not at once obeyed, Philometor, by his kind treatment and still kinder words, kept them more than forty days longer at Alexandria.

At last the Roman ambassadors left Egypt, and on their way home they went to Cyrene, to let Euergetes know that his brother had disobeyed the orders of the senate, and would not give up Cyprus; and Euergetes then sent two ambassadors to Rome to beg them to revenge their affronted dignity and to enforce their orders by arms. The senate of course declared the peace with Egypt at an end, and ordered the ambassadors from Philometor to quit Rome within five days, and sent their own ambassadors to Cyrene to tell Euergetes of their decree.

But while this was going on, the state of Cyrene had risen in arms against Euergetes; his vices and cruelty had made him hated, they had gained for him the nick-names of Kakergetes, or *mischief-maker*, and Physcon, or *bloated;* and while wishing to gain Cyprus he was in danger of losing his own kingdom. When he marched against the rebels, he was beaten and wounded, either in the battle or by an attack upon his life afterwards, and his success was for some time doubtful. When he had at last put down this rising, he sailed for Rome, to urge his complaints against Philometor, upon whom he laid the blame of the late rebellion, and to ask for help. The senate, after hearing both sides, sent a small fleet with Euergetes, not large enough to put him on the throne of Cyprus, but gave him, what they had before refused, leave to levy an army of his own, and to enlist their allies in Greece and Asia as mercenaries under his standard.

The Roman troops seem not to have helped Euer-getes; but he landed in Cyprus with his own mercenaries, and was there met by Philometor, who had brought over the Egyptian army in person. Euergetes, however, was beaten in several battles, he was soon forced to shut himself up in the city of Lapitho, and at last to lay down his arms before his elder brother.

If Philometor had upon this put his brother to death, the deed would have seemed almost blameless after the family murders already related in this history. But, with a goodness of heart, he a second time forgave his brother all that had passed, replaced him on the throne of Cyrene,

and promised to give him his daughter in marriage. We
are not told whether the firmness and forgiving mildness
of Philometor had turned the Roman senate in his fa-

GARDEN NEAR HELIOPOLIS.

vour, but their troops seemed wanted in other quarters;
at any rate they left off trying to enforce their decree;
Philometor kept Cyprus, and sent Euergetes a yearly
gift of grain from Alexandria.

During the wars in Syria between Philometor and
Antiochus Epiphanes, at the beginning of this reign,
the Jews were divided into two parties, one favouring
the Egyptians and one the Syrians. At last the Syrian
party drove their enemies out of Jerusalem; and Onias,
the high priest, with a large body of Jews, fled to Egypt.
There they were well received by Philometor, who allowed them to dwell in the neighbourhood of Heliopolis;
and he gave them leave to build a temple and ordain
priests for themselves. Onias built his temple at On
or Onion, a city about twenty-three miles from Memphis,
once the capital of the district of Heliopolis. It was on
the site of an old Egyptian temple of the goddess Pasht,
which had fallen into disuse and decay, and was built
after the model of the temple of Jerusalem. Though by
the Jewish law there was to be no second temple, yet
Onias defended himself by quoting, as if meant for his
own times, the words of Isaiah, who says that in that day
there shall be an altar to the Lord in the midst of the
land of Egypt. The building of this temple, and the
celebrating the Jewish feasts there, as in rivalry to the
temple of Jerusalem, were a never-failing cause of quarrel between the Hebrew and the Greek Jews. They each
altered the words of the Bible to make it speak their
own opinions. The Hebrew Bible now says that the new
temple was in the City of Destruction, and the Greek
Bible says that it was in the City of Righteousness;
whereas, from the Arabic version and some early com-
mentaries, it seems that Isaiah was speaking of the city
of Heliopolis, where there had been of old an altar to

the Lord. The leaders of the Greek party wished the
Jews to throw aside the character of strangers and foreign traders; to be at home and to become owners of
the soil. "Hate not laborious work," says the son of
Sirach; "neither husbandry, which the Most High hath
ordained."

About the same time the Jews brought before Ptolemy, as a judge, their quarrel with the Samaritans, as
to whether, according to the law of Moses, the temple
ought to have been built at Jerusalem, or on the green
and fertile Mount Gerizim, where the Samaritans built
their temple, or on the barren white crags of Mount Ebal,
where the Hebrew Bible says that it should be built; and
as to which nation had altered their copies of the Bible
in the twenty-seventh chapter of Deuteronomy and
eighth chapter of Joshua. This dispute had lately been
the cause of riots and rebellion. Ptolemy seems to have
decided the question for political reasons, and to please
his own subjects, the Alexandrian Jews; and without listening to the arguments as to what the law ordered, he
was content with the proof that the temple had stood
at Jerusalem for about eight hundred years, and he put
to death the two Samaritan pleaders, who had probably
been guilty of some outrage against the Jews in zeal
for Mount Gerizim, and for which they might then have
been on their trial.

Onias, the high priest, was much esteemed by Philometor, and bore high offices in the government; as also
did Dositheus, another Jew, who had been very useful
in helping the king to crush a rebellion. Dositheus called

himself a priest and a Levite, though his title to that
honour seems to have been doubted by his countrymen.
He had brought with him into Egypt the book of Esther,
written in Greek, which he said had been translated out
of the Hebrew in Jerusalem by Lysimachus. It contained some additions for which the Hebrew has never
been brought forward, and which are now placed among
the uncanonical books in the Apocrypha.

Since the Ptolemies had found themselves too weak
to hold Ethiopia, they had placed a body of soldiers on
the border of the two countries, to guard Egypt from
the inroads of the enemy. This station, twelve miles
to the south of Syënë, had by degrees grown into a city,
and was called Parembole, or *The Camp;* and, as most
of the soldiers were Greek mercenaries, it was natural
that the temple which Philometor built there should be
dedicated in the Greek language. Of the temples hitherto
built by the Ptolemies, in the Egyptian cities, every one
seems to have had the king's name and titles, and its
dedication to the gods, carved on its massive portico in
hieroglyphics; but this was in a Greek city, and it was
dedicated to Isis and Serapis, on behalf of Philometor
and his queen, in a Greek inscription.

Philometor also built a temple at Antæopolis to An-
tæus, a god of whom we know little, but that he gave
his name to the city; and another to Aroëris at Ombos;
and in the same way he carved the dedications on the
porticoes in the Greek language. This custom became
common after that time, and proves both the lessened
weight which the native Egyptians bore in the state,

TEMPLE OF APOLLINOPOLIS MAGNUS.

and that the kings had forgotten the wise rules of Ptolemy Soter, in regard to the religious feelings of the people. They must have been greatly shocked by this use of foreign writing in the place of the old characters of the country, which, from having been used in the temples, even for ages beyond the reach of history, had at last been called sacred. In the temple at Antæopolis we note a marked change in the style of building. The screen in front of the great portico is almost removed by having a doorway made in it between every pair of columns.

It is to this reign, also, that we seem to owe the great temple at Apollinopolis Magna, although it was not finished till one or two reigns later. It is one of the largest and least ruined of the Egyptian temples. Its front is formed of two huge square towers, with sloping sides, between which is the narrow doorway, the only opening in its massive walls. Through this the worshipper entered a spacious courtyard or cloister, where he found shade from the sun under a covered walk on either side. In front is the lofty portico with six large columns, the entrance to the body of the building. This last is flat-roofed, and far lower than the grand portico which hid it from the eyes of the crowd in the courtyard. The staircases in the towers are narrow. The sacred rooms within were small and dark, with only a glimmering flame here and there before an altar, except when lighted up with a blaze of lamps on a feast-day. As a castle it must have had great strength; from the top and loop-holes of the two towers, stones and darts might be hurled at the enemy; and as it was in the hands of the Egyptians, it is the strongest proof that they were either not distrusted or not feared by their Greek rulers. The city of Apollinopolis stands on a grand and lofty situation, overlooking the river and the valley; and this proud temple, rising over all, can only have been planned by military skill as a fortress to command the whole.

At this time the Greeks in Egypt were beginning to follow the custom of their Egyptian brethren, to take upon themselves monastic vows, and to shut themselves up in the temples in religious idleness. But these foreigners were looked upon with jealousy by the Egyptian monks as intruders on their endowments, and we meet with a petition addressed to Philometor by Ptolemy, the son of Glaucias, a monk in the temple of Serapis at Memphis, who styles himself a Macedonian, complaining that his cell had been violently entered and himself ill-treated because he was a Greek; and reminding the king that last year, when the king visited the Serapium, he had addressed the same petition to him through the bars of his window. The priests in temples of Egypt were maintained, partly by their own estates, and partly by the offerings of the pious; and we still possess a deed of sale made in this reign by the Theban priests, of one-half of a third of their collections for the dead who had been buried in Thynabunum, the Libyan suburb of Thebes. This sixth share of the collections consisted of seven or eight families of slaves; the price of it was four hundred pieces of brass; the bargain was made in the presence of sixteen witnesses, whose names are

given; and the deed was registered and signed by a
public notary in the city of Thebes. The custom of
giving offerings to the priests for the good of the dead
would seem to have been a cause of some wealth to the
temples. It was one among the many Egyptian customs
forbidden by the law of Moses.

From this deed of sale we also gain some knowledge
of the state of slavery in Egypt. The names of the slaves
and of their fathers are Koptic, and in some cases borrowed from the names of the gods; hence the slaves were
probably of the same religion, and spoke nearly the same
language as their masters. They sunk into that low
state rather by their own want of mind than by their
masters' power. In each case the slave was joined in
the same lot with his children; and the low price of four
hundred pieces of brass, perhaps about thirty-eight dollars for eight families, or even if it be meant for the half
of eight families, proves that they were of the nature of
serfs, and that the master, either by law or custom, could
have had no power of cruelly overworking them. On
the other hand, in the reign of Philadelphus, the prisoners taken in battle, who might be treated with greater
severity, were ransomed at fifteen dollars each. We see
by the monuments that there were also a few negroes
in the same unhappy state of slavery. They were probably not treated much worse than the lowest class of
those born on the soil, but they were much more valuable.
Other slaves of the Berber race were brought in coasting
vessels from Opone on the incense coast, near to the
island of Dioscorides.

Aristarchus, who had been the tutor of Euergetes II., and of a son of Philometor, was one of the ornaments of this reign. He had been a pupil of Aristophanes, the grammarian, and had then studied under Crates at Pergamus, the rival school to Alexandria. He died at Cyprus, whither he probably withdrew on the death of Philometor. He was chiefly known for his critical writings, in which his opinions of poetry were thought so just that few dared to disagree with them; and his name soon became proverbial for a critic. Aristarchus had also the good fortune to be listened to in his lecture-room by one whose name is far more known than those of his two royal pupils. Moschus of Syracuse, the pastoral poet, was one of his hearers; but his fame must not be claimed for Alexandria; he can hardly have learned from the critic that just taste by which he joined softness and sweetness to the rude plainness of the Doric muse. Indeed in this he only followed his young friend Bion, whose death he so beautifully bewails, and from whose poems he generously owns that he learned so much. It may be as well to add that the lines in which he says that Theocritus, who had been dead above one hundred years, joined with him in his sorrow for the death of Bion are later additions not found in the early manuscripts of his poems.

From our slight acquaintance with Bion's life, we are left in doubt whether he accompanied his friend Moschus to the court of Alexandria; but it is probable that he did. In his beautiful lamentation for the death of Adonis, we have an imitation of the melancholy chant of the Egyptians, named *maneros*, which they sang through the streets in the procession on the feast of Isis, when the crowd joined in the chorus, " Ah, hapless Isis, Osiris is no more." The tale has been a good deal changed by the Sicilian muse of Bion, but in the boar which killed Adonis, we have the wicked Typhon as carved on the monuments; we have also the wound in the thigh, and the consolations of the priests, who every year ended their mournful song with advising the goddess to reserve her sorrow for another year, when on the return of the festival the same lament would be again celebrated. The whole poem has a depth and earnestness of feeling which is truly Egyptian, but which was very little known in Alexandria.

To the Alexandrian grammarians, and more particularly to Aristophanes, Aristarchus, and their pupil, Ammonius, we are indebted for our present copies of Homer. These critics acted like modern editors, each publishing an edition, or rather writing out a copy, which was then re-copied in the museum as often as called for by the demands of the purchasers of books. Aristophanes left perhaps only one such copy or edition, while Aristarchus, in his efforts to correct the text of the great epic poet, made several such copies. These were in the hands of the later scholiasts, who appealed to them as their authority, and ventured to make no further alterations; we therefore now read the Iliad and Odyssey nearly as left by these Alexandrian critics. They no doubt took some liberties in altering the spelling and smoothing the lines; and, though we should value most

highly a copy in the rougher form in which it came into
their hands, yet, on the whole, we must be great gainers
by their labours. They divided the Iliad and Odyssey
into twenty-four books each, and corrected the faulty
metres; but one of their chief tasks was to set aside, or

put a mark against,
those more modern
lines which had crept
into the ancient poems.
It had been usual to call
every old verse Ho-
mer's or Homeric, and
these it was the busi-
ness of the critic to
mark as not genuine.
Aristarchus was jo-
cosely said to have
called every line spuri-
ous which he did not
like; but everything
that we can learn of

THE APOTHEOSIS OF HOMER.

him leads us to believe that he executed his task with
judgment. From these men sprang the school of Alexandrian grammarians, who for several centuries continued their minute and often unprofitable studies in
verbal criticism.

These were the palmy days of criticism. Never before
or since have critics held so high a place in literature.
The world was called upon to worship and do honour
to the poet, but chiefly that it might admire the skill of

the critic who could name the several sources of his beauties. The critic now ranked higher than a priest at the foot of Mount Parnassus. Homer was lifted to the skies that the critic might stand on a raised pedestal among the Muses. Such seems to be the meaning of the figures on the upper part of the well-known sculpture called the Apotheosis of Homer. It was made in this reign; and at the foot Ptolemy and his mother, in the characters of Time and the World, are crowning the statue of the poet, in the presence of ten worshippers who represent the literary excellences which shine forth in his poems. The figures of the Iliad and Odyssey kneel beside his seat, and the Frogs and Mice creep under his footstool, showing that the latter mock-heroic poem was already written and called the work of Homer.

Other celebrities who flourished under the fifth Ptolemy were Pamphilius, an Alexandrian physician who wrote on medical plants; Nicander, a poet and physician who studied poisons, and the great Hipparchus, the founder of mathematical astronomy. Hero, also, in this reign, invented a kind of primitive steam-engine. These men and their contemporaries were in the habit of writing their scientific observations in the form of poetry, but it was verse without earnest-

HERO'S ROTATING STEAM-ENGINE.

ness and feeling, and such of it as survives is valued not for its literary qualities or charms of diction, but for the side-lights it throws upon the manners and education of the age.

The portrait of the king is known from those coins which bear the name of "*King Ptolemy the mother-loving god.*" The eagle on the other side of the coins has a phœnix or palm-branch on its wing or by its side, which may be supposed to mean that they were struck in Phœnicia. We have not before met with the title of " *god,*" on the coins of the Ptolemies; but, as every one of them had been so named in the hieroglyphical inscriptions, it can scarcely be called new.

When Philometor quitted the island of Cyprus after beating his brother in battle, he left Archias as governor, who entered into a plot to give it up to Demetrius, King of Syria, for the sum of five hundred talents. But the plot was found out, and the traitor then put an end to his own life, to escape from punishment and self-reproach. By this treachery of Demetrius, Philometor was made his enemy, and he joined Attalus, King of Pergamus, and Ariarathes, King of Cappadocia, in setting up Alexander Balas as a pretender to the throne of Syria, who beat Demetrius in battle, and put him to death. Philometor two years afterwards gave his elder daughter, Cleopatra, in marriage to Alexander, and led her himself to Ptolemaïs, or Acre, where the marriage was celebrated with great pomp.

But even in Ptolemaïs, the city in which Alexander had been so covered with favours, Philometor was near falling under the treachery of his new son-in-law. He learned that a plot had been formed against his life by Ammonius, and he wrote to Alexander to beg that the traitor might be given up to justice. But Alexander

acknowledged the plot as his own, and refused to give
up his servant. On this, Philometor recalled his daughter, and turned against Alexander the forces which he
had led into Syria to uphold him. He then sent to the
young Demetrius, afterwards called Nicator, the son of
his late enemy, to offer him the throne and wife which
he had lately given to Alexander Balas. Demetrius was
equally pleased with the two offers. Philometor then
entered Antioch at the head of his army, and there he
was proclaimed by the citizens King of Asia and Egypt;
but with a forbearance then very uncommon, he called
together the council of the people, and refused the crown,
and persuaded them to receive Demetrius as their king.

COIN OF PTOLEMY V.

It is interesting to note
that Alexander Balas and
Demetrius Nicator each
in his turn acknowledged
his debt to the King of
Egypt by putting the
Ptolemaic eagle on his
coins, and adjusting them to the Egyptian standard of
weight: and in this they were afterwards followed by
Antiochus, the son of Demetrius. The Romans, on the
other hand, sometimes used the same eagle in boast of
their power over Egypt; but we cannot be mistaken
in what was meant by these Syrian kings, who none of
them, when their coins were struck, were seated safely
on the throne. With them, as with some of the Greek
cities of Asia Minor, the use of the Egyptian eagle on
the coins was an act of homage.

Philometor and Demetrius, as soon as the latter was acknowledged king at Antioch, then marched against Alexander, routed his army, and drove him into Arabia. But in this battle Philometor's horse was frightened by the braying of an elephant, and threw the king into the ranks of the enemy, and he was taken up covered with wounds. He lay speechless for five days, and the surgeons then endeavoured to cut out a piece of the broken bone from his skull. He died under the operation: but not before the head of Alexander had been brought to him as the proof of his victory.

Thus fell Ptolemy Philometor in the forty-second year of his age. His reign began in trouble; before he reached the years of manhood the country had been overrun by foreigners, and torn to pieces by civil war; but he left the kingdom stronger than he found it, a praise which he alone can share with Ptolemy Soter. He was alike brave and mild; he was the only one of the race who fell in battle, and the only one whose hands were unstained with civil blood. At an age and in a country when poison and the dagger were too often the means by which the king's authority was upheld, when goodness was little valued, and when conquests were thought the only measure of greatness, he spared the life of a brother taken in battle, he refused the crown of Syria when offered to him; and not only no one of his friends or kinsmen, but no citizen of Alexandria, was put to death during the whole of his reign. We find grateful inscriptions to his honour at the city of Citium in Cyprus, in the island of Theræ, and at Methone in Argolis.

Philometor had reigned thirty-five years in all; eleven years alone, partly while under age, then six years jointly with his brother, Euergetes II., and eighteen more alone while his brother reigned in Cyrene. He married his sister Cleopatra, and left her a widow, with two daughters, each named Cleopatra. The elder daughter we have seen offered to Euergetes, then married to Alexander Balas, and lastly to Demetrius. The younger daughter, afterwards known by the name of Cleopatra Cocce, was still in the care of her mother. He had most likely had three sons. One perhaps had been the pupil of Aristarchus, and died before his father; as the little elegy by Antipator of Sidon, which is addressed to the dead child, on the grief of his father and mother, would seem to be meant for a son of Philometor. A second son was murdered, and a third lived in Syria.

On the death of Philometor, his widow, Cleopatra, and some of the chief men of Alexandria proclaimed his young son king, most likely under the name of Ptolemy Eupator; but Euergetes, whose claim was favoured by the mob, marched from Cyrene to Alexandria to seize the crown of Egypt. Onias the Jew defended the city for Cleopatra; but a peace was soon made by the help of Thermus, the Roman ambassador, and on this the gates of Alexandria were opened. It was agreed that Euergetes should be king, and marry Cleopatra, his sister and his brother's widow. We may take it for granted that one article of the treaty was that her son should reign on the death of his uncle; but Euergetes, forgetting that he owed his own life to Philometor, and also disregarding the Romans who were a party to the treaty, had the boy put to death on the day of the marriage.

The Alexandrians, after the vices and murders of former kings, could not have been much struck by the behaviour of Euergetes towards his family; but he was not less cruel towards his people. Alexandria, which he had entered peaceably, was handed over to the unbridled cruelty of the mercenaries, and blood flowed in every street. The anger of Euergetes fell more particularly on the Jews for the help which they had given to Cleopatra, and he threatened them with utter destruction. The threat was not carried into execution; but such was the Jews' alarm, that they celebrated a yearly festival in Alexandria for several hundred years, in thankfulness for their escape from it. The population of the city, who looked upon it less as a home than as a place of trade in which they could follow their callings with the greatest gain, seemed to quit Alexandria as easily as they had come there under Ptolemy Soter; and Euergetes, who was afraid that he should soon be left to reign over a wilderness, made new laws in favour of trade and of strangers who would settle there.

In the lifetime of Philometor he had never laid aside his claim to the throne of Egypt, but had only yielded to the commands of Rome and to his brother's forces, and he now numbered the years of his reign from his former seizing of Alexandria. He had reigned six years with his brother, and then eighteen years in Cyrene, and he therefore called the first year of his real reign the twenty-fifth.

In the next year he went to Memphis to be crowned; and, while the pomps and rites were there being performed, his queen and sister bore him a son, whom, from the place and to please the people, he named Memphites. But his queen was already in disgrace; and some of those very friends who on his brother's death had marched with him against Alexandria were publicly put to death for speaking ill of his mistress Irene. He soon afterwards put away his wife and married her younger daughter, his niece, Cleopatra Cocce. The divorced Cleopatra was allowed to keep her title; and, as she was the widow of the late king, she held a rank in the state before the wife of the reigning king. Thus, the small temple of

TEMPLE OF HÂTHOR AT PHILÆ.

Hâthor in the island of Philæ was dedicated to the goddess in the name of King Ptolemy and Queen Cleopatra his sister, and Queen Cleopatra his wife, designated as the gods Euergetæ.

The Roman senate, however, felt its authority slighted by this murder of the young Eupator, and divorce of Cleopatra, both of whom were living under its protection. The late ambassador, Thermus, by whose treachery

or folly Euergetes had been enabled to crush his rivals
and gain the sovereign power, was on his return to Rome
called to account for his conduct. Cato the Censor, in
one of his great speeches, accused him of having been
seduced from his duty by the love of Egyptian gold, and
of having betrayed the queen to the bribes of Euergetes.
In the meanwhile Scipio Africanus the younger and two
other Roman ambassadors were sent by the senate to see
that the kingdom of their ally was peaceably settled.
Euergetes went to meet him with great pomp, and received him with all the honours due to his rank; and the
whole city followed him in crowds through the streets,
eager to catch a sight of the conqueror of Carthage, of the
greatest man who had been seen in Alexandria, of one
who by his virtues and his triumphs had added a new
glory even to the name of Scipio. He brought with him,
as his friend and companion (in the case of a modern
ambassador we should say, as his chaplain), the philosopher, Panætius, the chief of the Stoics, who had gained
a great name for his three books on the " Duty of Man,"
which were afterwards copied by Cicero.

Euergetes showed them over the palace and the treasury; but, though the Romans had already begun to run
the down-hill race of luxury, in which the Egyptians were
so far ahead of them, yet Scipio, who held to the old
fashions and plain manners of the republic, was not
dazzled by mere gold and purple. But the trade of Alexandria, the natural harbour, the forest of masts, and the
lighthouse, the only one in the world, surpassed anything
that his well-stored mind had looked for. He went by

COLORED RELIEFS CARVED IN THE GREAT TEMPLE AT PHILÆ.

boat to Memphis, and saw the rich crops on either bank, and the easy navigation of the Nile, in which the boats were sailing up the river by the force of the wind and floating down by the force of the stream. The villages on the river side were large and thickly set, each in the bosom of its own grove of palm-trees; and the crowded population was well fed and well clothed. The Roman statesman saw that nothing was wanting but a good government to make Egypt what it used to be, the greatest kingdom in the world.

Scipio went no higher than Memphis; the buildings of Upper Egypt, the oldest and the largest in the world, could not draw him to Thebes, a city whose trade had fallen off, where the deposits of bullion in the temples had lessened, and whose linen manufacture had moved towards the Delta. Had this great statesman been a Greek he would perhaps have gone on to this city, famous alike in history and in poetry; but, as it was, Scipio and his friends then sailed for Cyprus, Syria, and the other provinces or kingdoms under the power of Rome, to finish this tour of inspection.

For some time past, the Jews, taking advantage of the weakness of Egypt and Syria, had been struggling to make themselves free; and, at the beginning of this reign Simon Maccabæus, the high priest, sent an embassy to Rome, with a shield of gold weighing one thousand *minae*, as a present, to get their independence acknowledged by the Romans. On this the senate made a treaty of alliance with the family of the Maccabees, and, using the high tone of command to which they had for some

time past been accustomed, they wrote to Euergetes and
the King of Syria, ordering them not to make war upon
their friends, the Jews. But in an after decree the Romans recognise the close friendship and the trading inter-
course between Egypt and Judæa; and when they declared that they would protect the Jews in their right
to levy custom-house duties, they made an exception in
favour of the Egyptian trade. The people of Judæa in
these struggles were glad to forget the jealousy which
had separated them from their brethren in Egypt, and
the old quarrel between the Hebrews and the Hellenists;
the Sanhedrim of Jerusalem wrote to the Sanhedrim of
Alexandria, telling them that they were going to keep the
Feast of the Tabernacles in solemn thanksgiving to the
Almighty for their deliverance, and begging for the ben-
efit of their prayers.

The Jews, however, of Judæa, on their gaining their
former place as a nation, did not, as before, carry forward the chain of history in their sacred books. While
they had been under the yoke of the Babylonians, the
Persians, and the Syrians, their language had undergone
some changes; and when the Hebrew of the Old Testament was no longer the spoken language, they perhaps
thought it unworthy of them to write in any other. At
any rate, it is to their Greek brethren in Egypt that we
are indebted for the history of the bravery of the Maccabees. Jason of Cyrene wrote the history of the Maccabees, and of the Jewish wars against Antiochus Epiphanes and his son, Antiochus Eupator. This work, which
was in five books, is lost, and we now read only the short

history which was drawn from it by some unknown
Greek writer, which, with the letter from the Jews of
Judæa to their brethren of Egypt, forms the second book
of Maccabees.

In the list of Alexandrian authors, we must not forget to mention Jesus, the son of Sirach, who came into
Egypt in this reign, and translated into Greek the Hebrew work of his grandfather Jesus, which is named the
Book of Wisdom, or Ecclesiasticus. It is written in
imitation of the Proverbs of Solomon; and though its
pithy sayings fall far short of the deep wisdom and lofty
thoughts which crowd every line of that wonderful work,
yet it will always be read with profit and pleasure. In
this book we see the earliest example that we now possess
of a Jewish writer borrowing from the Greek philosophers; though how far the Greek thoughts were part
of the original Hebrew may be doubted, because the work
was left unfinished by Jesus the grandfather, and
completed by the Alexandrian translator, his grandson.
Hereafter we shall see the Alexandrian Jews engrafting
on the Jewish theology more and more of the Platonic
philosophy, which very well suited the serious earnestness of their character, and which had a most remarkable
effect in making their writings and opinions more fitted
to spread into the ancient schools.

This and other writings of the Alexandrian Jews were
by them added to the list of sacred books which together
made their Greek Bible; but they were never acknowledged at Jerusalem. The Hebrew books of the law and
the prophets were first gathered together by Nehemiah

after the return of the Hebrews from Babylon; but his library had been broken up during the Syrian wars. These Hebrew books, with some few which had since been written, were again got together by Judas Maccabæus; and after his time nothing more seems to have been added to them, though the Alexandrian Jews continued to add new books to their Greek Bible, while cultivating the Platonic philosophy with a success which made a change in their religious opinions. It was in Alexandria, and very much by the help of the Jews, that Eastern and Western opinions now met. Each made some change in the other, and, on the union of the two, Alexandria gave to the world a new form of philosophy.

The vices and cruelty of Euergetes called for more than usual skill in the minister to keep down the angry feelings of the people. This skill was found in the general Hierax, who was one of those men whose popular manners, habits of business, and knowledge of war, make them rise over every difficulty in times of trouble. On him rested the whole weight of the government; his wise measures in part made up for the vices of his master; and, when the treasure of the state had been turned to the king's pleasures, and the soldiers were murmuring for want of pay, Hierax brought forward his own money to quiet the rebellion. But at last the people could bear their grievances no longer; the soldiers without pay, instead of guarding the throne, were its greatest enemies, and the mob rose in Alexandria, set fire to the palace, and Euergetes was forced to leave the city and withdraw to Cyprus.

The Alexandrians, when free from their tyrant, sent for Cleopatra, his sister and divorced queen, and set her upon the throne. Her son by Philometor, in whose name she had before claimed the throne, had been put to death by Euergetes; Memphites, one of her sons by Euergetes, was with his father in the island of Cyprus; and Euergetes, fearing that his first wife Cleopatra and her advisers might make use of his son's name to strengthen her throne, had the child at once put to death. The birthday of Cleopatra was at hand, and it was to be celebrated in Alexandria with the usual pomp; and Euergetes, putting the head, hands, and feet of his son Memphites into a box, sent it to Alexandria by a messenger, who had orders to deliver it to Cleopatra in the midst of the feast, when the nobles and ambassadors were making their accustomed gifts. The grief of Cleopatra was only equalled by the anger of the Alexandrians, who the more readily armed themselves under Marsyas to defend the queen against the invasion for which Euergetes was then making preparations.

The queen's forces shortly marched against the army of Euergetes that was entering Egypt under the command of Hegelochus; but the Egyptian army was beaten on the Syrian frontier. Marsyas was sent prisoner to Euergetes; and the king then showed the only act of mercy which can be mentioned to his praise, and spared the life of a prisoner whom he thought he could make use of. Cleopatra then sent to Syria, to her son-in-law Demetrius, to ask for help, which was at first readily granted, but Demetrius was soon called home again by

a rising in Antioch. But great indeed must be the cruelty
which a people will not bear from their own king rather
than call in a foreign master to relieve them. The return
of the hated and revengeful Euergetes was not dreaded
so much by the Alexandrians as the being made a province of Syria. Cleopatra received no help from Demetrius, but she lost the love of her people by asking for
it, and she was soon forced to fly from Alexandria. She
put her treasures on board a ship, and joined her son
Ptolemy and her son-in-law Demetrius in Syria, while
Euergetes regained his throne. As soon as Euergetes
was again master of Egypt, it was his turn to be revenged
upon Demetrius; and he brought forward Zabbineus, a
young Egyptian, the son of Protarchus, a merchant, and
sent him into Syria with an army to claim the throne
under the name of Alexander, the adopted son of Antiochus. Alexander easily conquered and then put to
death Demetrius, but, when he found that he really was
King of Syria, he would no longer receive orders from
Egypt; and Euergetes found that the same plots and
forces were then wanted to put down this puppet, which
he had before used to set him up. He began by making
peace with his sister Cleopatra, who was again allowed
to return to Egypt; and we find her name joined with
those of Euergetes and his second queen in one of the
public acts of the priests. He then sent an army and
his daughter Tryphæna in marriage to Antiochus Grypus,
one of the sons of Demetrius, who gladly received his
help, and conquered Alexander and gained the throne
of his father.

OBELISK AT HELIOPOLIS.

We possess a curious inscription upon an obelisk that once stood in the island of Philæ, recording, as one of the grievances that the villagers smarted under, the necessity of finding supplies for the troops on their marches, and also for all the government messengers and public servants, or those who claimed to travel as such. The cost of this grievance was probably greater at Philæ than in other places, because the traveller was there stopped in his voyage by the cataracts on the Nile, and he had to be supplied with labourers to carry his luggage where the navigation was interrupted. Accordingly the priests at Philæ petitioned the king that their temple might be relieved from this heavy and vexatious charge, which they said lessened their power of rightly performing their appointed sacrifices; and they further begged to be allowed to set up a monument to record the grant which they hoped for. Euergetes granted the priests' prayer, and accordingly they set up a small obelisk; and the petition and the king's answer were carved on the base of this monument.

The gold mines near the Nubian or Golden Berenicë, though not so rich as they used to be, were worked with full activity by the unhappy prisoners, criminals, and slaves, who were there condemned to labour in gangs under the lash of their taskmasters. Men and women alike, even old men and children, each at such work as his overstretched strength was equal to, were imprisoned in these caverns tunnelled under the sea or into the side of the mountain; and there by torchlight they suffered the cruel tortures of their overseers without having power to make their groans heard above ground. No lot upon earth could be more wretched than that of these unhappy men; to all of them death would have been thought a boon.

The survey of the coast of the Red Sea, which was undertaken in this or the last reign, did not reach beyond the northern half of that sea. It was made by Agatharcides, who, when the philosopher Heracleides Lembus filled the office of secretary to the government under Philometor, had been his scribe and reader. Agatharcides gives a curious account of the half-savage people on these coasts, and of the more remarkable animals and products of the country. He was a most judicious historian, and gave a better guess than many at the true cause of why there was most water in the Nile in the dryest season of the year; which was a subject of never-ceasing inquiry with the travellers and writers on physics. Thales said that its waters were held back at its mouths by the Etesian winds, which blow from the north during the summer months; and Democritus of Abdera said that these winds carried heavy rain-clouds to Ethiopia; whereas the north winds do not begin to blow till the Nile has risen, and the river has returned to its usual size before the winds cease. Anaxagoras, who was followed by Euripides, the poet, thought that the large supply of water came from the melting of snow in Ethiopia. Ephorus thought that there were deep springs in the river's bed, which gushed forth with greater force in summer than in winter. Herodotus and Œnopides both thought that the river was in its natural state when the

country was overflowed; and the former said that its
waters were lessened in winter by the attraction of the
sun, then over Southern Ethiopia; and the latter said
that, as the earth grew cool, the waters were sucked into
its pores. The sources of the Nile were hidden by the
barbarism of the tribes on its banks; but by this time
travellers had reached the region of tropical rains; and
Agatharcides said that the overflow in Egypt arose from
the rains in Upper Ethiopia. But the Abyssinian rains
begin to fall at midsummer, too late to cause the inundation in Egypt; and therefore the truth seemed after
all to lie with the priests of Memphis, who said the Nile
rises on the other side of the equator, and the rain falling
in what was winter on that side of the globe made the
Nile overflow in the Egyptian summer.

From the very earliest times, says Ebers, the Pharaohs had understood the necessity of measuring exactly
the amount or deficiency of the inundations of the Nile,
and Nilometers are preserved which were erected high
up the river in Nubia by kings of the Old Empire, by
princes, that is to say, who reigned before the invasion
of the Hyksos. Herodotus tells us that the river must
rise sixteen ells for the inundation to be considered a
favourable one. If it remained below this mark, the
higher fields failed in obtaining a due supply of water,
and a dearth was the result. If it greatly exceeded it,
it broke down the dykes, damaged the villages, and had
not retired into its bed by the time for sowing the seed.
Thus the peasant, who could expect no rain, and was
threatened neither by frosts nor storms, could have his

prospects of a good or bad harvest read off by the priests
with perfect certainty by the scale of the Nilometer, and
not by the servants of the divinities only, but by the
officers of the realm, who calculated the amount of taxes
to be paid to them in proportion to the rising of the river.

The standard was protected by the magic power of
unapproachable sanctity, and the husbandman has been
strictly interdicted from
the earliest time to this
very day from casting a
glance at it during the time
when the river is rising; for
what sovereign could bear
to disclose without reserve
the decrees of Providence
as to the most important
of his rights, that of esti-
mating the amount of taxes
to be imposed? In the time
of the Pharaohs it was the
priesthood that declared to
the king and to the people
their estimate of the inundations, and at the present
day, the sheik, who is
sworn to secrecy, is under

NILOMETER AT RHODHA.

the control of the police of Cairo, and has his own Nilometer, the zero point of which is said to be somewhat
below that of the ancient standard. The engineers of
the French expedition first detected the fraud, by means

of which the government endeavoured every year to secure the full amount of taxes.

When the Nile has reached a height of a little over fifteen old Arabic ells, it exceeds its lowest level by more than eight ells, and has reached the height requisite to enable it to irrigate the highest fields. This happy event is announced to the people, who await it with breathless anxiety, and the opening of the dykes may be proceeded with. A festival to celebrate this occasion has been held from the remotest times. At the present time customs prevail which can, it is alleged, be traced by direct descent to the times of the Pharaohs, and yet during the dominion of Christianity in Egypt, and later again under sovereigns governing a nation wholly converted to Islam, the old worship of the Nile, with all its splendour, its display, and its strange ceremonies, was extirpated with the utmost rigour. But some portion of every discarded religion becomes merged in the new one that has supplanted it as a fresh form of superstition, and thus we discover from a Christian document dating from the sixth century, that the rising of the Nile "in its time" was no longer attributed to Osiris, but to a certain Saint Orion, and, as the priest of antiquity taught that a tear of Isis led to the overflowing of the Nile, so we hear the Egyptians of the present day say that "a divine tear" has fallen into the stream and caused the flood.

The trade of the Egyptians had given them very little knowledge of geography. Indeed the whole trade of the ancients was carried on by buying goods from their nearest neighbours on one side, and selling them to those on the other side of them. Long voyages were unknown; and, though the trading wealth of Egypt had mainly arisen from carrying the merchandise of India and Arabia Felix from the ports on the Red Sea to the ports on the Mediterranean, the Egyptians seem to have gained no knowledge of the countries from which these goods came. They bought them of the Arab traders, who came to Cosseir and the Troglodytic Berenicê from the opposite coast; the Arabs had probably bought them from the caravans that had carried them across the desert from the Persian Gulf; and that these land journeys across the desert were both easier and cheaper than a coasting voyage, we have before learned, from Philadelphus thinking it worth while to build watering and resting-houses in the desert between Koptos and Berenicê, to save the voyage between Berenicë and Cosseir.

India seems to have been only known to the Greeks as a country that by sea was to be reached by the way of the Euphrates and the Persian Gulf; and though Scylax had, by the orders of Darius, dropped down the river Indus, coasted Arabia, and thence reached the Red Sea, this voyage was either forgotten or disbelieved, and in the time of the Ptolemies it seems probable that nobody thought that India could be reached by sea from Egypt. Arrian indeed thought that the difficulty of carrying water in their small ships, with large crews of rowers, was alone great enough to stop a voyage of such a length along a desert coast that could not supply them with fresh water.

The long voyages of Solomon and Necho had been limited to coasting Africa; the voyage of Alexander the Great had been from the Indus to the Persian Gulf; hence it was that the court of Euergetes was startled by the strange news that the Arabian guards on the coast of the Red Sea had found a man in a boat by himself, who could not speak Koptic, but who they afterwards found was an Indian, who had sailed straight from India, and had lost his shipmates. He was willing to show any one the route by which he had sailed; and Eudoxus of Cyzicus in Asia Minor came to Alexandria to persuade Euergetes to give him the command of a vessel for this voyage of discovery. A vessel was given him; and, though he was but badly fitted out, he reached a country, which he called India, by sea, and brought back a cargo of spices and precious stones. He wrote an account of the coasts which he visited, and it was made use of by Pliny. But it is more than probable the unknown country called India, which Eudoxus visited, was on the west coast of Africa. Abyssinia was often called India by the ancients.

In these attempts at maritime discovery, and efforts after a cheaper means of obtaining the Indian products, the Greek sailors of Euergetes made a settlement in the island of Dioscorides, now called Socotara, in the Indian Ocean, forty leagues eastward of the coast of Africa; and there they met the trading vessels from India and Ceylon. This little island continued a Greek colony for upwards of seven centuries, and Greek was the only language spoken there till it fell under the

Arabs in the twilight of history, when all the European
possessions in Africa were overthrown. But the art of
navigation was so far unknown that but little use was
made of this voyage; the goods of India, which were
all costly and of small weight, were still for the most
part carried across the desert on camels' backs, and we
may remark that at a later period hardly more than
twenty small vessels ever went to India in one year
during the reigns of the Ptolemies, and that it was not
till Egypt was a province of Rome that the trade-winds
across the Arabian Sea were found out by Hippalus,
a pilot in the Indian trade. The voyage was little known
in the time of Pliny; even the learned Propertius seems
to have thought that silk was a product of Arabia; and
Palmyra and Petra, the two chief cities in the desert,
whose whole wealth rested and whose very being hung
upon their being watering-places for these caravans,
were still wealthy cities in the second century of our
era, when the voyage by the Arabian Sea became for
the first time easier and cheaper than the journeys across
the desert.

Euergetes had been a pupil of Aristobolus, a learned
Jew, a writer of the peripatetic sect of philosophers,
one who had made his learning respected by the pagans
from his success in cultivating their philosophy; and
also of Aristarchus, the grammarian, the editor of
Homer; and, though the king had given himself up to
the lowest pleasures, yet he held with his crown that
love of letters and of learning which had ennobled his
forefathers. He was himself an author, and wrote, like

Ptolemy Soter, his Memorabilia, or an account of what he had seen most remarkable in his lifetime. We may suppose that his writings were not of a very high order; they were quoted by Athenæus, who wrote in the reign of Marcus Aurelius; but we learn little else from them than the names of the mistresses of Ptolemy Philadelphus, and that a flock of pheasants was kept in the palace of Alexandria. He also wrote a commentary on Homer, of which we know nothing. When busy upon literature, he would allow his companions to argue with him till midnight on a point of history or a verse of poetry; but not one of them ever uttered a word against his tyranny, or argued in favour of a less cruel treatment of his enemies.

In this reign the schools of Alexandria, though not holding the rank which they had gained under Philadelphus, were still highly thought of. The king still gave public salaries to the professors; and Panaretus, who had been a pupil of the philosopher Arcesilaus, received the very large sum of twelve talents, or ten thousand dollars a year. Sositheus and his rival, the younger Homer, the tragic poets of this reign, have even been called two of the Pleiades of Alexandria; but that was a title given to many authors of very different times, and to some of very little merit. Such indeed was the want of merit among the poets of Alexandria that many of their names would have been unknown to posterity had they not been saved in the pages of the critics and grammarians, and pieced together by the skill of nineteenth century investigators.

But, unfortunately, the larger number of the men
of letters had in the late wars taken part with Philometor against the cruel and luxurious Euergetes. Hence,
when the streets of Alexandria were flowing with the
blood of those whom he called his enemies, crowds of

TEMPLE OF KOM OMBO.

learned men left Egypt, and were driven to earn a livelihood by teaching in the cities to which they then fled.
They were all Greeks, and few of them had been born
in Alexandria. They had been brought there by the
wealth of the country and the favour of the sovereign;
and they now withdrew when these advantages were
taken away from them. The isles and coasts of the

Mediterranean were so filled with grammarians, philosophers, geometers, musicians, schoolmasters, painters, and physicians from Alexandria that the cruelty of Euergetes II., like the taking of Constantinople by the Turks, may be said to have spread learning by the ill-treatment of its professors.

The city which was then rising highest in arts and letters was Pergamus in Asia Minor, which, under Eumenes and Attalus, was almost taking the place which Alexandria had before held. Its library already held two hundred thousand volumes, and raised a jealousy in the mind of Euergetes. Not content with buying books and adding to the size of his own library, he wished to lessen the libraries of his rivals; and, nettled at the number of volumes which Eumenes had got together at Pergamus, he made a law, forbidding the export of the Egyptian papyrus on which they were written. On this the copiers employed by Eumenes wrote their books upon sheepskins, which were called *charta pergamena*, or parchment, from the name of the city in which they were written. Thus our own two words, parchment from *Pergamus*, and paper from *papyrus*, remain as monuments of the rivalry in book-collecting between the two kings.

Euergetes was so bloated with disease that his body was nearly six feet round, and he was made weak and slothful by this weight of flesh. He walked with a crutch, and wore a loose robe like a woman's, which reached to his feet and hands. He gave himself up very much to eating and drinking, and on the year that he was chosen priest of Apollo by the Cyrenians, he showed his pleasure at the honour by a memorable feast which he gave in a costly manner to all those who had before filled that office. He had reigned six years with his brother, then eighteen years in Cyrene, and lastly twenty-nine years after the death of his brother, and he died in the fifty-fourth year of his reign, and perhaps the sixty-ninth of his age. He left a widow, Cleopatra Cocce; two sons, Ptolemy and Ptolemy Alexander; and three daughters, Cleopatra, married to her elder brother; Tryphæna, married to Antiochus Grypus; and Selene unmarried; and also a natural son, Ptolemy Apion, to whom by will he left the kingdom of Cyrene; while he left the kingdom of Egypt to his widow and one of his sons, giving her the power of choosing which should be her colleague. The first Euergetes earned and deserved the name, which was sadly disgraced by the second; but such was the fame of Egypt's greatness that the titles of its kings were copied in nearly every Greek kingdom. We meet with the flattering names of Soter, Philadelphus, Euergetes, and the rest, on the coins of Syria, Parthia, Cappadocia, Paphlagonia, Pontus, Bactria, and Bithynia; while that of Euergetes, *the benefactor*, was at last used as another name for a tyrant.

CHAPTER VI

THE GROWTH OF ROMAN INFLUENCE IN EGYPT

The weakness of the Ptolemies : Egypt bequeathed to Rome : Pompey, Cæsar, and Antony befriend Egypt.

ON the death of Ptolemy Euergetes II., his widow, Cleopatra Cocce, would have chosen her younger son, Ptolemy Alexander, then a child, for her partner on the throne, most likely because it would have been longer in the course of years before he would have claimed his share of power; but she was forced, by a threatened rising of the Alexandrians, to make her elder son king. Before, however, she would do this she made a treaty with him, which would strongly prove, if anything were still wanting, the vice and meanness of the Egyptian court. It was, that, although married to his sister Cleopatra, of whom he was very fond, he should put her away, and marry his younger sister Selene; because the mother hoped that Selene would be false to her husband's cause, and weaken his party in the state by her treachery.

CARTOUCHE OF SOTER II.

Ptolemy took the name of Soter II., though he is more often called Lathyrus, from a stain upon his face in the form of an ivy-leaf, pricked into his skin in honour of Osiris. He was also called Philometor; and we learn from an inscription on a temple at Apollinopolis Parva, that both these names formed part of the style in which the public acts ran in this reign; it is dedicated by " the Queen Cleopatra and King Ptolemy, gods Philometores, Soteres, and his children," without mentioning his wife. Here, as in Persia and Judæa, the king's mother often held rank above his wife. The name of Philometor was given to him by his mother, because, though he had reached the years of manhood, she wished to act as his guardian; but her unkindness to him was so remarkable that historians have thought that it was a nickname. The mother and the son were jointly styled sovereigns of Egypt; but they lived apart, and in distrust of one another, each surrounded by personal friends; while Cleopatra's stronger mind and greater skill in king-craft gained for her the larger share of power, and the effective control of Egypt.

Cleopatra, the daughter, put away by her husband at the command of her mother, soon made a treaty of marriage with Antiochus Cyzicenus, the friend of her late husband, who was struggling for the throne of Syria with his brother, Antiochus Grypus, the husband of her sister Tryphæna; and on her way to Syria she stopped at Cyprus, where she raised a large army and took it with her as her dower, to help her new husband against his brother and her sister.

With this addition to his army Cyzicenus thought his forces equal to those of his brother; he marched against him and gave him battle. But he was beaten, and he fled with his wife Cleopatra; and they shut themselves up in the city of Antioch. Grypus and Tryphæna then laid siege to the city, and the astute Tryphæna soon took her revenge on her sister for coming into Syria to marry the brother and rival of her husband. The city was taken; and Tryphæna ordered her sister to be torn from the temple into which she had fled, and to be put to death. In vain Grypus urged that he did not wish his victory to be stained by the death of a sister; that Cleopatra was by marriage his sister as well as hers; that she was the aunt of their children; and that the gods would punish them if they dragged her from the altar. But Tryphæna was merciless and unmoved; she gave her own orders to the soldiers, and Cleopatra was killed as she clung with her arms to the statue of the goddess. This cruelty, however, was soon overtaken by punishment: in the next battle Cyzicenus was the conqueror, and he put Tryphæna to death, to quiet, as was said, the ghost of her murdered sister.

In the third year of her reign Cleopatra Cocce gave the island of Cyprus to her younger son, Alexander, as an independent kingdom, thinking that he would be of more use to her there, in upholding her power against his brother Lathyrus, than he could be at Alexandria.

In the last reign Eudoxus had been entrusted by Euergetes with a vessel and a cargo for a trading voyage of discovery towards India; and in this reign he was again sent by Cleopatra down the Red Sea to trade with the unknown countries in the east. How far he went may be doubted, but he brought back with him from the coast of Africa the prow of a ship ornamented with a horse's head, the usual figurehead of the Carthaginian ships. This he showed to the Alexandrian pilots, who knew it as belonging to one of the Phœnician ships of Cadiz or Gibraltar. Eudoxus justly argued that this prow proved that it was possible to sail round Africa and to reach India by sea from Alexandria. The government, however, would not fit him out for a third voyage; but his reasons were strong enough to lead many to join him, and others to help him with money, and he thereby fitted out three vessels on this attempt to sail round Africa by the westward voyage. He passed the Pillars of Hercules, or Straits of Gibraltar, and then turned southward. He even reached that part of Africa where the coast turns eastward. Here he was stopped by his ships wanting repair. The only knowledge that he brought back for us is, that the natives of that western coast were of nearly the same race as the Ethiopians on the eastern coast. He was able to sail only part of the way back, and he reached Mauritania with difficulty by land. He thence returned home, where he met with the fate not unusual to early travellers. His whole story was doubted; and the geographers at home did not believe that he had ever visited the countries that he attempted to describe.

The people of Lower Egypt were, as we have seen, of several races; and, as each of the surrounding nations was in its turn powerful, that race of men was uppermost in Lower Egypt. Before the fall of Thebes the Kopts ruled in the Delta; when the free states of Greece held the first rank in the world, even before the time of Alexander's conquests, the Greeks of Lower Egypt were masters of their fellow-countrymen; and now that Judæa, under the bravery of the Maccabees, had gained among nations a rank far higher than what its size entitled it to, the Egyptian Jews found that they had in the same way gained weight in Alexandria. Cleopatra had given the command of her army to two Jews, Chelcias and Ananias, the sons of Onias, the priest of Heliopolis; and hence, when the civil war broke out between the Jews and Samaritans, Cleopatra helped the Jews, and perhaps for that reason Lathyrus helped the Samaritans. He sent six thousand men to his friend, Antiochus Cyzicenus, to be led against the Jews, but this force was beaten by the two sons of Hyrcanus, the high priest.

By this act Lathyrus must have lost the good-will of the Jews of Lower Egypt, and hence Cleopatra again ventured to choose her own partner on the throne. She raised a riot in Alexandria against him, in the tenth year of their reign, on his putting to death some of her friends, or more likely, as Pausanias says, by showing to the people some of her eunuchs covered with blood, who she said were wounded by him; and she forced him to fly from Egypt. She took from him his wife, Selene, whom she had before thrust upon him, and who had borne him two children; and she allowed him to withdraw to the kingdom of Cyprus, from which place she recalled her favourite son, Alexander, to reign with her in Egypt.

During these years the building was going forward of the beautiful temple at the city, afterwards named by the Romans Contra-Latopolis, on the other side of the Nile from Latopolis or Esne. Little now remains of it but its massive portico, upheld by two rows of four columns each,, having the globe with outstretched wings carved on the overhanging eaves. The earliest names

TEMPLE PORTICO AT CONTRA - LATOPOLIS.

found among the hieroglyphics with which its walls are covered are those of Cleopatra Cocce and her son, Ptolemy Soter, while the latest name is that of the Emperor Commodus. Even under Cleopatra Cocce, who was nearly the worst of the family, the building of these great temples did not cease.

The two sons were so far puppets in the hands of their clever mother, that on the recall of Alexander no change was seen in the government beyond that of the names which were placed at the head of the public acts. The former year was called the tenth of Cleopatra and

Ptolemy Soter, and this year was called the eleventh
of Cleopatra and eighth of Ptolemy Alexander; as Alexander counted his years from the time when he was
sent with the title of king to Cyprus. As he was, like
his brother, under the guidance of his mother, he was
like him in the hieroglyphical inscriptions called *mother-
loving*.

While the kingdoms of Egypt and Syria were alike
weakened by civil wars and by the vices of their kings,
Judæa, as we have seen, had risen under the wise government of the Maccabees to the rank of an independent
state; and latterly Aristobulus, the eldest son of Hyrcanus, and afterwards Alexander Jannæus, his second
son, had made themselves kings. But Gaza, Ptolemaïs,
and some other cities, bravely refused to part with their
liberty, and sent to Lathyrus, then King of Cyprus, for
help. This was not, however, done without many mis-
givings; for some were wise enough to see that, if Lathyrus helped them, Cleopatra would, on the other hand,
help their king, Jannæus; and when Lathyrus landed
at Sicaminos with thirty thousand men, the citizens of
Ptolemaïs refused even to listen to a message from him.

The city of Gaza then eagerly sent for the help which
the city of Ptolemaïs refused. Lathyrus drove back
Jannæus, and marched upon Asochis, a city of Galilee,
where he scaled the walls on the Sabbath Day, and took
ten thousand prisoners and a large booty. He then sat
down before the city of Saphoris, but left it on hearing
that Jannæus was marching against him on the other
side of the Jordan, at the head of a force larger than

his own. He crossed the river in face of the Jewish army, and routed it with great slaughter. The Jewish historian adds, that between thirty and fifty thousand men were slain upon the field of battle, and that the women and children of the neighbouring villages were cruelly put to death.

Cleopatra now began to fear that her son Lathyrus would soon make himself too powerful, if not checked in his career of success, and that he might be able to march upon Egypt. She therefore mustered her forces, and put them under the command of Chelcias and Ananias, her Jewish generals. She sent her treasure, her will, and the children of Alexander, to the island of Cos, as a place of safety, and then marched with the army into Palestine, having sent forward her son Alexander with the fleet. By this movement Lathyrus was unable to keep his ground in Cœle-Syria, and he took the bold step of marching towards Egypt. But he was quickly followed by Chelcias, and his army was routed, though Chelcias lost his life in the battle. Cleopatra, after taking Ptolemaïs, sent part of her army to help that which had been led by Chelcias; and Lathyrus was forced to shut himself up in Gaza. Soon after this the campaign ended, by Lathyrus returning to Cyprus, and Cleopatra to Egypt.

On this success, Cleopatra was advised to seize upon the throne of Jannæus, and again to add to Egypt the provinces of Palestine and Cœle-Syria, which had so long made part of the kingdom of her forefathers. She yielded, however, to the reasons of her general Ananias, for the Jews of Lower Egypt were too strong to be treated with slight. It was by the help of the Jews that Cleopatra had driven her son Lathyrus out of Egypt; they formed a large part of the Egyptian armies, which were no longer even commanded by Greeks; and it must have been by these clear and unanswerable reasons that Ananias was able to turn the queen from the thoughts of this conquest, and to renew the league between Egypt and Judæa.

Cleopatra, however, was still afraid that Lathyrus would be helped by his friend Antiochus Cyzicenus to conquer Egypt, and she therefore kept up the quarrel between the brothers by again sending troops to help Antiochus Grypus; and lastly, she gave him in marriage her daughter Selene, whom she had before forced upon Lathyrus. She then sent an army against Cyprus; and Lathyrus was beaten and forced to fly from the island.

In the middle of this reign died Ptolemy Apion, King of Cyrene. He was the half-brother of Lathyrus and Alexander, and, having been made King of Cyrene by his father Euergetes II., he had there reigned quietly for twenty years. Being between Egypt and Carthage, then called the Roman province of Africa, and having no army which he could lead against the Roman legions, he had placed himself under the guardianship of Rome; he had bought a truce during his lifetime, by making the Roman people his heirs in his will, so that on his death they were to have his kingdom. Cyrene had been part of Egypt for above two hundred years, and was usually governed by a younger son or brother of the king. But on the death of Ptolemy Apion, the Roman senate, who had latterly been grasping at everything within their reach, claimed his kingdom as their inheritance, and in the flattering language of their decree by which the country was enslaved, they declared Cyrene free. From that time forward it was practically a province of Rome.

Ptolemy Alexander, who had been a mere tool in the hands of his mother, was at last tired of his gilded chains; but he saw no means of throwing them off, or of gaining that power in the state which his birth and title, and the age which he had then reached, ought to have given him. The army was in favour of his mother, and an unsuccessful effort would certainly have been punished with death; so he took perhaps the only path open to him: he left Egypt by stealth, and chose rather to quit his throne and palace than to live surrounded by the creatures of his mother and in daily fear for his life.

Cleopatra might well doubt whether she could keep her throne against both her sons, and she therefore sent messengers with fair promises to Alexander, to ask him to return to Egypt. But he knew his mother too well ever again to trust himself in her hands; and while she was taking steps to have him put to death on his return, he formed a plot against her life by letters. In this double game Alexander had the advantage of his mother; her character was so well known that he needed not to be told of what was going on; while she perhaps thought that the son whom she had so long ruled as a child would not dare to act as a man. Alexander's plot was of the two the best laid, and on his reaching Egypt his mother was put to death.

But Alexander did not long enjoy the fruits of his murder. The next year the Alexandrians rose against him in a fury. He was hated not so much perhaps for the murder of his mother as for the cruelties which he had been guilty of, or at least had to bear the blame of, while he reigned with her. His own soldiers turned against him, and he was forced to seek his safety by flying on board a vessel in the harbour, and he left Egypt with his wife and daughter. He was followed by a fleet under the command of Tyrrhus, but he reached Myræ, a city of Lycia, in safety; and afterwards, in crossing over to Cyprus, he was met by an Egyptian fleet under Chæreas, and killed in battle.

Though others may have been guilty of more crimes, Alexander had perhaps the fewest good qualities of any of the family of the Lagidæ. During his idle reign of twenty years, in which the crimes ought in fairness to be laid chiefly to his mother, he was wholly given up to the lowest and worst of pleasures, by which his mind and body were alike ruined. He was so bloated with vice and disease that he seldom walked without crutches; but at his feasts he could leap from his raised couch and dance with naked feet upon the floor with the companions of his vices. He was blinded by flattery, ruined by debauchery, and hated by the people.

His coins are not easily known from those of the other kings, which also bore the name of " *Ptolemy the king* " round the eagle. Some of the coins of his mother have

the same words round the eagle on the one side, while
on the other is her head, with a helmet formed like the
head of an elephant, or her head with the name of
" *Queen Cleopatra.*" There are other coins with the
usual head of Jupiter, and with two eagles to point out
the joint sovereignty of herself and son.

Few buildings or parts of buildings mark the reign
of Ptolemy Alexander; but his name is not wholly unknown among the sculptures of
Upper Egypt. On the walls of
the temple of Apollinopolis
Magna he is represented as
making an offering to the god
Horus. There the Egyptian
artist has carved a portrait of this Greek king, whom
he perhaps had never seen, clothed in a dress which he
never wore, and worshipping a god whom he may have
hardly known by name.

COIN OF CLEOPATRA AND
ALEXANDER.

History has not told us who was the first wife of
Alexander, but he left a son by her named after himself Ptolemy Alexander, whom we have seen sent by his
grandmother for safety to the island of Cos, the fortress
of the family, and a daughter whom he carried with
him in his flight to Lycia. His second wife was Cleopatra Berenicê, the daughter of his brother Lathyrus,
by whom he had no children, and who is called in the
hieroglyphics his queen and sister.

On the flight of Alexander, the Alexandrians sent
an embassy to Cyprus to bring back Soter II., or Lathyrus, as he is called; and he entered Egypt without any

opposition. He had reigned ten years with his mother, and then eighteen years by himself in Cyprus; and during those years of banishment had shown a wisdom and good behaviour which must have won the esteem of the Alexandrians, when compared with his younger brother Alexander. He had held his ground against the fleets and armies of his mother, but either through weakness or good feeling had never invaded Egypt.

His reign is remarkable for the rebellion and ruin of the once powerful city of Thebes. It had long been falling in trade and in wealth, and had lost its superiority in arms; but its temples, like so many citadels, its obelisks, its colossal statues, and the tombs of its great kings still remained, and with them the memory of its glory then gone by. The hieroglyphics on the walls still recounted to its fallen priests and nobles the provinces in Europe, Asia, and Africa which they once governed, and the weight of gold, silver, and corn which these provinces sent as a yearly tribute. The paintings and sculptures showed the men of all nations and of all colours, from the Tatar of the north to the Negro

COIN OF CLEOPATRA AND ALEXANDER, WITH EAGLES.

of the south, who had graced the triumphs of their kings: and with these proud trophies before their eyes they had been bending under the yoke of Euergetes II. and Cleopatra Cocce for about fifty years. So small a measure of justice has usually been given to a conquered people

by their rulers, that their highest hopes have risen to
nothing more than an escape from excess of tyranny.
If life, property, female honour, national and religious
feelings have not been constantly and wantonly out-
raged, lesser evils have been patiently endured. Political servitude, heavy taxes, daily ill-treatment, and occa-
sional cruelty the Thebans had borne for two centuries
and a half under their Greek masters, as no less the

THE MEMNONIUM AT THEBES.

lot of humanity than poverty, disease, and death. But
under the government of Cleopatra Cocce the measure
of their injuries overflowed, and taking advantage of
the revolutions in Alexandria, a large part of Upper
Egypt rose in rebellion.

We can therefore hardly wonder that when Lathyrus
landed in Egypt, and tried to recall the troubled cities to
quiet government and good order, Thebes should have
refused to obey. The spirit of the warriors who followed
Ramses to the shores of the Black Sea was not quite

dead. For three years the brave Kopts, entrenched within their temples, every one of which was a castle, withstood his armies; but the bows, the hatchets, and the chariots could do little against Greek arms; while the overthrow of the massive temple walls, and the utter ruin of the city, prove how slowly they yielded to greater skill and numbers, and mark the conqueror's distrust lest the temples should be again so made use of. Perhaps the only time before when Thebes had been stormed after a long siege was when it first fell under the Persians; and the ruin which marked the footsteps of Cambyses had never been wholly repaired. But the wanton cruelty of the foreigners did little mischief, when compared with the unpitying and unforgiving distrust of the native conquerors. The temples of Tentyra, Apollinopolis, Latopolis, and Philæ show that the massive Egyptian buildings, when let alone, can withstand the wear of time for thousands of years; but the harder hand of man works much faster, and the wide acres of Theban ruins prove alike the greatness of the city and the force with which it was overthrown; and this is the last time that Egyptian Thebes is met with in the pages of history.

The traveller, whose means and leisure have allowed him to reach the spot, now counts the Arab villages which have been built within the city's bounds, and perhaps pitches his tent in the open space in the middle of them. But the ruined temples still stand to call forth his wonder. They have seen the whole portion of time of which history keeps the reckoning roll before them; they have seen kingdoms and nations rise and fall: Babylonians,

Assyrians, Hebrews, Persians, Greeks, and Romans. They have seen the childhood of all that we call ancient; and they still seem likely to stand, to tell their tale to those who will hereafter call us ancients. After this rebellion, Lathyrus reigned in quiet, and was even able to be of use to his Greek allies; and the Athenians, in gratitude, set up statues of bronze to him and Berenicë, his daughter.

During this reign, the Romans were carrying on a war with Mithridates, King of Pontus, in Asia Minor; and Sulla, who was then at the head of the republic, sent Lucullus, the soldier, the scholar, and the philosopher, as ambassador to Alexandria, to ask for help against the enemy. The Egyptian fleet moved out of harbour to meet him, a pomp which the kings of Egypt had before kept for themselves alone. Lathyrus received him on shore with the greatest respect, lodged him in the palace, and invited him to his own table, an honour which no foreigner had enjoyed since the kings of Egypt had thrown aside the plain manners of the first Ptolemies. Lucullus had brought with him the philosopher Antiochus of Athens, who had been the pupil of Philo, and they found time to enjoy the society of Dion, the academic philosopher, who was then teaching at Alexandria; and there they might have been seen with Heraclitus of Tyre, talking together about the changes which were creeping into the Platonic philosophy, and about the two newest works of Philo, which had just come to Alexandria. Antiochus could not read them without showing his anger: such sceptical opinions had never before been heard of in the Academy; but they knew the handwriting of Philo, they were certainly his. Selius and Tetrilius, who were there, had heard him teach the same opinions at Rome, whither he had fled, and where he was then teaching Cicero. The next day, the matter was again talked over with Lucullus, Heraclitus, Aristus of Athens, Ariston, and Dion; and it ended in Antiochus writing a book, which he named Sosus, against those new opinions of his old master, against the new Academy, and in behalf of the old Academy.

Lathyrus understood the principles of the balance of power and his own interest too well to help the Romans to crush Mithridates, and he wisely wished not to quarrel with either. He therefore at once made up his mind not to grant the fleet which Lucullus had been sent to ask for. It had been usual for the kings of Egypt to pay the expenses of the Roman ambassadors while living in Alexandria; and Lathyrus offered four times the usual allowance to Lucullus, beside eighty talents of silver. Lucullus, however, would take nothing beyond his expenses, and returned the gifts, which were meant as a civil refusal of the fleet; and, having failed in his embassy, he sailed hastily for Cyprus, leaving the wonders of Egypt unvisited. Lathyrus sent a fleet of honour to accompany him on his voyage, and gave him his portrait cut in an emerald. Mithridates was soon afterwards conquered by the Romans; and it was only by skilful embassies and well-timed bribes that Lathyrus was able to keep off the punishment which seemed to await him for having thus disobeyed the orders of Sulla. Egypt was then the only kingdom, to the west of Persia, that had not yet bowed its neck under the Roman yoke.

The coins of Lathyrus are not easily or certainly known from those of the other Ptolemies; but those of his second wife bear her head on the one side, with the name of " *Queen Selene*," and on the other side the eagle, with the name of " *King Ptolemy*." He had before reigned ten years with his mother, and after his brother's death he reigned six years and a half more; but, as he counted the years that he had reigned in Cyprus, he died in the thirty-seventh year of his reign. He left a daughter named Berenicë, and two natural sons, each named Ptolemy, one of whom reigned in Cyprus, and the other, nicknamed Auletes, *the piper*, afterwards gained the throne of Egypt.

COIN OF PTOLEMY LATHYRUS AND SELENE.

On the death of Lathyrus, or Ptolemy Soter II., his daughter Cleopatra Berenicê, the widow of Ptolemy Alexander, mounted the throne of Egypt in B. c. 80; but it was also claimed by her stepson, the young Alexander, who was then living in Rome. Alexander had been sent to the island of Cos, as a place of safety, when his grandmother Cleopatra Cocce followed her army into Cœle-Syria. But, as the Egyptians had lost the command of the sea, the royal treasure in Cos was no longer out of danger, and the island was soon afterwards taken by Mithridates, King of Pontus, who had conquered Asia Minor. Among the treasures in that island the Alexandrians lost one of the sacred relics of the kingdom, the chlamys or war-cloak which had belonged to Alexander the Great, and which they had kept with religious care as the safeguard of the empire. It then fell into the hands of Mithridates, and on his overthrow it became the prize of Pompey, who wore it in his triumph at the end of the Mithridatic war. With this chlamys, as had always been foretold by the believers in wonders, Egypt lost its rank among nations, and the command. of the world passed to the Romans, who now possessed this time-worn symbol of sovereignty.

Alexander also at that time fell into the hands of Mithridates; but he afterwards escaped, and reached the army of Sulla, under whose care he lived for some time in Rome. The Alexandrian prince hoped to gain the throne of his father by means of the friendship of one who could make and unmake kings at his pleasure; and Sulla might have thought that the wealth of Egypt would be at his command by means of his young friend. To these reasons Alexander added the bribe which was then becoming common with the princes who held their thrones by the help of Rome, he made a will, in which he named the Roman people as his heirs; and the senate then took care that the kingdom of Egypt should be a part of the wealth which was afterwards to be theirs by inheritance. After Berenicê, his stepmother, had been queen about six months, they sent him to Alexandria, with orders that he should be received as king; and, to soften the harshness of this command, he was told to marry Berenicë, and reign jointly with her.

The orders of Sulla, the Roman dictator, were of course obeyed; and the young Alexander landed at Alexandria, as King of Egypt and the friend of Rome. He married Berenicë; and on the nineteenth day of his reign, with a cruelty unfortunately too common in this history, he put her to death. The marriage had been forced upon him by the Romans, who ordered all the political affairs of the kingdom; but, as they took no part in the civil or criminal affairs, he seems to have been at liberty to murder his wife. But Alexander was hated by the people as a king thrust upon them by foreign arms; and Berenicë, whatever they might have before thought of her, was regretted as the queen of their choice. Hence his crime met with its reward. His own guards immediately rose upon him; they dragged him from the palace to the gymnasium, and there put him to death.

Though the Romans had already seized the smaller kingdom of Cyrene under the will of Ptolemy Apion, they could not agree among themselves upon the wholesale robbery of taking Egypt under the will which Alexander had made in their favour. They seized, however, a paltry sum of money which he had left at Tyre as a place of safety; and it was a matter of debate for many years afterwards in Rome, whether they should not claim the kingdom of Egypt. But the nobles of Rome, who sold their patronage to kings for sums equal to the revenues of provinces, would have lost much by handing the kingdom over to the senate. Hence the Egyptian monarchy was left standing for two reigns longer.

On the death of Ptolemy Alexander, the Alexandrians might easily have changed their weak and wicked rulers, and formed a government for themselves, if they had known how. The legitimate male line of the Ptolemies came to an end on the death of the young Alexander II. The two natural sons of Soter II. were then the next in succession; and, as there was no other claimant, the crown fell to the elder. He was young, perhaps even a minor under the age of fourteen. His claims had been wholly overlooked at the death of his father; for though by the Egyptian law every son was held to be equally legitimate, it was not so by the Macedonian law. He took the name of Neus Dionysus, or the young Osiris, as we find it written in the hieroglyphics, though he is usually called Auletes, *the piper;* a name afterwards given him because he was more proud of his skill in playing on the flute than of his very slender knowledge of the art of governing.

It was in this reign that the historian Diodorus Siculus travelled in Egypt, and wrote his account of the manners and religion of the people. What he tells us of the early Egyptian history is of little value when compared with the history by Manetho, who was a native of the country and could read the hieroglyphic records, or even with that by Herodotus; but nevertheless he deserves great praise, and our warmest thanks, for being nearly the first Greek writer when Egyptian learning could no longer be thought valuable; when the religion, though looked down upon, might at any rate be studied with ease—for being nearly the first writer who thought the manners of this ancient people, after they had almost passed off the page of history, worth the notice of a philosopher.

Diodorus never quotes Manetho, but follows Herodotus in making one great hero for the chief actions of antiquity, whom he calls Sesoosis or Sesonchosis. To him he assigns every great work of which the author was unknown, the canals in the Delta, the statue of Amenhôthes III., the obelisks of Ramses II., the distant navigation under Necho, the mounds and trenches dug against Assyrian and Persian invasion, and even the great ship of Ptolemy Philopator; and not knowing that Southern Arabia and even Ethiopia had by the Alexandrians been sometimes called India, he says that this hero conquered even India beyond the Ganges. On the other hand, the fabulous conquest of the great serpent, the enemy of the human race, which we see sculptured on the sarcophagus of Oimenepthah, he describes as an historic fact of the reign of Ptolemy Philadelphus. He tells us how this huge beast, forty-five feet long, was beaten down by troops of archers, slingers, and cavalry, and brought alive in a net to Alexandria, where Eve's old enemy was shown in a cage for the amusement of the curious citizens.

Memphis was then a great city; in its crowded streets, its palaces and temples, it was second only to Alexandria. A little to the west stood the pyramids, which were thought one of the seven wonders of the world. Their broad bases, sloping sides, and solid masonry had withstood the weather for ages; and their

huge unwieldy stones were a less easy quarry for after
builders than the live rock when nearer to the river's
side. The priests of Memphis knew the names of the
kings who, one after the other, had built a new portico
to their great temple of Phtah; but as to when or by
whom the pyramids were built, they had perhaps less
knowledge than the present day historian. The modern
Egyptologist, with his patient investigation, assigns the
largest of these three pyramids to Khûfûi or Kheops, a
famous ruler of the fourth dynasty, and the others were
erected by his immediate successors. The temple of
Phtah, and every other building of Memphis, is now
gone, and near the spot stands the great city of Cairo,
whose mosques and minarets have been quarried of its
ruins, but the pyramids still stand, after fifty-six centuries of broken and changing history, unbroken and
unchanged. They have outlived any portion of time that
their builders could have dreamed of, but their worn
surface no longer declares to us their builders' names
and history. Their sloping sides, formed to withstand
attacks, have not saved the inscriptions which they once
held; and the builders, in thus overlooking the reed
which was growing in their marshes, the papyrus, to
which the great minds of Greece afterwards trusted their
undying names, have only taught us how much safer it
would have been, in their wish to be thought of and
talked of in after ages, to have leaned upon the poet and
historian.

The beautiful temples of Dendera and Latopolis,
which were raised by the untiring industry of ages and

finished under the Roman emperors, were begun about this reign. Though some of the temples of Lower Egypt had fallen into decay; and though the throne was then tottering to its fall, the priests in Upper Egypt were still building for immortality. The religion of the Kopts was still flourishing.

The Egyptian's opinion of the creation was the growth of his own river's bank. The thoughtful man, who saw the Nile every year lay a body of solid manure upon his field, was able to measure against the walls of the old temples that the ground was slowly but certainly rising. An increase of the earth was being brought about by the river. Hence he readily believed that the world itself had of old been formed out of water, and by means of water. The philosophers were nearly of the same opinion. They held that matter was itself eternal, like the other gods, and that our world, in the beginning, before it took any shape upon itself, was like thin mud, or a mass of water containing all things that were afterwards to be brought forth out of it. When the water had by its divine will separated itself from the earth, then the great Ra, the sun, sent down his quickening heat, and plants and animals came forth out of the wet land, as the insects are spawned out of the fields, before the eyes of the husbandman, every autumn after the Nile's overflow has retreated. The crafty priests of the Nile declared that they had themselves visited and dwelt in the caverns beneath the river, where these treasures, while yet unshaped, were kept in store and waiting to come into being. And on the days sacred to

the Nile, boys, the children of priestly families, werë
every year dedicated to the blue river-god that they
might spend their youth in monastic retirement, and

HORUS ON THE CROCODILES. BULAK MUSEUM.

as it was said in these caverns beneath his waves. These
early Egyptian myths seem to have influenced the compilers of the Hebrew Scriptures. The author of the book
of Genesis tells us that the Hebrew God formed the earth
and its inhabitants by dividing the land from the water,

and then commanding them both to bring forth living
creatures; and again one of the Psalmists says that his
substance, while yet imperfect, was by the Creator curiously wrought in the lowest depths of the earth. The
Hebrew writer, however, never thinks that any part of
the creation was its own creator. But in the Egyptian
philosophy sunshine and the river Nile are themselves
the divine agents; and hence fire and water received
divine honours, as the two purest of the elements; and
every day when the temple of Serapis in Alexandria was
opened, the singer standing on the steps of the portico
sprinkled water over the marble floor while he held forth
the fire to the people; and though he and most of his
hearers were Greeks, he called upon the god in the Egyptian language.

The inner walls of the temples glittered with gold
and silver and amber, and sparkled with gems from
Ethiopia and India; and the recesses were veiled with
rich curtains. The costliness was often in striking contrast with the chief inmate, much to the surprise of the
Greek traveller, who, having leave to examine a temple,
had entered the sacred rooms, and asked to be shown
the image of the god for whose sake it was built. One
of the priests in waiting then approached with a solemn
look, chanting a hymn, and pulling aside the veil allowed him to peep in at a snake, a crocodile, or a cat,
or some other beast, fitter to inhabit a bog or cavern
than to lie on a purple cushion in a stately palace. The
funerals of the sacred animals were celebrated with great
pomp, particularly that of the bull Apis; and at a cost,

in one case, of one hundred talents, or eighty-five thousand dollars, which was double what Ptolemy Soter, in his wish to please his new subjects, spent upon the Apis of his day. After the funeral the priests looked for a calf with the right spots, and when they had found one they fattened it for forty days, and brought it to Memphis in a boat under a golden awning, and lodged it safely in the temple. The religious feelings of the Egyptians were much warmer and stronger than those of the Greeks or Romans; they have often been accused of

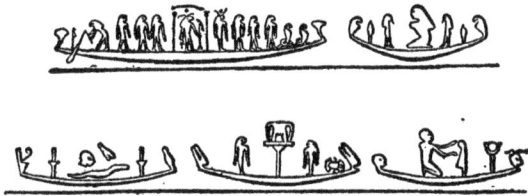

RELIGIOUS PROCESSION ON THE NILE.

eating one another, but never of eating a sacred animal. Once a year the people of Memphis celebrated the birthday of Apis with great pomp and expense, and one of the chief ceremonies on the occasion was the throwing a golden dish into the Nile. During the week that these rejoicings lasted, while the sacred river was appeased by gifts, the crocodile was thought to lose its fierceness, its teeth were harmless, and it never attempted to bite; and it was not till six o'clock on the eighth day that this animal again became an object of fear to those whose occupations brought them to the banks of the Nile. Once a year also the statues of the gods were removed from their pedestals and placed in barges, and thus carried in solemn procession along the Nile, and only brought back to the temples after some days. It was supposed that the gods were passing these days on a visit to the righteous Ethiopians.

The cat was at all times one of the animals held most sacred by the Egyptians. In the earliest and latest times we find the statues of their goddesses with cats' heads. The cats of Alexandria were looked upon as so many images of Neith or the Minerva of Saïs, a goddess worshipped both by Greeks and Egyptians; and it passed into a proverb with the Greeks, when they spoke of any two things being unlike, to say that they were as much like one another as a cat was to Minerva. It is to Alexandria also that we trace the story of a cat turned into a lady to please a prince who had fallen in love with it. The lady, however, when dressed in her bridal robes, could not help scampering about the room after a mouse seen upon the floor; and when Plutarch was in Egypt it had already become a proverb, that any one in too much finery was as awkward as a cat in a crocus-coloured robe.

So deeply rooted in the minds of the Egyptians was the worship of these animals that, when a Roman soldier had killed a cat unawares, though the Romans were masters of the country, the people rose against him in a fury. In vain the king sent a message to quiet the mob, to let them know that the cat was killed by accident; and, though the fear of Rome would most likely have saved a Roman soldier unharmed whatever other crime he might have been guilty of, in this case nothing would quiet the people but his death, and he was killed before the eyes of Diodorus, the historian. One nation rises above another not so much from its greater strength or skill in arms as from its higher aim and stronger wish for power. The Egyptians, we see, had not lost their courage, and when the occasion called them out they showed a fearlessness not unworthy of their Theban forefathers; on seeing a dead cat in the streets they rose against the king's orders and the power of Rome;

EGYPTIAN FUNERAL CEREMONIES.

had they thought their own freedom or their country's greatness as much worth fighting for, they could perhaps have gained them. But the Egyptians had no civil laws or rights that they cared about; they had nothing left that they valued but their religion, and this the Romans took good care not to meddle with. Had the Romans made war upon the priests and temples, as the Persians had done, they would perhaps in the same way have been driven out of Egypt: but they never shocked the religious feelings of the people, and even after Egypt had become a Roman province, when the beautiful temples of Esne, Dendera, and other cities, were dedicated in the names of the Roman emperors, they seldom copied

the example of Philometor, and put Greek, much less
Roman, writing on the portico, but continued to let the
walls be covered with hieroglyphical inscriptions.

The Egyptians, when rich enough to pay for it, still
had the bodies of their friends embalmed at their death,
and made into mummies; though the priests, to save
part of the cost, often put the mummy of a man just
dead into a mummy-case which had been made and used
in the reign of a Thûtmosis or an Amenhôthes. They
thought that every man at his death took upon himself
the character of Osiris, that the nurses who laid out the
dead body represented the goddesses Isis and Nepthys,
while the man who made the mummy was supposed to
be the god Anubis. When the embalming was finished,
it was part of the funeral to bring the dead man to trial
for what he had done when living, and thus to determine
whether he was entitled to an honourable burial. The
mummy was ferried across the lake belonging to the
temple, and taken before the judge Osiris. A pair of
scales was brought forth by the dog-headed Anubis and
the hawk-headed Horus; and with this they weighed
the past life of the deceased. The judge, with the advice
of a jury of forty-two, then pronounced the solemn ver-
dict, which was written down by the ibis-headed Thot.
But human nature is the same in all ages and in all
countries, and, whatever might have been the past life
of the dead, the judge, not to hurt the feelings of the
friends, always declared that he was " a righteous and
a good man: " and, notwithstanding the show of truth
in the trial, it passed into a proverb to say of a wicked

man, that he was too bad to be praised even at his funeral. This custom of embalming was thought right by all; but from examining the mummies that have come down to us, it would seem to have been very much confined to the priestly families, and seldom used in the case of children. The mummies, however, were highly valued by the survivors of the family, and when from poverty any man was driven to borrow money, the mum-

MUMMY, MUMMY - CASES, AND CASKET.

mies were thought good security by the lender, and taken as such for the loan. The mummy-cases indeed could be sold for a large sum, as when made of wood they were covered with painting, and sometimes in part gilt, and often three in number, one enclosing the other. The stone mummy-cases were yet more valuable, as they were either of white alabaster or hard black basalt, beautifully polished, in either case carved with hieroglyphics, and modelled to the shape of the body like the inner wooden cases.

It is interesting to note here that the pigment known to modern art by the name of mummy is, in many cases, actually prepared from the bituminous substances preserved within the wrappings of the ancient mummies. The grinding up of mummies imported from Thebes or Memphis for the purpose of enabling the twentieth century painter to paint the golden tresses of contemporary belles is of course not very extensively carried on, for one mummy will make several thousand tubes of paint, but the practice exists, and of late has been protested against both in England and France.

Though the old laws of Egypt must very much have fallen into disuse during the reigns of the latter Ptolemies, they had at least been left unchanged; and they teach us that the shadow of freedom may be seen, as in Rome under the Cæsars, and in Florence under the Medici, long after the substance has been lost. In quarrels between man and man, the thirty judges, from the cities of Thebes, Memphis, and Heliopolis, were still guided by the eight books of the law. The king, the priests, and the soldiers were the only landholders in the country, while the herdsmen, husbandmen, and handicraftsmen were thought of lower caste. Though the armies of Egypt were for the most part filled with Greek mercenaries, and the landholders of the order of soldiers could then have had as little to do with arms as knights and esquires have in our days, yet they still boasted of the wisdom of their laws, by which arms were only to be trusted to men who had a stake in the country worth fighting for. The old manners had long since

passed away. The priests alone obeyed the old marriage law, that a man should have only one wife. Other
men, when rich enough, married several. All children
were held equally legitimate, whatever woman was the
mother.

It is to these latter reigns of the Ptolemies, when high
feeling was sadly wanting in all classes of society, when
literature and art were alike in a very low state, that
we may place the rise of caricature in Egypt. We find

DEVELOPMENT OF EGYPTIAN CARICATURE.

drawings made on papyrus to scoff at what the nation
used to hold sacred. The sculptures on the walls of the
temples are copied in little; and cats, dogs, and monkeys
are there placed in the attitudes of the gods and kings
of old. In one picture we have the mice attacking a
castle defended by the cats, copied from a battle-scene
of Ramses II. fighting against the Ethiopians. In another the king on his throne as a dog, with a second dog
behind him as a fan-bearer, is receiving the sacred offerings from a cat. In a third the king and queen are seen

playing at chess or checkers in the form of a lion playing with a unicorn or horned ass.

We may form some opinion of the wealth of Egypt in its more prosperous times when we learn from Cicero that in this reign, when the Romans had good means of knowing, the revenues of the country amounted to twelve thousand five hundred talents, or ten million dollars; just one-half of which was paid by the port of Alexandria. This was at a time when the foreign trade had, through the faults of the government, sunk down to its lowest ebb; when not more than twenty ships sailed each year from the Red Sea to India; when the free population of the kingdom had so far fallen off that it was not more than three millions, which was only half of what it had been in the reign of Ptolemy Soter, though Alexandria alone still held three hundred thousand persons.

But, though much of the trade of the country was lost, though many of the royal works had ceased, though the manufacture of the finer linen had left the country, the digging in the gold mines, the favourite source of wealth to a despot, never ceased. Night and day in the mines near the Golden Berenicë did slaves, criminals, and prisoners of war work without pause, chained together in gangs, and guarded by soldiers, who were carefully chosen for their not being able to speak the language of these unhappy workmen. The rock which held the gold was broken up into small pieces; when hard it was first made brittle in the fire; the broken stone was then washed to separate the waste from the heavier

NEAR THE MINES OF MAGHARAH.

grains which held the gold; and, lastly, the valuable parts when separated were kept heated in a furnace for five days, at the end of which time the pure gold was found melted into a button at the bottom. But the mines were nearly worn out; and the value of the gold was a very small part of the thirty-five million dollars which they are said to have yielded every year in the reign of Ramses II.

As Auletes felt himself hardly safe upon the throne, his first wish was to get himself acknowledged as king by the Roman senate. For this end he sent to Rome a large sum of money to buy the votes of the senators, and he borrowed a further sum of Rabirius Posthumus, one of the richest farmers of the Roman taxes, which he spent on the same object. But though the Romans never tried to turn him out of his kingdom, he did not get the wished-for decree before he went to Rome in the twenty-fourth year of his reign. But we know nothing of the first years of his reign. A nation must be in a very demoralised state when its history disproves the saying, that the people are happy while their annals are short. There was more virtue and happiness, and perhaps even less bloodshed, with the stir of mind while Ptolemy Soter was at war with Antigonus than during this dull, un-warlike, and vicious time. The king gave himself up to his natural bent for pleasure and debauchery. At times when virtue is uncopied and unrewarded it is usually praised and let alone; but in this reign sobriety was a crime in the eyes of the king, a quiet behaviour was thought a reproach against his irregularities. The

Platonic philosopher Demetrius was in danger of being put to death because it was told to the king that he never drank wine, and had been seen at the feast of Bacchus in his usual dress, while every other man was in the dress of a woman. But the philosopher was allowed to disprove the charge of sobriety, or at least to make amends for his fault; and, on the king sending for him the next day, he made himself drunk publicly in the sight of all the court, and danced with cymbals in a loose dress of Tarentine gauze. But so few are the deeds worth mentioning in the falling state that we are pleased even to be told that, in the one hundred and seventy-eighth Olympiad, Strato of Alexandria conquered in the Olympic games and was crowned in the same day for wrestling, and for *pancratium*, or wrestling and boxing joined, these sports being considered among the most honourable in which athletes could contend.

In the thirteenth year of this reign (B. C. 68), when the war against the pirates called for the whole naval force of Rome, Pompey sent a fleet under Lentulus Marcellinus to clear the coast and creeks of Egypt from these robbers. The Egyptian government was too weak to guard its own trade; and Lentulus in his consulship put the Ptolemaic eagle and thunderbolt on his coins, to show that he had exercised an act of sovereignty. Three years later, we again meet with the eagle and thunderbolt on the consular coins of Aurelius Cotta; and we learn from Cicero that in that year it was found necessary to send a fleet to Alexandria to enforce the orders of the senate.

We next find the Roman senate debating whether they should not seize the kingdom as their inheritance under the will of Ptolemy Alexander II., but, moved by the bribes of Auletes, and perhaps by other reasons which we are not told, they forbore to grasp the prize. In this difficulty Auletes was helped by the great Pompey, to whom he had sent an embassy with a golden crown worth four thousand pieces of gold, which met him at Damascus on his Syrian campaign. He then formed a secret treaty with Mithridates, King of Pontus, who was engaged in warfare with the Romans, their common enemy. Auletes was now a widower with six young children, and Mithridates had two daughters; and accordingly it was agreed that one daughter should be married to Auletes, and the other to his brother, the King of Cyprus. But the ruin and death of Mithridates broke off the marriages; and Auletes was able to conceal from the Romans that he had ever formed an alliance with their enemy.

In the year which was made famous by the consulship of Cicero, Jerusalem was taken by the Roman army under Pompey; and Judæa, which had enjoyed a short-lived freedom of less than one hundred years under the Maccabees, was then put under a Roman governor. The fortifications of the temple were destroyed. This was felt by the Jews of Lower Egypt as a heavy blow, and from this time their sufferings in that country began. While their brethren had been lords of Judæa, they had held up their heads with the Greeks in Alexandria, but upon the fall of Jerusalem they sunk down to the rank of the Egyptians. They thought worse of themselves, and they were thought worse of by others. The Egyptian Jews were very closely allied to the people of the Delta. Though they had been again and again warned by their prophets not to mix with the Egyptians, they seem not to have listened to the warning. They were in many religious points less strict than their brethren in Judæa. The living in Egypt, the building a second temple, and the using a Greek Bible, were all breaches, if not of the law, at least of the tradition. They surrounded their synagogues with sacred groves, which were clearly forbidden by Moses. Though they were not guilty of worshipping images, yet they did not think it wrong to have portraits and statues of themselves. In their dislike of pork, in their washings, and in other Eastern customs, they were like the Egyptians; and hence the Greeks, who thought them both barbarians, very grudgingly yielded to them the privileges of choosing their own magistrates, of having their own courts of justice, and the other rights of citizenship which the policy of the Ptolemies had granted. The Jews, on the other hand, in whose eyes religion was everything, saw the Greeks and Egyptians worshipping the same gods and the same sacred animals, and felt themselves as far above the Greeks in those branches of philosophy which arise out of religion as they were below them in that rank which is gained by success in war. Hence it was with many heartburnings, and not without struggles which shed blood in the streets of Alexandria, that they found themselves, in the years which ushered in the Christian era, sinking down to the level of the Egyptians, and losing one by one the rights of Macedonian citizenship.

During these years Auletes had been losing his friends and weakening his government, and, at last, when he refused to quarrel with the senate about the island of Cyprus, the Egyptians rose against him in arms, and he was forced to fly from Alexandria. He took ship for Rome, and in his way there he met Cato, who was at Rhodes on his voyage to Cyprus. He sent to Cato to let him know that he was in the city, and that he wished to see him. But the Roman sent word back that he was unwell, and that if the king wanted to speak to him he must come himself. This was not a time for Auletes to quarrel with a senator, when he was on his way to Rome to beg for help against his subjects; so he was forced to go to Cato's lodgings, who did not even rise from his seat when the king entered the room. But this treatment was not quite new to Auletes; in his flight from Alexandria, in disguise and without a servant, he had had to eat brown bread in the cottage of a peasant; and he now learned how much more irksome it was to wait upon the pleasure of a Roman senator. Cato gave him the best advice; that, instead of going to Rome, where he would find that all the wealth of Egypt would be thought a bribe too small for the greediness of the senators whose votes he wanted, he would do better to return to Alexandria, and make peace with his rebellious subjects. Auletes, however, went on to Italy, and he arrived at Rome in the twenty-fourth year of his reign; and in the three years that he spent there in courting and bribing the senators, he learned the truth of Cato's statements, and the value of his advice.

His brother Ptolemy, who was reigning in Cyprus, was not even so well treated. The Romans passed a law making that wealthy island a Roman province, no doubt upon the plea of the will of Alexander II. and the king's illegitimacy; and they sent Cato, rather against his will, to turn Ptolemy out of his kingdom. Ptolemy gave up the island without Cato being called upon to use force, and in return the Romans made him high priest in the temple of the Paphian Venus; but he soon put himself to death by poison. Canidius Crassus, who had been employed by Cato in this affair, may have had some fighting at sea with the Egyptians, as on one of his coins we see on one side a crocodile, and on the other the prow of a ship, as if he had beaten the Egyptian fleet in the mouth of the Nile.

On the flight of their king, the rebellious Alexandrians set on the throne the two eldest of his daughters, Cleopatra Tryphæna and Berenicê, and sent an embassy, at the head of which was Dion, the academic philosopher, to plead their cause at Rome against the king. But the gold of Auletes had already gained the senate; and Cicero spoke, on his behalf, one of his great speeches, now unfortunately lost, in which he rebutted the charge that Auletes was at all to be blamed for the death of Alexander, whom he thought justly killed by his guards for the murder of his queen and kinswoman. Cæsar, whose year of consulship was then drawing to an end, took his part warmly; and Auletes became in debt to

him in the sum of seventeen million drachmæ, or nearly
two and a half million dollars, either for money lent to
bribe the senators, or for bonds then given to Cæsar instead of money. By these means Auletes got his title
acknowledged; the door of the senate was shut against
the Alexandrian ambassadors; and the philosopher Dion,
the head of the embassy, was poisoned in Rome by the
slaves of his friend Lucceius, in whose house he was
dwelling. But nevertheless, Auletes was not able to get
an army sent to help him against his rebellious subjects
and his daughters; nor was Cæsar able to get from the
senate, for the employment of his proconsular year, the
task of replacing Auletes on the throne.

This high employment was then sought for both by
Lentulus and by Pompey. The senate at first leaned in
favour of the former; and he would perhaps have gained
it if the Roman creditors of Auletes, who were already
trembling for their money, had not bribed openly in
favour of Pompey, as the more powerful of the two. On
Pompey, therefore, the choice of the senate at last fell.
Pompey then took Auletes into his house, as his friend
and guest, and would have got orders to lead him back
into his kingdom at the head of a Roman army had not
the tribunes of the people, fearing any addition to Pompey's great power, had recourse to their usual state-
engine, the Sibylline books; and the pontifex, at their
bidding, publicly declared that it was written in those
sacred pages that the King of Egypt should have the
friendship of Rome, but should not be helped with an
army.

But though Lentulus and Pompey were each strong enough to stop the other from having this high command, Auletes was not without hopes that some Roman general would be led, by the promise of money, and by the honour, to undertake his cause, though it would be against the laws of Rome to do so without orders from the senate. Cicero then took him under his protection, and carried him in a litter of state to his villa at Baiæ, and wrote to Lentulus, the proconsul of Cilicia and Cyprus, strongly urging him to snatch the glory of replacing Auletes on the throne, and of being the patron of the King of Egypt. But Lentulus seems not to have chosen to run the risk of so far breaking the laws of his country.

Auletes then went, with pressing letters from Pompey, to Gabinius, the proconsul of Syria, and offered him the large bribe of ten thousand talents, or seven and a half million dollars, if he would lead the Roman army into Egypt, and replace him on the throne. Most of the officers were against this undertaking; but the letters of Pompey, the advice of Mark Antony, the master of the horse, and perhaps the greatness of the bribe, outweighed those cautious opinions.

While Auletes had been thus pleading his cause at Rome and with the army, Cleopatra Tryphæna, the elder of the two queens, had died; and, as no one of the other children of Auletes was old enough to be joined with Berenicë on the throne, the Alexandrians sent to Syria for Seleucus, the son of Antiochus Grypus and of Selene, the sister of Lathyrus, to come to Egypt and marry Berenicê. He was low-minded in all his pleasures and tastes, and got the nickname of Cybiosactes, *the scullion.* He was even said to have stolen the golden sarcophagus in which the body of Alexander was buried; and was so much disliked by his young wife that she had him strangled on the fifth day after their marriage. Berenicë then married Archelaus, a son of Mithridates Eupator, King of Pontus; and she had reigned one year with her sister and two years with her husbands when the Roman army brought back her father, Ptolemy Auletes, into Egypt.

Gabinius, on marching, gave out as an excuse for quitting the province entrusted to him by the senate, that it was in self-defence; and that Syria was in danger from the Egyptian fleet commanded by Archelaus. He was accompanied by a Jewish army under the command of Antipator, sent by Hyrcanus, whom the Romans had just made governor of Judæa. Mark Antony was sent forward with the horse, and routed the Egyptian army near Pelusium, and then entered the city with Auletes. The king, in the cruelty of his revenge, wished to put the citizens to the sword, and was only stopped by Antony's forbidding it. The Egyptian army was at this time in the lowest state of discipline; it was the only place where the sovereign was not despotic. The soldiers, who prized the lawlessness of their trade even more than its pay, were a cause of fear only to their fellow-citizens. When Archelaus led them out against the Romans, and ordered them to throw up a trench around their camp, they refused to obey; they said that ditch-making was not work for soldiers, but that it ought to be done at the cost of the state. Hence, when on this first success Gabinius followed with the body of the army, he easily conquered the rest of the country and put to death Berenicë and Archelaus. He then led back the army into his province of Syria, but left behind him a body of troops under Lucius Septimius to guard the throne of Auletes and to check the risings of the Alexandrians.

Gabinius had refused to undertake this affair, which was the more dangerous because against the laws of Rome, unless the large bribe were first paid down in money. He would take no promises; and Auletes, who in his banishment had no money at his command, had to borrow it of some one who would listen to his large promises of after payment. He found this person in Rabirius Posthumus, who had before lent him money, and who saw that it would be all lost unless Auletes regained the throne. Rabirius therefore lent him all he was worth, and borrowed the rest from his friends; and as soon as Auletes was on the throne, he went to Alexandria to claim his money and his reward. While Auletes still stood in need of Roman help, and saw the advantage of keeping faith with his foreign creditors, Rabirius was allowed to hold the office of royal *diœcetes*, or paymaster-general, which was one of great state and profit, and one by which he could in time have repaid himself his loan. He wore a royal robe; the taxes of Alexandria went through his hands; he was indeed master of the city. But when the king felt safe on his throne, he sent away his troublesome creditor, who

returned to Rome with the loss of his money, to stand his trial as a state criminal for having lent it. Rabirius had been for a time mortgagee in possession of the revenues of Egypt; and Auletes had felt more indebted for his crown to a Roman citizen than to the senate. But in the dealings of Rome with foreign kings, these evils had often before arisen, and at last been made criminal; and while Gabinius was tried for treason, *de majestate*, for leading his army out of his province, Rabirius was tried, under the *Lex Julia de pecuniis repetundis*, for lending money and taking office under Auletes.

One of the last acts of Gabinius in Syria was to change the form of the Jewish government into an aristocracy, leaving Hyrcanus as the high priest. The Jews thereon began to rebuild the walls of Jerusalem, that had been thrown down by Pompey. Among the prisoners sent to Rome by Gabinius was Timagenes, the son of the king's banker, who probably lost his liberty as a hostage on Ptolemy's failure to repay the loan. But he was afterwards ransomed from slavery by a son of Sulla, and he remained at Rome teaching Greek eloquence in the schools, and writing his numerous works.

The climate of Egypt is hardly suited to Europeans, and perhaps at no time did the births in the Greek families equal the deaths. That part of the population was kept up by newcomers; and latterly the Romans had been coming over to share in the plunder that was there scattered among the ruling class. For some time past Alexandria had been a favourite place of settlement for

such Romans as either through their fault or their misfortune were forced to leave their homes. All who were
banished for their crimes or who went away to escape

THE SPHINX.

from trial, all runaway slaves, all ruined debtors, found
a place of safety in Alexandria; and by enrolling them
selves in the Egyptian army they joined in bonds of

fellowship with thousands like themselves, who made it a point of honour to screen one another from being overtaken by justice or reclaimed by their masters. With such men as these, together with some bands of robbers from Syria and Cilicia, had the ranks of the Egyptian army latterly been recruited. These were now joinëd by a number of soldiers and officers from the army of Gabinius, who liked the Egyptian high pay and lawlessness better than the strict discipline of the Romans. As, in this mixed body of men, the more regular courage and greater skill in war was found among the Romans, they were chiefly chosen as officers, and the whole had something of the form of a Roman army. These soldiers in Alexandria were above all law and discipline.

The laws were everywhere badly enforced, crimes passed unpunished, and property became unsafe. Robberies were carried on openly, and the only hope of recovering what was stolen was by buying it back from the thief. In many cases, whole villages lived upon plunder, and for that purpose formed themselves into a society, and put themselves under the orders of a chief; and, when any merchant or husbandman was robbed, he applied to this chief, who usually restored to him the stolen property on payment of one-fourth of its value.

As the country fell off in wealth, power, and population, the schools of Alexandria fell off in learning, and we meet with few authors whose names can brighten the pages of this reign. Apollonius of Citium, indeed, who had studied surgery and anatomy at Alexandria under Zopyrus, when he returned to Cyprus, wrote a

treatise on the joints of the body, and dedicated his work
to Ptolemy, king of that island.   The work is still remaining in manuscript.

Beside his name of Neus Dionysus, the king is in
the hieroglyphics sometimes called Philopator and Philadelphus; and in a Greek inscription on a statue at Philæ
he is called by the three names, Neus Dionysus, Philopator, Philadelphus.   The coins which are usually
thought to be his are in a worse style of art than those
of the kings before him.   He died in B. C. 51, in the
twenty-ninth year of his reign, leaving four children,
namely, Cleopatra, Arsinoë, and two Ptolemies.

CLEOPATRA ON THE CYDNUS.

CHAPTER VII

CLEOPATRA AND HER BROTHERS

Pompey, Cæsar, and Antony in Egypt — Cleopatra's extravagance and intrigues — Octavianus annexes Egypt — Retrospect.

PTOLEMY NEUS DIONYSUS had by his will left his kingdom to Cleopatra and Ptolemy, his elder daughter and elder son, who, agreeably to the custom of the country, were to marry one another and reign with equal power. He had sent one copy of his will to Rome, to be lodged in the public treasury, and in it he called upon the Roman people, by all the gods and by the treaties by which they were bound, to see that it was obeyed. He had also begged them to undertake the guardianship of his son. The senate voted Pompey tutor to the young king, or governor of Egypt; and the Alexandrians in the third year of his reign sent sixty ships of war to help

the great Pompey in his struggle against Julius Cæsar
for the chief power in Rome. But Pompey's power was
by that time drawing to an end, and the votes of the
senate could give no strength to the weak: hence the
eunuch Pothinus, who had the care of the elder Ptolemy,
was governor of Egypt, and his first act was to declare
his young pupil king, and to set at nought the will of
Auletes, by which Cleopatra was joined with him on the
throne.

Cleopatra fled into Syria, and, with a manly spirit
which showed what she was afterwards to be, raised an
army and marched back to the borders of Egypt, to claim
her rights by force of arms. It was in the fourth year
of her reign, when the Egyptian troops were moved to
Pelusium to meet her, and the two armies were within
a few leagues of one another, that Pompey, who had been
the friend of Auletes when the king wanted a friend,
landed on the shores of Egypt in distress, and almost
alone. His army had just been beaten at Pharsalia, and
he was flying from Cæsar, and he hoped to receive from
the son the kindness which he had shown to the father.
But gratitude is a virtue little known in palaces, and
Ptolemy had been cradled in princely selfishness. In
this civil war between Pompey and Cæsar, the Alexandrians would have been glad to be the friends of both,
but that was now out of the question; Pompey's coming made it necessary for them to choose which they
should join, and Ptolemy's council, like cowards, only
wished to side with the strong. Pothinus the eunuch,
Achilles the general, who was a native Egyptian, and

ALEXANDRIA.

Theodotus of Chios, who was the prince's tutor in rhetoric, were the men by whom the fate of this great Roman
was decided. " By putting him to death," said Theodotus, " you will oblige Cæsar, and have nothing to fear
from Pompey; " and he added with a smile, " Dead men
do not bite." So Achilles and Lucius Septimius, the head
of the Roman troops in the Egyptian army, were sent
down to the seaside to welcome him, to receive him as
a friend, and to murder him. They handed him out of
his galley into their boat, and put him to death on his
landing. They then cut off from his lifeless trunk the
head which had been three times crowned with laurels
in the capitol; and in that disfigured state the young
Ptolemy saw for the first time, and without regret, the
face of his father's best friend.

When Cæsar, following the track of Pompey, arrived
in the roadstead of Alexandria, all was already over.
With deep agitation he turned away when the murderer
brought to his ship the head of the man who had been his
son-in-law and for long years his colleague in rule, and
to get whom alive into his power he had come to Egypt.
The dagger of the rash assassin precluded an answer
to the question, how Cæsar would have dealt with the
captive Pompey; but, while the human sympathy which
still found a place in the great soul of Cæsar, side by
side with ambition, enjoined that he should spare his
former friend, his interest also required that he should
annihilate Pompey otherwise than by the executioner.
Pompey had been for twenty years the acknowledged
ruler of Rome; a dominion so deeply rooted does not

end with the ruler's death. The death of Pompey did not break up the Pompeians, but gave to them instead of an aged, incapable, and worn-out chief, in his sons Gnacus and Sextus, two leaders, both of whom were young and active, and the second of them of decided capacity. To the newly founded hereditary monarchy, hereditary pretendership attached itself at once like a parasite, and it was very doubtful whether by this change of persons Cæsar did not lose more than he gained.

Meanwhile in Egypt Cæsar had now nothing further to do, and the Romans and Egyptians expected that he would immediately set sail and apply himself to the subjugation of Africa, and to the huge task of organisation which awaited him after the victory. But Cæsar, faithful to his custom—wherever he found himself in the wide Empire—of finally regulating matters at once and in person, and firmly convinced that no resistance was to be expected either from the Roman garrison or from the court; being, moreover, in urgent pecuniary embarrassment, landed in Alexandria with the two amalgamated legions accompanying him to the number of thirty-two hundred men and eight hundred Celtic and German cavalry, took up his quarters in the royal palace, and proceeded to collect the necessary sums of money and to regulate the Egyptian succession, without allowing himself to be disturbed by the saucy remark of Pothinus that Cæsar should not for such petty matters neglect his own so important affairs. In his dealings with the Egyptians he was just and even indulgent. Although the aid which they had given to Pompey justified the imposing of a war contribution, the exhausted land was spared from this; and, while the arrears of the sums stipulated for in B. C. 59, and since then only about half paid, were remitted, there was required merely a final payment of ten million denarii (two million dollars). The belligerent brother and sister were enjoined immediately to suspend hostilities, and were invited to have their dispute investigated and decided before the arbiter. They submitted; the royal boy was already in the palace and Cleopatra also presented herself there. Cæsar adjudged the kingdom of Egypt, agreeably to the testament of Auletes, to the intermarried brother and sister Cleopatra and Ptolomoreus Dionysus, and further gave unasked the kingdom of Cyprus—cancelling the earlier act of annexation—as the appanage of the second-born of Egypt to the younger children of Auletes, Arsinoë and Ptolemy the younger.

But a storm was secretly preparing. Alexandria was a cosmopolitan city as well as Rome, hardly inferior to the Italian capital in the number of its inhabitants, far superior to it in stirring commercial spirit, in skill of handicraft, in taste for science and art: in the citizens there was a lively sense of their own national importance, and, if there was no political sentiment, there was at any rate a turbulent spirit, which induced them to indulge in their street riots regularly and heartily. We may conceive their feelings when they saw the Roman general ruling in the palace of the Lagids, and their kings accepting the award of his tribunal. Pothinus and the boy-king, both, as may be conceived, very dissatisfied at once with the peremptory requisition of all debts and with the intervention in the throne-dispute which could only issue, as it did, in the favour of Cleopatra, sent—in order to pacify the Roman demands—the treasures of the temple and the gold plate of the king with intentional ostentation to be melted at the mint; with increasing indignation the Egyptians—who were pious even to superstition, and who rejoiced in the world-renowned magnificence of their court as if it were a possession of their own—beheld the bare walls of their temples and the wooden cups on the table of their king. The Roman army of occupation also, which had been essentially denationalised by its long abode in Egypt and the many intermarriages between the soldiers and Egyptian women, and which moreover numbered a multitude of the old soldiers of Pompey and runaway Italian criminals and slaves in its ranks, was indignant at Cæsar, by whose orders it had been obliged to suspend its action on the Syrian frontier, and at his handful of haughty legionaries. The tumult even at the landing, when the multitude saw the Roman axes carried into the old palace, and the numerous instances in which his soldiers were assassinated in the city, had taught Cæsar the immense danger in which he was placed with his small force in presence of the exasperated multitude. But it was difficult to return on account of the northwest winds prevailing at this season of the year, and the attempt of embarkation might easily become a signal for the outbreak of the insurrection; besides, it was not the nature of Cæsar to take his departure without having accomplished his work. He accordingly ordered up at once reinforcements from Asia, and meanwhile, till these arrived, made a show of the utmost self-possession. Never was there greater gaiety in his camp than during this rest at Alexandria, and while the beautiful and clever Cleopatra was not sparing of her charms in general and least of all towards her judge, Cæsar also appeared among all his victories to value most those won over beautiful women. It was a merry prelude to graver scenes. Under the leadership of Achilles and, as was afterwards proved, by the secret orders of the king and his guardian, the Roman army of occupation stationed in Egypt appeared unexpectedly in Alexandria, and, as soon as the citizens saw that it had come to attack Cæsar, they made common cause with the soldiers.

With a presence of mind, which in some measure justifies his foolhardiness, Cæsar hastily collected his scattered men; seized the persons of the king and his ministers; entrenched himself in the royal residence and adjoining theatre; and gave orders, as there was no time to place in safety the war-fleet stationed in the principal harbour immediately in front of the theatre, that it should be set on fire and that Pharos, the island with the light-tower commanding the harbour, should be occupied by means of boats. Thus at least a restricted position for defence was secured, and the way was kept open to procure supplies and reinforcements. At the same time orders were issued to the commandant of Asia Minor as well as to the nearest subject countries, the Syrians and the Nabatæans, the Cretans and the

Rhodians, to send men and ships in all haste to Egypt. The insurrection, at the head of which the Princess Arsinoë and her confidant, the eunuch Ganymedes, had placed themselves, meanwhile had free course in all Egypt and in the greater part of the capital. In the streets of the latter there was daily fighting, but without success either on the part of Cæsar in gaining freer scope and breaking through to the fresh water lake of Mariut which lay behind the town, where he could have provided himself with water and forage; or on the part of the Alexandrians in acquiring superiority in besieging and depriving them of all drinking water; for, when the Nile canals in Cæsar's part of the town had been spoiled by the introduction of salt water, drinkable water was unexpectedly found in wells dug on the beach.

As Cæsar was not to be overcome from the landward side, the exertions of the besiegers were directed to destroy his fleet and cut him off from the sea, by which supplies reached him. The island with the lighthouse and the mole by which this was connected with the mainland divided the harbour into a western and an eastern half, which were in communication with each other through two arch-openings in the mole. Cæsar commanded the island and the east harbour, while the mole and the west harbour were in possession of the citizens; and, as the Alexandrian fleet was burnt, his vessels sailed in and out without hindrance. The Alexandrians, after having vainly attempted to introduce fire-ships from the western into the eastern harbour, equipped with the remnant of their arsenal a small squadron, and with this blocked up the way of Cæsar's vessels, when these were towing in a fleet of transports with a legion that had arrived from Asia Minor; but the excellent Rhodian mariners of Cæsar mastered the enemy. Not long afterwards, however, the citizens captured the lighthouse-island, and from that point totally closed the narrow and rocky mouth of the east harbour for larger ships; so that Cæsar's fleet was compelled to take its station in the open roads before the east harbour, and his communication with the sea hung only on a weak thread. Cæsar's fleet, attacked in that roadstead repeatedly by the superior naval force of the enemy, could neither shun the unequal strife, since the loss of the lighthouse-island closed the inner harbour against it, nor yet withdraw, for the loss of the roadstead would have debarred Cæsar wholly from the sea. Though the brave legionaries, supported by the dexterity of the Rhodian sailors, had always hitherto decided these conflicts in favour of the Romans, the Alexandrians renewed and augmented their naval armaments with unwearied perseverance; the besieged had to fight as often as it pleased the besiegers, and, if the former should be on a signal occasion vanquished, Cæsar would be totally hemmed in and probably lost.

It was absolutely necessary to make an attempt to recover the lighthouse-island. The double attack, which was made by boats from the side of the harbour and by the war-vessels from the seaboard, in reality brought not only the island but also the lower part of the mole into his power; it was only at the second arch-opening of the mole that Cæsar ordered the attack to be stopped, and the mole to be there closed towards the city by a transverse wall. But while a violent conflict arose here round the entrenchers, the Roman troops left the lower part of the mole adjoining the island bare of defenders; a division of Egyptians landed there unexpectedly, attacked in the rear the Roman soldiers and sailors crowded together on the mole of the transverse wall, and drove the whole mass in wild confusion into the sea. A part were taken on board by the Roman ships; but more were drowned. Some four hundred soldiers and a still greater number of men belonging to the fleet were sacrificed on this day; the general himself, who had shared the fate of his men, had been obliged to seek refuge in his ship, and, when this sank from having been overloaded with men, he had to save himself by swimming to another. But, severe as was the loss suffered, it was amply compensated by the recovery of the lighthouse-island, which along with the mole as far as the first arch-opening remained in the hands of Cæsar.

At length the longed-for relief arrived, Mithridates of Pergamus, an able warrior of the school of Mithridates Eupator, whose natural son he claimed to be, brought up by land from Syria a motley army,—the Iduræans of the prince of the Libanus, the Bedouins of Jamblichus, son of Sampsiceramus, the Jews under the minister Antipater, and the contingents generally of the petty chiefs and communities of Cilicia and Syria. From Pelusium, which Mithridates had the fortune to occupy on the day of his arrival, he took the great road towards

Memphis, with the view of avoiding the intersected ground of the Delta and crossing the Nile before its division; during which movement his troops received manifold support from the Jewish peasants who were settled in this part of Egypt. The Egyptians, with the young king Ptolemy now at their head, whom Cæsar had released to his people in the vain hope of allaying the insurrection by his means, despatched an army to the Nile, to detain Mithridates on its farther bank. The army fell in with the enemy even beyond Memphis at the so-called Jews' camp, between Onion and Heliopolis; nevertheless Mithridates, trained in the Roman fashion of manœuvring and encamping, amidst successful conflicts gained the opposite bank at Memphis. Cæsar, on the other hand, as soon as he obtained news of the arrival of the relieving army, conveyed a part of his troops in ships to the end of the lake of Morea to the west of Alexandria, and marched round this lake and down the Nile to meet Mithridates advancing up the river.

The junction took place without the enemy attempting to hinder it. Cæsar then marched into the Delta, whither the king had retreated, overthrew, notwithstanding the deeply cut canal in their front, the Egyptian vanguard at the first onset, and immediately stormed the Egyptian camp itself. It lay at the foot of a rising ground between the Nile—from which only a narrow path separated it—and marshes difficult of access. Cæsar caused the camp to be assailed simultaneously from the front and from the flank on the path along the Nile; and during this assault ordered a third detachment to ascend unseen the heights of the camp. The victory was complete; the camp was taken, and those of the Egyptians who did not fall beneath the sword of the enemy were drowned in the attempt to escape to the fleet on the Nile. With one of the boats, which sank overladen with men, the young king also disappeared in the waters of his native stream.

Immediately after the battle Cæsar advanced at the head of his cavalry from the land side straight into the portion of the capital occupied by the Egyptians. In mourning attire, with the images of their gods in their hands, the enemy received him and sued for peace; and his troops, when they saw him return as victor from the side opposite to that by which he had set forth, welcomed him with boundless joy. The fate of the town, which had ventured to thwart the plans of the master of the world and had brought him within a hair's-breadth of destruction, lay in Cæsar's hands; but he was too much of a ruler to be sensitive, and dealt with the Alexandrians as with the Massiliots. Cæsar—pointing to their city severely devastated and deprived of its granaries, of its world-renowned library, and of other important public buildings on the occasion of the burning of the fleet— exhorted the inhabitants in future earnestly to cultivate the arts of peace alone, and to heal the wounds inflicted on themselves; for the rest, he contented himself with granting to the Jews settled in Alexandria the same rights which the Greek population of the city enjoyed, and with placing in Alexandria instead of the previous Roman army of occupation—which nominally at least obeyed the kings of Egypt, a Roman garrison—two of the legions besieged there, and a third which afterwards arrived from Syria—under a commander nominated by himself. For this position of trust a man was purposely selected whose birth made it impossible for him to abuse it—Rufio, an able soldier, but the son of a freed man. Cleopatra and her younger brother Ptolemy obtained the sovereignty of Egypt under the supremacy of Rome; the Princess Arsinoë was carried off to Italy, that she might not serve once more as a pretext for insurrections to the Egyptians, who were after the Oriental fashion quite as much devoted to their dynasty as they were indifferent towards the individual dynasts; and Cyprus became again a part of the Roman province of Cilicia.

Cæsar's love for Cleopatra, who had just borne him a son named Cæsarion, was not so strong as his ambition; and after having been above a year in Egypt he left her to govern the kingdom in her own name, but on his behalf; and sailed for Italy, taking with him the sixth legion. While engaged in this warfare in Alexandria, Cæsar had been appointed dictator in Rome, where his power was exercised by Mark Antony, his master of the horse; and for above six months he had not written one letter home, as though ashamed to write about the foolish difficulty he had entangled himself in, until he had got out of it.

On reaching Rome Cæsar amused the people and himself with a grand triumphal show, in which, among the other prisoners of war, the Princess Arsinoë followed his car in chains; and, among the works of art and nature which were got together to prove to the gazing crowd the greatness of his conquests, was that remarkable African animal the camelopard, then for the first time seen in Rome. In one chariot was a statue of the Nile god; and in another the Pharos lighthouse on fire, with painted flames. Nor was this the last of Cæsar's triumphs, for soon afterwards Cleopatra, and her brother Ptolemy, then twelve years old, who was called her husband, came to Rome as his guests, and dwelt for some time with him in his house.

The history of Egypt, at this time, is almost lost in that of Rome. Within five years of Cæsar's landing in Alexandria, and finding that by the death of Pompey he was master of the world, he paid his own life as the forfeit for crushing his country's liberty. The Queen of Egypt, with her infant son Cæsarion about four years old, was then in Rome, living with Cæsar in his villa on the farther side of the Tiber. On Cæsar's death her first wish was to get the child acknowledged by the Roman senate as her colleague on the throne of Egypt, and as a friend of the Roman people. With this view she applied to Cicero for help, making him an offer of some books or works of art; but he was offended at her haughtiness and refused her gifts. Besides, she was more likely to thwart than to help the cause for which he was struggling. He was alarmed at hearing that she was soon to give birth to another child. He did not want any more Cæsars. He hoped she would miscarry, as he wished she had before miscarried. So he bluntly refused to undertake her cause. On this she thought herself unsafe in Rome, she fled privately, and reached Egypt in safety with Cæsarion; but we hear of no second child by Julius. The Romans were now the masters of Egypt, and Cleopatra could hardly hope to reign but by the help of one of the great generals who were struggling for the sovereignty of the republic. Among these was the young Sextus Pompeius, whose large fleet made him for a time master of Sicily and of the sea; and he was said to have been admitted by the Queen of Egypt as a lover. But he was able to be of but little use to her in return for her favours, as his fleet was soon defeated by Octavianus.

Cæsar had left behind him, in the neighbourhood of Alexandria, a large body of Roman troops, in the pay and nominally under the orders of Cleopatra, but in reality to keep Egypt in obedience. There they lived as if above all Egyptian law or Roman discipline, indulging in the vices of that luxurious capital. When some of them in a riot, in the year 45 B. C., killed two sons of Bibulus the consul, Cleopatra was either afraid or unable to punish the murderers; the most she could do was to get them sent in chains into Syria to the grieving father, who with true greatness of mind sent them back to the Egyptian legions, saying that it was for the senate to punish them, not for him.

While Ptolemy her second husband was a boy and could claim no share of the government, he was allowed to live with all the outward show of royalty, but as soon as he reached the age of fifteen, in B. C. 44, at which he might call himself her equal and would soon be her master, Cleopatra had him put to death. She had then reigned four years with her elder brother and four years with her younger brother, and from that time forward she reigned alone, calling her child by Cæsar her colleague on the throne.

At a time when vice and luxury claimed the thoughts of all who were not busy in the civil wars, we cannot hope to find the fruits of genius in Alexandria; but the mathematics are plants of a hardy growth, and are not choked so easily as poetry and history. Sosigenes was then the first astronomer in Egypt, and Julius Cæsar was guided by his advice in setting right the Roman Calendar. He was a careful and painstaking mathematician, and, after fixing the length of the year at three hundred and sixty-five days and a quarter, he three times changed the beginning of the year, in his doubts as to the day on which the equinox fell; for the astronomer could then only make two observations in a year with a view to learn the time of the equinox, by seeing when the sun shone in the plane of the equator. Photinus the mathematician wrote both on arithmetic and geometry, and was usually thought the author of a mathematical work published in the name of the queen, called the Canon of Cleopatra.

Didymus was another of the writers that we hear of at that time. He was a man of great industry, both in reading and writing; but when we are told that he wrote three thousand five hundred volumes, or rolls, it rather teaches us that a great many rolls of papyrus would be wanted to make a modern book, than what number of books he wrote. These writings were mostly on verbal criticism, and all have long since perished except some notes or scholia on the Iliad and Odyssey which bear his name, and are still printed in some editions of Homer.

Dioscorides, the physician of Cleopatra, has left a work on herbs and minerals, and on their uses in medicine; also on poisons and poisonous bites. To these he has added a list of prescriptions. His works have been much read in all ages, and have only been set aside by

RUINS OF HERMONTHIS.

the discoveries of the last few centuries. Serapion, another physician, was perhaps of this reign. He followed medicine rather than surgery; and, while trusting chiefly to his experience gained in clinical or bedside practice, was laughed at by the surgeons as an empiric.

The small temple at Hermonthis, near Thebes, seems to have been built in this reign, and it is dedicated to Mandoo, or the sun, in the name of Cleopatra and Cæsarion. It is unlike the older Egyptian temples in being much less of a fortress; for what in them is a strongly walled courtyard, with towers to guard the narrow doorway, is here a small space between two double rows of columns, wholly open, without walls, while the roofed building is the same as in the older temples. Near it is a small pool, seventy feet square, with stone sides, which was used in the funerals and other religious rites.

The murder of Cæsar did not raise the character of the Romans, or make them more fit for self-government. It was followed by the well-known civil war; and when, by the battle of Philippi and the death of Brutus and Cassius, his party was again uppermost, the Romans willingly bowed their necks to his adopted son Octavianus, and his friend Mark Antony.

It is not easy to determine which side Cleopatra meant to take in the war between Antony and the murderers of Cæsar; she did not openly declare herself, and she probably waited to join that which fortune favoured. Allienus had been sent to her by Dolobella to ask for such troops as she could spare to help Antony, and he led a little army of four Roman legions out of Egypt into Syria; but when there he added them to the force which Cassius had assembled against Antony. Whether he acted through treachery to the queen or by her orders is doubtful, for Cassius felt more gratitude to Allienus than to Cleopatra. Serapion also, the Egyptian governor of Cyprus, joined what was then the stronger side, and sent all the ships that he had in his ports to the assistance of Cassius. Cleopatra herself was getting ready another large fleet, but since the war was over, and Brutus and

Cassius dead before it sailed, she said it was meant to
help Octavianus and Antony. Thus, by the acts of her
generals and her own hesitation, Cleopatra fairly laid
herself open to the reproach of ingratitude to her late
friend Cæsar, or at least of thinking that the interests
of his son Cæsarion were opposed to those of his nephew
Octavianus; and accordingly, as Antony was passing
through Cilicia with his army, he sent orders to her to
come from Egypt and meet him at Tarsus, to answer the
charge of having helped Brutus and Cassius in the late
military campaign.

Dellius, the bearer of the message, showed that he
understood the meaning of it, by beginning himself to
pay court to her as his queen. He advised her to go,
like Juno in the Iliad, " tricked in her best attire," and
told her that she had nothing to fear from the kind and
gallant Antony. On this she sailed for Cilicia laden with
money and treasures for presents, full of trust in her
beauty and power of pleasing. She had won the heart
of Cæsar when, though younger, she was less skilled in
the arts of love, and she was still only twenty-five years
old; and, carrying with her such gifts and treasures as
became her rank, she entered the river Cydnus with the
Egyptian fleet in a magnificent galley. The stern was
covered with gold; the sails were of scarlet cloth: and
the silver oars beat time to the music of flutes and harps.
The queen, dressed like Venus, lay under an awning
embroidered with gold, while pretty dimpled boys, like
Cupids, stood on each side of the sofa fanning her. Her
maidens, dressed like sea-nymphs and graces, handled

the silken tackle and steered the vessel. As she approached the town of Tarsus the winds wafted the perfumes and the scent of the burning incense to the shores, which were lined with crowds who had come out to see her land; and Antony, who was seated on the tribunal waiting to receive her, found himself left alone.

Tarsus on the river Cydnus was situated at the foot of the wooded slopes of Mount Taurus, and it guarded the great pass in that range between the Phrygian tribes and the Phœnician tribes. It was a city half-Greek and half-Asiatic, and had from the earliest days been famed for ship-building and commerce. Mount Taurus supplied it with timber, and around the mouth of its river, as it widens into a quiet lake, were the ancient dockyards which had made the ships of Tarshish proverbial with the Hebrew writers. Its merchants, enriched by industry and enlightened by foreign trade, had ornamented their city with public buildings, and established a school of Greek learning. Its philosophers, however, were more known as travelling teachers than as scholars. No learned men came to Tarsus; but it sent forth its rhetoricians in its own ships, who spread themselves as teachers over the neighbouring coasts. In Rome there were more professors of rhetoric, oratory, and poetry from Tarsus than from Alexandria or Athens. Athenodorus Cordylion, the stoic, taught Cato; Athenodorus, the son of Sandon, taught Cæsar; Nestor a little later taught the young Marcellus; while Demetrius was one of the first men of learning who sailed to the distant island of Britain. This school, in the next generation,

sent forth the apostle Paul, who taught Christianity
throughout the same coasts.

Tarsus was now to be amused by the costly follies
and extravagances of Cleopatra. As an initial display,
soon after landing, she invited Antony and his generals
to a dinner, at which the whole of the dishes placed before
them were of gold, set with precious stones, and the room
and the twelve couches were ornamented with purple
and gold. On his praising the splendour of the sight, as
passing anything he had before seen, she said it was a
trifle, and begged that he would take the whole of it as
a gift from her. The next day he again dined with her,
and brought a larger number of his friends and generals,
and was of course startled to see a costliness which made
that of the day before seem nothing; and she again gave
him the whole of the gold upon the table, and gave to
each of his friends the couch upon which he sat.

These costly and delicate dinners were continued
every day; and one evening, when Antony playfully
blamed her wastefulness, and said that it was not possible to fare in a more costly manner, she told him that
the dinner of the next day should cost ten thousand sestertia, or three hundred thousand dollars. This he would
not believe, and laid her a wager that she would fail in
her promise. When the day came the dinner was as
grand and dainty as those of the former days; but when
Antony called upon her to count up the cost of the meats
and wines, she said that she did not reckon them, but
that she should herself soon eat and drink the ten thousand sestertia. She wore in her ears two pearls, the

largest known in the world, which, like the diamonds of
European kings, had come to her with her crown and
kingdom, and were together valued at that large sum.
On the servants removing the meats, they set before her

EGYPTIAN PICTURE OF CLEOPATRA.

a glass of vinegar, and she took one of these earrings
from her ear and dropped it into the glass, and when
dissolved drank it off. Plancus, one of the guests, who
had been made judge of the wager, snatched the other
from the queen's ear, and saved it from being drunk up
like the first, and then declared that Antony had lost his

bet. The pearl which was saved was afterwards cut in two and made into a pair of earrings for the statue of Venus in the Pantheon at Rome; and the fame of the wager may be said to have made the two half pearls at least as valuable as the two whole ones.

The beauty, sweetness, and gaiety of this young queen, joined to her great powers of mind, which were all turned to the art of pleasing, had quite overcome Antony; he had sent for her as her master, but he was now her slave. Her playful wit was delightful; her voice was as an instrument of many strings; she spoke readily to every ambassador in his own language; and was said to be the only sovereign of Egypt who could understand the languages of all her subjects: Greek, Egyptian, Ethiopic, Troglodytic, Hebrew, Arabic, and Syriac. With these charms, at the age of five-and-twenty, the luxurious Antony could deny her nothing. The first favour which she asked of her lover equals any cruelty that we have met with in this history: it was, that he would have her sister Arsinoë put to death. Cæsar had spared her life, after his triumph, through love of Cleopatra; but he was mistaken in the heart of his mistress; she would have been then better pleased at Arsinoë's death; and Antony, at her bidding, had her murdered in the temple of Diana, at Ephesus.

Though Fulvia, the faithful wife of Antony, could scarcely keep together his party at Rome against the power of Octavianus, his colleague in the triumvirate, and though Labienus, with the Parthian legions, was ready to march into Syria against him, yet he was so entangled

in the artful nets of Cleopatra, that she led him captive
to Alexandria; and there the old warrior fell into every
idle amusement, and offered up at the shrine of pleasure
one of the greatest of sacrifices, the sacrifice of his time.
The lovers visited each other every day, and the waste
of their entertainments passed belief. Philotas, a physician who was following his studies at Alexandria, told
Plutarch's grandfather that he was once invited to see
Antony's dinner cooked, and among other meats were
eight wild boars roasting whole; and the cook explained
to him that, though there were only twelve guests, yet
as each dish had to be roasted to a single turn of the spit,
and Antony did not know at what hour he should dine,
it was necessary to cook at least eight dinners. But the
most costly of the luxuries then used in Egypt were the
scents and the ointments. Gold, silver, and jewels, as
Pliny remarks, will pass to a man's heirs, even clothes
will last a few months or weeks, but scents fly off and
are lost at the first moment that they are admired; and
yet ointments, like the attar of roses, which meltëd and
gave out their scent, and passed into air when placed
upon the back of the hand, as the coolest part of the body,
were sold for four hundred denarii the pound. But the
ointment was not meant to be used quite so wastefully.
It was usually sealed up in small alabaster jars, which
were made in the town of Alabastron, on the east of the
Nile, and thence received their name. These were long
in shape, without a foot, and had a narrow mouth. They
were meant never to be opened, but to let the scent escape
slowly and sparingly through the porous stone. In these

Egyptian jars scented ointment was carried by trade to the banks of the Tigris and to the shores of the Mediterranean.

The tenth and eleventh years of the queen's reign were marked by a famine through the land, caused by the Nile's not rising to the wished-for height and by the want of the usual overflow; and an inscription which was written both in the Greek and Egyptian languages declares the gratitude of the Theban priests and elders and citizens to Callimachus, the prefect of the Theban taxes, who did what he could to lessen the sufferings in that city. The citizens of Alexandria on those years received from the government a smaller gift of corn than usual, and the Jews then felt their altered rank in the state. They were told that they were not citizens, and accordingly received no portion whatever out of the public granaries, but were left like the Egyptians to take care of themselves. From this time forward there was an unceasing quarrel between Greeks and Jews in the city of Alexandria.

Cleopatra, who held her power at the pleasure of the Roman legions, spared no pains to please Antony. She had borne him first a son named Ptolemy, and then a son and daughter, twins, Alexander Helius and Cleopatra Selene, or *Sun* and *Moon*. She gamed, she drank, she hunted, she reviewed the troops with him, and, to humour his coarser tastes, she followed him, in his midnight rambles through the city, in the dress of a servant; and nothing that youth, beauty, wealth, and elegance could do to throw a cloak over the grossness of vice and crime

was forgotten by her. The biographer thought it waste
of time to mention all Cleopatra's arts and Antony's
follies, but the story of his fishing was not to be
forgotten. One day, when sitting in the boat with her, he
caught but little, and was vexed at her seeing his want
of success. So he ordered one of his men to dive into
the water and put upon his hook a fish which had been
before taken. Cleopatra, however, saw what was being
done, and quietly took the hint for a joke of her own.
The next day she brought a larger number of friends
to see the fishing, and, when Antony let down his line,
she ordered one of her divers to put on the hook a salted
fish. The line was then drawn up and the fish landed
amid no little mirth of their friends; and Cleopatra playfully consoled him, saying: " Well, general, you may
leave fishing to us petty princes of Pharos and Canopus;
your game is cities, provinces, and kingdoms."

Antony's eldest son by Fulvia came to Alexandria at
this time, and lived in the same princely style with his
father. Philotas the physician lived in his service, and
one day at supper when Philotas silenced a tiresome
talker with a foolish sophism the young Antony gave him
as a reward the whole sideboard of plate. But in the
middle of this gaiety and feasting Antony was recalled
to Europe by letters which told him that his wife and
brother had been driven out of Rome by Octavianus.
Before, however, he reached Rome his wife Fulvia was
dead; and, wishing to strengthen his party, he at once
married Octavia, the sister of Octavianus and widow of
Marcellus.

In that year Herod passed through Egypt on his way
to Rome to claim Judæa as his kingdom. He came
through Arabia to Pelusium, and thence he sailed to
Alexandria. Cleopatra, who wanted his services, gave
him honourable entertainment in her capital, and made
him great offers in order to persuade him to take the
command of her army. But the Jewish prince saw that a
kingdom was to be gained by offering his services to
Antony and Octavianus; and he went on to Rome. There
through the friendship of Antony he was declared King
of Judæa by the senate. He then returned to Syria to
collect an army and to win the kingdom which had been
granted to him; and by the help of Sosius, Antony's
lieutenant, he had conquered Jerusalem when the war
broke out between Antony and Octavianus.

In the next year (B. C. 38) Antony was himself in
Syria, carrying on the war which ended with the battle
of Actium; and he sent to Alexandria to beg Cleopatra
to join him there. On her coming, he made her perhaps
the largest gift which lover ever gave to his mistress:
he gave her the wide provinces of Phœnicia, Cœle-Syria,
Cyprus, part of Cilicia, part of Judæa, and part of Arabia
Nabatæa. These large gifts only made her ask for more,
and she begged him to put to death Herod, King of
Judæa, and Malichus, King of Arabia Nabatæa, the
former of whom had advised Antony to break through
the disgraceful ties which bound him to Cleopatra, as the
only means of saving himself from being crushed by the
rising power of Octavianus. She asked to have the whole
of Arabia and Judæa given to her. But Antony had not

so far forgotten himself as to yield to these commands; and he only gave her the balsam country around Jericho, and a rent-charge of two hundred talents, or one hundred and fifty thousand dollars, a year, on the revenues of Judæa. On receiving this large addition to her kingdom, and perhaps in honour of Antony, who had then lost all power in Italy but was the real king of Egypt and its Greek provinces, Cleopatra began to count the years of her reign afresh: what was really the sixteenth of her reign, and had been called the sixteenth of Ptolemy, her elder brother, she called the first of her own reign, and she reckoned them in the same way till her death. Cleopatra had accompanied Antony on his expedition against Armenia, as far as the river Euphrates, and returned through Damascus to Judæa. There she was politely received by her enemy Herod, who was too much in fear of Antony to take his revenge on her. She farmed out to him the revenues of her parts of Arabia and Judæa, and was accompanied by him on her way towards Egypt.

But after wondering at the wasteful feasts and gifts, in which pearls and provinces were alike trifled with, we are reminded that even Cleopatra was of the family of the Lagidæ, and that she was well aware how much the library of the museum had added to the glory of Alexandria. It had been burnt by the Roman troops under Cæsar, and, to make amends for this, Antony gave her the large library of the city of Pergamus, by which Eumenes and Attalus had hoped to raise a school that should equal the museum of Alexandria. Cleopatra placed these two hundred thousand volumes in the temple

of Serapis; and Alexandria again held the largest library
in the world; while Pergamus ceased to be a place of
learning. By the help of this new library, the city still
kept its trade in books and its high rank as a school of
letters; and, when the once proud kingdom of Egypt was
a province of Rome, and when almost every trace of the
monarchy was lost, and half a century afterwards Philo,
the Jewish philosopher of Alexandria, asked, " Where
are now the Ptolemies? " the historian could have found
an answer by pointing to the mathematical schools and
the library of the Serapeum.

But to return to our history. When Antony left Cleopatra, he marched against the Parthians, and on his return he again entered Alexandria in triumph, leading
Artavasdes, King of Armenia, chained behind his chariot
as he rode in procession through the city. He soon afterwards made known his plans for the government of
Egypt and the provinces. He called together the Alexandrians in the Gymnasium, and, seating himself and
Cleopatra on two golden thrones, he declared her son
Cæsarion her colleague, and that they should hold Egypt,
Cyprus, Africa, and Cœle-Syria. To her sons by himself
he gave the title of kings the children of kings; and to
Alexander, though still a child, he gave Armenia and
Media, with Parthia when it should be conquered; and
to Ptolemy he gave Phœnicia, Syria, and Cilicia. Cleopatra wore the sacred robe of Isis, and took the title of
the New Isis, while the young Alexander wore a Median
dress with turban and tiara, and the little Ptolemy a
long cloak and slippers, with a bonnet encircled by a

diadem, like the successors of Alexander. Antony himself wore an Eastern scimetar by his side, and a royal diadem round his head, as being not less a sovereign than Cleopatra. To Cleopatra he then gave the whole of his Parthian booty, and his prisoner Tigranes.

But notwithstanding Antony's love for Cleopatra, her falsehood and cruelty were such that when his power in Rome fell he could no longer trust her. He even feared that she might have him poisoned, and would not eat or drink in her palace without having the food first tasted herself. But she had no such thoughts, and only laughed at him for his distrust. One day to prove her power, and

COIN OF CLEOPATRA AND ANTONY.

at the same time her good faith, she had the flowers with which he was to be crowned, as he reclined at her dinner-table, dipped in deadly poison. Antony dined with these round his head, while she wore a crown of fresh flowers. During the dinner Cleopatra playfully took off her garland and dipped it in her cup to flavour the wine, and Antony did the same with his poisoned flowers, steeping them in his own cup of wine. He even raised it to his lips to drink, when she hastily caught hold of his hand. " Now," said she, " I am the enemy against whom you have latterly been so careful. If I could have endured to live without you, that draught would have given me the opportunity." She then ordered the wine to be taken to one of the condemned criminals, and sent Antony out to see that the man died on drinking it.

On the early coins of Cleopatra we see her head on the one side and the eagle or the cornucopia on the other side, with the name of " *Queen Cleopatra.*" After she had borne Antony children, we find the words round their heads, " *Of Antony, on the conquest of Armenia;* " " *Of Cleopatra the queen, and of the kings the children of kings.*" On the later coins we find the head of Antony joined with hers, as king and queen, and he is styled " *the emperor* " and she " *the young goddess.*" Cleopatra was perhaps the last Greek sovereign that bore the title of god. Nor did it seem unsuitable to her, so common had thë Greeks of Asia and Egypt made that epithet, by giving it to their kings, and even to their kings' families and favourites. But the use of the word made no change in their religious opinions; they never for a moment supposed that the persons whom they so styled had any share in the creation and government of the world.

The death of Julius Cæsar and afterwards of Brutus and Cassius had left Antony with the chief sway in the Roman world; but his life of pleasure in Egypt had done much to forfeit it; and Octavianus, afterwards called

LATER COIN OF CLEOPATRA AND ANTONY.

Augustus, had been for some time rising in power against him. His party, however, was still strong enough in Rome to choose for consul his friend Sosius, who put the head of Antony on one side of his coins, and the Egyptian eagle and thunderbolt on the other. Soon afterwards Antony was himself chosen as consul elect for the coming year, and he then struck his last coins in Egypt. The rude copper coins have on one side the name of " *The queen, the young goddess,*" and on the other side of " *Antony, Consul a third time.*" But he never was consul for the third time; before the day of entering on the office he was made an enemy of Rome by the senate. Octavianus, however, would not declare war against him, but declared war against Cleopatra, or rather, as he said, against Mardion her slave, Iris her waiting - woman, and Charmion, another favourite woman; for these had the chief management of Antony's affairs.

At the beginning of the year B. C. 31, which was to end with the battle of Actium, Octavianus held Italy, Gaul, Spain, and Carthage, with an army of eighty thou-

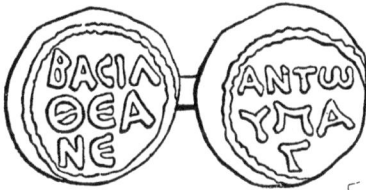

CONSULAR COIN OF ANTONY.

sand foot, twelve thousand horse, and a fleet of two hundred and fifty ships: Antony held Egypt, Ethiopia, and Cyrene, with one hundred thousand foot, twelve thousand horse, and five hundred ships; he was followed by the kings of Africa, Upper Cilicia, Cappadocia, Paphlagonia, Commagene, and Thrace; and he received help from the kings of Pontus, Arabia, Judæa, Lycaonia, Galatia, and Media. Thus Octavianus held Rome, with its western provinces and hardy legions, while Antony held the Greek kingdom of Ptolemy Philadelphus. Cleopatra was confident of success and as boastful as she was confident. Her most solemn manner of

promising was: " As surely as I shall issue my decrees
from the Roman Capitol." But the mind of Antony was
ruined by his life of pleasure. He carried her with him
into battle, at once his strength and his weakness, and
he was beaten at sea by Octavianus, on the coast of
Epirus, near Actium. This battle, which sealed the fate
of Antony, of Egypt, and of Rome, would never have
been spoken of in history if he had then had the courage
to join his land forces; but he sailed away in a fright
with Cleopatra, leaving an army larger than that of
Octavianus, which would not believe that he was gone.
They landed at Parætonium in Libya, where he remained
in the desert with Aristocrates the rhetorician and one
or two other friends, and sent Cleopatra forward to
Alexandria. There she talked of carrying her ships
across the isthmus to the head of the Red Sea, along the
canal from Bubastis to the Bitter Lakes, and thence
flying to some unknown land from the power of the conqueror. Antony soon however followed her, but not to
join in society. He locked himself up in his despair
in a small fortress by the side of the harbour, which he
named his Timonium, after Timon, the Athenian philosopher who forsook the society of men. When the news,
however, arrived that his land forces had joined Octavianus, and his allies had deserted him, he came out
of his Timonium and joined the queen.

In Alexandria, Antony and Cleopatra only so far regained their courage as to forget their losses, and to
plunge into the same round of costly feasts and shows
that they had amused themselves with before their fall;

but, while they were wasting these few weeks in pleasure, Octavianus was moving his fleet and army upon Egypt.

When he landed on the coast, Egypt held three millions of people; he might have been met by three hundred thousand men able to bear arms. As for money, which has sometimes been called the sinews of war, though there might have been none in the treasury, yet it could not have been wanting in Alexandria. But the Egyptians, like the ass in the fable, had nothing to fear from a change of masters; they could hardly be kicked and cuffed worse than they had been; and, though they themselves were the prize struggled for, they looked on with the idle stare of a bystander. Some few of the garrisons made a show of holding out; but, as Antony had left the whole of his army in Greece when he fled away after the battle of Actium, he had lost all chance of safety.

When Pelusium was taken, it was said by some that Seleucus the commander had given it up by Cleopatra's orders; but the queen, to justify herself, put the wife and children of Seleucus into the hands of Antony to be punished if he thought fit. When Octavianus arrived in front of Alexandria he encamped not far from the hippodrome, a few miles from the Canopic or eastern gate. On this Antony made a brisk sally, and, routing the Roman cavalry, returned to the city in triumph. On his way to the palace he met Cleopatra, whom he kissed, armed as he was, and recommended to her favour a brave soldier who had done good service in the battle. She gave the man a cuirass and helmet of gold; but he saw that Antony's cause was ruined; his new-gotten treasure made him selfish, and he went over to the enemy's camp that very night. The next morning Antony ordered out his forces, both on land and sea, to engage with those of Octavianus; but he was betrayed by his generals: his fleet and cavalry deserted him without a

blow being struck; and his infantry, easily routed, retreated into the city.

Cleopatra had never acted justly towards her Jewish subjects; and, during a late famine, had denied to them their share of the wheat distributed out of the public granaries to the citizens of Alexandria. The Jews in return showed no loyalty to Cleopatra, nor regret at her enemy's success; and on this defeat of her troops her rage fell upon them. She made a boast of her cruelty towards them, and thought if she could have killed all the Jews with her own hand she should have been repaid for the loss of the city. On the other hand, Antony thought that he had been betrayed by Cleopatra, as she had received many messengers from Octavianus. To avoid his anger, therefore, she fled to a monument which she had built near the temple of Isis, and in which she had before placed her treasure, her gold, silver, emeralds, pearls, ebony, ivory, and cinnamon, together with a large quantity of flax and a number of torches, as though to burn herself and her wealth in one flame. Here she retired with two of her women, and secured herself with bars and bolts, and sent word to Antony that she was dead. Antony, when he heard it, believing that she had killed herself, and wishing not to be outdone in courage by a woman, plunged his sword into his breast. But the wound was not fatal, and when Cleopatra heard of it she sent to beg that he would come to her. Accordingly his servants carried him to the door of her monument. But the queen, in fear of treachery, would not suffer the door to be opened; but she let a cord down from the window, and she with her two women drew him up. Nothing could be more affecting than the sight to all who were near; Antony covered with blood, in the agonies of death, stretching out his hands to Cleopatra, and she straining every nerve and every feature of her face with the effort she was making. He was at last lifted in at the window, but died soon afterwards. By this time the city was in the power of Octavianus; he had not found it necessary to storm the walls, for Antony's troops had all joined him, and he sent in Gallus to endeavour to take Cleopatra alive. This he succeeded in doing by drawing her into conversation at the door of her monument, while three men scaled the window and snatched out of her hand the dagger with which she would have stabbed herself.

Octavianus, henceforth called Augustus, began by promising his soldiers two hundred and fifty drachmas each as prize money, for not being allowed to plunder Alexandria. He soon afterwards entered the city, not on horseback armed at the head of his victorious legions, but on foot, leaning on the arm of the philosopher Arius; and, as he wished to be thought as great a lover of learning as of mercy, he gave out that he spared the place to the prayers of his Alexandrian friend. He called the Greek citizens together in the gymnasium, and, mounting the tribunal, promised that they should not be hurt. Cleopatra's three children by Antony, who had not the misfortune to be of the same blood with the conqueror, were kindly treated and taken care of; while Cæsarion, her son by Julius Cæsar, who was betrayed by his tutor Rhodon while flying towards Ethiopia, was put to death as a rival. The flatterers of the conqueror would of course say that Cæsarion was not the son of Julius, but of Ptolemy, the elder of the two boys who had been called Cleopatra's husbands. The feelings of humanity might have answered that, if he was not the only son of the uncle to whom Octavianus owed everything, he was at least helpless and friendless, and that he never could trouble the undisputed master of the world; but Augustus, with the heartless cruelty which murdered Cicero, and the cold caution which marked his character through life, listening to the remark of Arius, that there ought not to be two Cæsars, had him at once put to death.

Augustus gave orders that Cleopatra should be carefully guarded lest she should put an end to her own life; he wished to carry her with him to Rome as the ornament of his triumph. He paid her a visit of condolence and consolation. He promised her she should receive honourable treatment. He allowed her to bury Antony. He threatened that her children should be punished if she hurt herself; but she deceived her guards and put herself to death, either by poison, or, as was more commonly thought, by the bite of an asp brought to her in a basket of fruit. She was thirty-nine years of age, having reigned twenty-two years, of which the last seven were in conjunction with Antony; and she was buried in his tomb with all regal splendour.

The death of Cleopatra was hailed at Rome as a relief from a sad disgrace by others besides the flatterers of the conqueror. When governed by Julius Cæsar, and afterwards by Antony, the Romans sometimes fancied they were receiving orders from the barbarian queen to whom their master was a slave. When Antony was in arms against his countrymen, they were not without alarm at Cleopatra's boast that she would yet make her power felt in the Capitol; and many feared that even when Antony was overthrown the conqueror might himself be willing to wear her chains. But the prudent

Augustus was in no danger of being dazzled by beauty. He saw clearly all that was within his reach; he did not want her help to the sovereignty of Egypt; and from the day that he entered the empty palace in Alexandria, his reign began as sole master of Rome and its dependent provinces.

While we have in this history been looking at the Romans from afar, and only seen their dealings with foreign kings, we have been able to note some of the changes in their manners nearly as well as if we had stood in the Forum. When Epiphanes, Philometor, and Euergetes II. owed their crowns to Roman help, Rome gained nothing but thanks, and that weight in their councils which is fairly due to usefulness: the senate asked for no tribute, and the citizens took no bribes. But with the growth of power came the love of conquest and of its spoils. Macedonia was conquered in what might be called self-defence; in the reign of Cleopatra Cocce, Cyrene was won by fraud, and Cyprus was then seized without a plea. The senators were even more eager for bribes than the senate for provinces. The nobles who governed these wide provinces grew too powerful for the senate, and found that they could heap up ill-gotten wealth faster by patronising kings than by conquering them; and the Egyptian monarchy was left to stand in the reigns of Auletes and Cleopatra, because the Romans were still more greedy than when they seized Cyrene and Cyprus. And, lastly, when the Romans were worn out by quarrels and the want of a steady government, and were ready to obey any master who could put a stop to civil bloodshed, they made Octavianus autocrat of Rome; he then gained for himself whatever he seized in the name of the republic, and he at once put an end to the Egyptian monarchy.

Thus fell the family of the Ptolemies, a family that had perhaps done more for arts and letters than any that can be pointed out in history. Like other kings who have bought the praises of poets, orators, and historians, they may have misled the talents which they wished to guide, and have smothered the fire which they seemed to foster; but, in rewarding the industry of the mathematicians and anatomists, of the critics, commentators, and compilers, they seem to have been highly successful. It is true that Alexandria never sent forth works with the high tone of philosophy, the lofty moral aim and the pure taste which mark the writings of Greece in its best ages, and which ennoble the mind and mend the heart; but it was the school to which the world long looked for knowledge in all those sciences which help the body and improve the arts of life, and which are sometimes called useful knowledge. Though great and good actions may not have been unknown in Alexandria, so few valued them that none took the trouble to record them. The well-paid writers never wrote the lives of the Ptolemies. The muse of history had no seat in the museum, but it was almost the birthplace of anatomy, geometry, conic sections, geography, astronomy, and hydrostatics.

If we retrace the steps by which this Græco-Egyptian monarchy rose and fell, we shall see that virtue and vice,

wisdom and folly, care and thoughtlessness, were for the most part followed by the rewards which to us seem natural. The Egyptian gold which first tempted the Greeks into the country, and then helped their energies to raise the monarchy, afterwards undermined those same energies, and became one of the principal causes of its final overthrow.

In Ptolemy Soter we see plain manners, careful plans, untiring activity, and a wise choice of friends. By him talents were highly paid wherever they were found; no service left unrewarded; the people trusted and taught the use of arms; their love gained by wise laws and even-handed justice; docks, harbours, and .fortresses built, schools opened; and by these means a great monarchy founded. Ptolemy was eager to fill the ranks of his armies with soldiers, and his new city with traders. Instead of trying to govern against the will of the people, to thwart or overlook their wishes and feelings, his utmost aim was to guide them, and to make Alexandria a more agreeable place of settlement than the cities of Asia Minor and Syria, for the thousands who were then pouring out of Greece on the check given to its trading industry by the overthrow of its freedom. Though every thinking man might have seen that the new government, when it gained shape and strength, would be a military despotism; yet his Greek subjects must have felt, while it was weak and resting on their good-will rather than on their habits, that they were enjoying many of the blessings of freedom. Had they then claimed a share in the government, they would most likely have gained

it, and thereby they would have handed down those blessings to their children.

Before the death of Ptolemy Soter, the habits of the
people had so closely entwined themselves round the
throne, that Philadelphus was able to take the kingdom
and the whole of its wide provinces at the hands of his
father as a family estate. He did nothing to mar his
father's wise plans, which then ripened into fruit-bear-
ing. Trade crowded the harbours and markets, learning
filled the schools, conquests rewarded the discipline of
the fleets and armies; power, wealth, and splendour followed in due order. The blaze thus cast around the
throne would by many kings have been made to stand
in the place of justice and mildness, but under Philadelphus it only threw a light upon his good government.
He was acknowledged both at home and abroad to be
the first king of his age; Greece and its philosophers
looked up to him as a friend and patron; and though
as a man he must take rank far below his father, by whose
wisdom the eminence on which he stood was raised, yet
in all the gold and glitter of a king Philadelphus was
the greatest of his family.

The Egyptians had been treated with kindness by
both of these Greek kings. As far as they had been able
or willing to copy the arts of Greece they had been raised
to a level with the Macedonians. The Egyptian worship
and temples had been upheld, as if in obedience to the
oft-repeated answer of the Delphic oracle, that the gods
should everywhere be worshipped according to the laws
of the country. But Euergetes was much more of an

Egyptian, and while he was bringing back the ancient splendour to the temples, the priests must have regained something of their former rank. But they had no hold on the minds of the soldiers. Had the mercenaries, upon whom the power of the king rested, been worshippers in the Egyptian temples, the priests might, as in the earlier times, like a body of nobles, have checked his power when too great, and at other times upheld it. But it was not so; and upon the whole, little seems to have been gained by the court becoming more Egyptian, while the army must have lost something of its Greek discipline and plainness of manners.

But in the next reign the fruits of this change were seen to be most unfortunate. Philopator was an Eastern despot, surrounded by eunuchs, and drowned in pleasures. The country was governed by his women and vicious favourites. The army, which at the beginning of his reign amounted to seventy-three thousand men, beside the garrisons, was at first weakened by rebellion, and before the end of his reign it fell to pieces. Nothing, however, happened to prove his weakness to surrounding nations; Egypt was still the greatest of kingdoms, though Rome on the conquest of Carthage, and Syria under Antiochus the Great, were fast gaining ground upon it; but he left to his infant son a throne shaken to the very foundations.

The ministers of Epiphanes, the infant autocrat, found the government without a head and without an army, the treasury without money, and the people without virtue or courage; and they placed the kingdom under the hands of the Romans to save it from being shared between the kings of Syria and Macedonia. Thus passed the first five reigns, the first one hundred and fifty years, the first half of the three centuries that the kingdom of the Ptolemies lasted. It was then rotten at the core with vice and luxury. Its population was lessening, its trade falling off, its treasury empty, its revenue too small for the wasteful expenses of the government; but,

CLEOPATRA'S NEEDLE.

nevertheless, in the eyes of surrounding nations, its trade and wealth seemed boundless. Taste, genius, and poetry had passed away; but mathematics, surgery, and grammar still graced the museum. The decline of art is shown upon the coins, and even in the shape of the letters upon the coins. On those of Cleopatra the engraver followed the fashion of the penman; the S is written like our C, the E has a round back, and the long O is formed like an M reversed.

During the reigns of the later Ptolemies the kingdom was under the shield, but also under the sceptre of Rome. Its kings sent to Rome for help, sometimes against their enemies, and sometimes against their subjects; sometimes they humbly asked the senate for advice, and at other times were able respectfully to disobey the Roman orders. One by one the senate seized the provinces; Cœle-Syria, the coast of Asia Minor, Cyrene, and the island of Cyprus; and lastly, though the Ptolemies still reigned, they were counted among the clients of the Roman patrician, to whom they looked up for patronage. From this low state Egypt could scarcely be said to fall when it became a part of the great empire of Augustus.

During the reigns of the Ptolemies, the sculpture, the style of building, the religion, the writing, and the language of the Kopts in the Thebaid were nearly the same as when their own kings were reigning in Thebes, with even fewer changes than usually creep in through time. They had all become less simple; and though it would be difficult, and would want a volume by itself to trace these changes, and to show when they came into use, yet a few of them may be pointed out. The change of fashion must needs be slower in buildings which are only raised by the untiring labour of years, and which when built stand for ages; but in the later temples we find less strength as fortresses, few obelisks or sphinxes, and no colossal statues; we no longer meet with vast caves or pyramids. The columns in a temple have several new patterns. The capitals which used to be copied from the papyrus plant are now formed of lotus flowers, or palm branches. In some cases, with a sad want of taste, the weight of the roof rests on the weak head of a woman. The buildings, however, of the Ptolemies are such that, before the hieroglyphics on them had been read by Doctor Young, nobody had ever guessed that they were later than the time of Cambyses, while three or four pillars at Alexandria were almost the only proof that the country had ever been held by Greeks.

In the religion we find many new gods or old gods in new dresses. Hapimou, the Nile, now pours water out of a jar like a Greek river god. The moon, which before ornamented the heads of gods, is now a goddess under the name of Ioh. The favourite Isis had appeared in so many characters that she is called the goddess with ten thousand names. The gods had also changed their rank; Phtah and Serapis now held the chief place. Strange change had also taken place in the names of men and cities. In the place of Pet-isis, Pet-amun, Psammo, and Serapion, we find men named Eudoxus, Hermophantus, and Polycrates; while of the cities, Oshmoo-nayn is called Hermopolis; Esne, Latopo-lis; Chemmis, Panopolis; and Thebes, Diospolis; and Ptolemais, Phylace, Par-embole, and others had sprung into being. Many new characters crept into the hieroglyphics, as the camelopard, the mummy lying on a couch, the ships with sails, and the chariot with horses; there were more words spelled with letters, the groups were more crowded, and the titles of the kings within the ovals became much longer.

GRÆCO EGYPTIAN COLUMN.

With the papyrus, which was becoming common about the time of the Persian invasion, we find the running hand, the enchorial or common writing, as it was called, coming into use, in which there were few symbols, and most of the words were spelt with letters. Each letter was of the easy sloping form, which came from its being made with a reed or pen, instead of the stiff form of the hieroglyphics, which were mostly cut in stone. But there is a want of neatness, which has thrown a difficulty over them, and has made these writings less easy to read than the hieroglyphics.

When the country fell into the hands of Augustus, the Kopts were in a much lower state than when conquered by Alexander. Of the old moral worth and purity of manners very little remained. All respect for women was lost; and, when men degrade those who should be their helps towards excellence, they degrade themselves also. Not a small part of the nation was sunk in vice. They had been slaves for three hundred years, sometimes trusted and well-treated, but more often trampled on and ground down with taxes and cruelty. They had never held up their heads as freemen, or felt themselves lords of their own soil; they had fallen off in numbers, in wealth, and in knowledge; nothing was left to them but their religion, their temples, their hieroglyphics, and the painful remembrance of their faded glories.

END OF VOL. X.

INDEX

A

Abydos (Abouthis), 70
Abyssinia, 159
Academy, of Plato, 6
Actium, Battle of, 349
Æschylus, 24
Agatharcides, 252
Agathocles, 185, 189-193
Alabastron, 340
Alexander Ægus, 57
Alexander Balas, 236, 237
Alexander Jannæus, 269, 270
Alexander the Great, 3, 4, 15, 22-37, 51
Alexandria, 5, 7, 22-28, 33, 56, 73, 102, 111, 117, 151, 216, 240, 259, 321, 356
Alexandrian Library, 344, 345
Allienus, 334
Amasis, 18
Ammon, 22
Ammonius, 233
Amon-Ra (Kneph-Ra, Jupiter-Ammon), 4, 22, 51
Amon, temple, 37
Anacleteria, 203
Anatomy, 87, 88
Animal worship, 25, 51, 52, 288-290
Anniceris, 90
Antæopolis, 226
Antigonus, 57, 58, 61, 62, 66, 75-77
Antioch, 61
Antiochus Cyzicenus, 264, 265
Antiochus Epiphanes, 214-218
Antiochus the Great, 179, 180, 194
Antiochus Theos, 145
Antipatros, 36
Antiphilus, 91, 92
Apelles, 84
Apis, 4, 21, 51, 52, 288, 289
Apis-Osiris, 4
Apollinopolis Magna, 229
Apollodorus Gelòus, 128
Apollonia, 34
Apollonius, 6, 24, 209
Apollonius of Citium, 313, 314
Apollonius of Perga, 173

Apollonius Rhodius, 171
Arabia, 24
Arabia Petræa, 65
Aratus, 126, 139, 140
Archelaus, 307
Archimedes, 173, 174, 184
Architecture, 363, 364
Arete, 90
Aristarchus, 126, 232, 233, 258
Aristippus, 89
Aristobolus, 258
Aristomenes, 200, 206, 207
Aristophanes, the grammarian, 167, 232, 233
Aristotle, 7, 22
Arius, 353
Army, Egypt, 147, 148, 307, 313, 361
Arridæus. See Philip Arridæus
Arsinoè, 96, 339
Arsinoèum, 143
Art, Egypt, 8, 136, 137, 162, 362
Artapanos, 12
Astronomy, 125-127, 332
Augustus. See Octavianus

B

Babylonia, 19
Balacrus, 24
Berenicê, 94, 95, 175
Bible, Hebrew, 245, 246
Bion, 232, 233
Britain, 336
Burial customs, 292-294

C

Cæsar Julius, 304, 305, 316, 319-331
Cæsarion, 329, 353
Calendar, Roman, 332
Callimachus, 121, 171
Camelopard, 330
Cambyses, 4, 52
Canals, 113
Canon of Cleopatra, 322
Canopus, 22, 26, 70

INDEX

INDEX

INDEX

INDEX

www.ingramcontent.com/pod-product-compliance
Lightning Source LLC
Chambersburg PA
CBHW040421110426
42814CB00007B/320

.